THE AMERICAN NATION
A HISTORY

FROM ORIGINAL SOURCES BY ASSOCIATED SCHOLARS

EDITED BY

ALBERT BUSHNELL HART, LL.D.
PROFESSOR OF HISTORY IN HARVARD UNIVERSITY

ADVISED BY
VARIOUS HISTORICAL SOCIETIES

THE AMERICAN NATION

A HISTORY

LIST OF AUTHORS AND TITLES

GROUP I

FOUNDATIONS OF THE NATION

GROUP II

TRANSFORMATION INTO A NATION

GROUP III

DEVELOPMENT OF THE NATION

GROUP IV

TRIAL OF NATIONALITY

GROUP V

NATIONAL EXPANSION

ANDREW JACKSON

(From a painting by Amans, 1840, in Sayles Hall, Brown University)

THE AMERICAN NATION: A HISTORY

VOLUME 15

JACKSONIAN DEMOCRACY

1829–1837

BY

WILLIAM MacDONALD, LL.D.

PROFESSOR OF HISTORY IN BROWN UNIVERSITY

WITH MAPS

NEW YORK AND LONDON
HARPER & BROTHERS PUBLISHERS

CONTENTS

CONTENTS

MAPS

EDITOR'S INTRODUCTION

HARDLY any year in American history so distinctly marks the transition from one era to
another as 1829; yet here as elsewhere the new dis-
pensation can be traced back to its foundations
in the previous state of things. Hence, Professor
MacDonald, after a brief chapter describing the conditions of the country in 1829, devotes chapter ii.
to Jackson's early public life. This chapter necessarily traverses the same period, though from a
different point of view, as Babcock's *American
Nationality*, chapter xvii., and Turner's *New West*,
chapter vi. The systematic narrative begins with
chapter iii., election of 1828. Chapter iv. is a discussion of the introduction of the spoils system into
national politics. Chapters v., vi., and ix. go into
the nullification episode, taking up the story where
Turner (*New West*, chapter xvii.) leaves it off, and
include the Webster-Hayne debate. Chapters vii.,
viii., and x. describe in succession the three important episodes of the Bank, internal improvements, and Indian affairs.

The election of 1832 (chapter xi.) introduces a
different group of questions: foreign affairs (chapter

xii.); removal of the deposits (chapter xiii.); and the
hitherto rather neglected subject of Jackson's interesting though somewhat blundering attempts at
reform (chapter xiv.).   Chapter xv. passes out of national affairs into a discussion of the changes which
the state governments were undergoing in this period of constitutional unrest.   Chapters xvi. and
xvii. describe the complicated questions of the public
lands and surplus revenue, and lead up to chapter
xvii., on the election of 1836.   The text concludes
with an interesting chapter (xviii.) on Jackson as
president and man, which reviews his public service.
The Critical Essay on Authorities is a convenient
selection from the mass of literature on the period.

The character of Andrew Jackson is so distinct
and so aggressive that few writers upon the period
can resist the temptation to group the events of his
administration around his personality.   This temptation Professor MacDonald has resisted.   His conception of the period is that it witnessed the fruition
of national policies, nearly all of which would have
come up and would have divided the nation had
there been no Andrew Jackson.   At the same time,
he shows how that dominant personality determined
when and how most of the great questions should
arise; and how Jackson hammered out a series of
political principles which became the foundation of
a new democratic party.

AUTHOR'S PREFACE

AUTHOR'S PREFACE

THE present narrative has been kept, for the
most part, strictly within the limits of the eight
years of Jackson's administrations. It has not, however, been possible in all cases to avoid summariz-
ing the early course of movements having important
development within this period, though I have tried
to avoid undue overlapping. The subject of slavery
is, by the plan of the series, excluded altogether.
As I am not writing a life of Jackson, but an account
of his time, many personal details have also been
omitted.

The volume is, in part, the outcome of special
studies, of which the fruit has been presented in
lectures given in the ordinary course of instruction
at Bowdoin College and Brown University, and to
summer classes at Harvard, Cornell, and the University of Chicago. I am under obligation to many
students at all of these institutions for aid in the
collection and sifting of data. I am also particularly indebted to Mr. Worthington C. Ford, of the
manuscript division of the Library of Congress, for
generous privileges in the consultation of the Jackson and Van Buren papers under his charge. As

these papers, when examined, were as yet uncalendared and unbound, they are referred to here as *Jackson MSS.* and *Van Buren MSS.*

WILLIAM MACDONALD.

JACKSONIAN DEMOCRACY

JACKSONIAN DEMOCRACY

CHAPTER I

THE UNITED STATES IN THE THIRTIES
(1829–1837)

THE administration of Andrew Jackson marks, with greater distinctness than does the administration of any other president, the beginning of a new period in the political history of the United States. Down to the close of the second war with Great Britain, American politics presented tolerably uniform characteristics: the administrative organization of the government under the Constitution, the development of a theory of constitutional law under the force of new problems, and the struggle with Great Britain and France for political and commercial recognition, were for each succeeding administration the questions of chief prominence. When, in 1814, the treaty of Ghent assured to the United States commercial independence, and freed the country once for all from serious intermeddling by any foreign power, there set in a period of political, economic, and social reorganization which rapidly prepared the way for that clear break with tradition, precedent, and form for which the Jacksonian period will always be distinguished.   There was to be still the same Constitution, but a new theory of it; the same administrative organization, but a new and un-heard-of spirit animating it; the same confidence in national honor and resource, but a more striking assertion of them; the same vigorous social life, but with strange and startling manifestations.   The United States of 1830 presented few radical differ-ences from the nation of a generation before; the United States of 1840 had almost forgotten that its past was more than a decade in extent.

The United States at the beginning of Jackson's administration comprised three distinct parcels of territory.   The original area of 843,799 square miles, as established by the treaty of 1783, had been more than doubled by the purchase of Louisiana in 1803; while in 1819 the acquisition of the Floridas added 58,680 square miles to the national possessions.   Al-together, the area of the United States in 1829, leaving Oregon out of account, aggregated 1,793,400 square miles.[1]   All of the most fertile portion of the continent, between the St. Lawrence and the Great Lakes on the north, the Gulf of Mexico on the south, the Atlantic Ocean on the east, and the Rocky Moun-tains on the west, was under American jurisdiction. No country in the world was better fitted, by geo-

[1] Twelfth Census (1900) *Statistical Atlas*, 25.

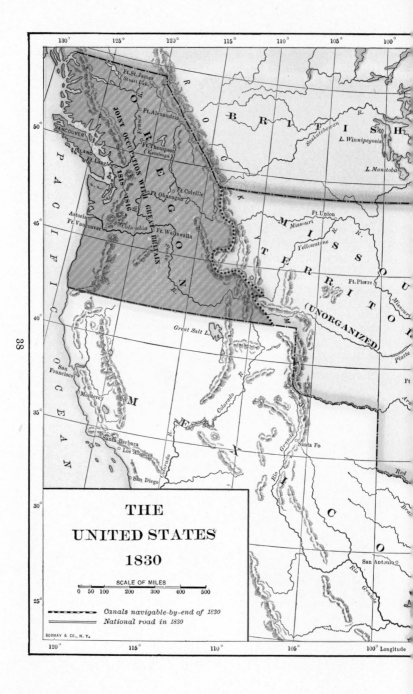

130° 125° 120° 115° 110° 105° 100°

B R I T I S H

L. Winnipegosis

L. Manitoba

Saskatchewan R.

Ft.St.James
Stuart Lake

Ft.Alexandria

VANCOUVER

Ft.Thompson
(Kamloops)

JOINT OCCUPATION WITH GREAT BRITAIN 1818-1846

O R E G O N

Ft.Langley

Ft.Colville

Ft.Okanagan

Astoria
Ft.Vancouver

Columbia R.

Ft.Wallawalla

PACIFIC

Ft.Union
Missouri

Yellowstone R.

M I S S O U R I

Ft.Pierre

T E R R I T O R Y

(UNORGANIZED)

Platte

Great Salt L.

San Francisco

Monterey

Santa Barbara
Los Angeles

San Diego

San Diego

M E X I C O

Colorado R.

Colorado R.

Rio Grande

Santa Fe

OCEAN

Ft

San Antonio

Red

Rio Grande

THE
UNITED STATES
1830

SCALE OF MILES
0 50 100   200   300   400   500

Canals navigable-by-end of 1830
National road in 1830

BORMAY & CO., N.Y.

120° 115° 110° 105° 100° Longitude

50° 45° 40° 35° 30° 25°

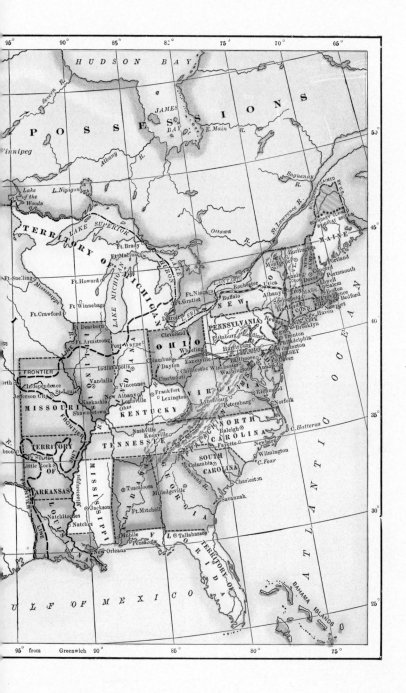

graphical position, climate, soil, and natural resources, to become the home of a great industrial
nation.

The political subdivisions of the country included
twenty-four states and four territories, besides the
District of Columbia. Of the new states, three—
Ohio, Indiana, and Illinois—had been formed within
the Northwest Territory created by the Ordinance
of 1787; three—Alabama, Louisiana, and Mississippi
—included territory bordering on the Gulf of Mexico
acquired subsequent to 1783; one—Maine—formed
from territory previously a part of Massachusetts;
and one—Missouri—from the eastern part of the
Louisiana cession. Two new states were admitted
during Jackson's second term. Michigan territory,
formed in 1805 from the northern part of the then
territory of Indiana, had its western boundary
extended to the Mississippi River in 1818, and to
the Missouri in 1834, thus including within its limits the vast region between Lake Huron and the
Missouri, north of the states of Ohio, Indiana,
Illinois, and Missouri, and south of the British possessions. The eastern part of this area was admitted, with some readjustment of boundaries,
as the state of Michigan in 1837.[1] Arkansas,
formed from the territory of Louisiana, received a
territorial government in 1819. In 1822 the region
ceded to the United States by Spain, and known

[1] *United States Stats. at Large*, II., 309; III., 428–431; IV.,
682, 701; V., 144.

as East and West Florida, was organized as Florida
territory. The territory of Wisconsin was organized in 1836.[1] The larger part of the Louisiana
purchase still remained without political organization, being commonly called the "Indian country."

Neither the external nor the internal boundaries of the United States were in 1829 finally determined. The northeast boundary, though fixed
in terms by the treaty of 1783,[2] had long been a
matter of diplomatic negotiation, and was not
settled until 1842. A dispute with Great Britain
regarding the northwest boundary, adjusted from
time to time by conventions for joint occupancy
of the disputed region, remained open until 1846.
The western limits of Louisiana were never accurately defined, and there was an uncomfortable
impression that, under the treaties of 1803 and
1819 with France and Spain, the United States had
somehow surrendered a valid claim to territory in
Texas. Beyond the assured western limits of the
United States, acceptance by Spain of the forty-
second parallel as the northern limit of its possessions on the Pacific coast, and the fixing of 54° 40′
as the southern limit of the Russian possessions,
by treaties of that country, of 1824 and 1825, with
the United States and Great Britain respectively,[3]

---

[1] *United States Stats. at Large*, III., 493, 654–659; V., 10–16
[2] *U. S. Treaties and Conventions* (ed. of 1887), 376.
[3] *Ibid.*, 931–933; *British and For. State Papers*, XII., 38–43.

had cleared the way for the assertion of a claim to the "Oregon country" by the United States, grounded also on discovery and occupation. Within the United States there were still many unsettled boundary controversies between the states, some of them of long standing; while it had not always been thought essential that the boundaries of a new state should be identical with those of the territory from which it was formed. With the exception of Virginia, however, which included what is now West Virginia, and Missouri, whose western boundary was not extended to the Missouri River until 1836,[1] the boundaries of the states existing in 1829 were substantially the same as now.

The population of the United States in 1830 was 12,866,020, an increase of 3,227,567, or 33.5 per cent., since 1820.[2] The rate of increase, though higher than for the decade 1810–1820, was less than from 1800 to 1810. From 1830 to 1840, also, the rate further declined, the population of 17,069,453 in the latter year showing a gain of 32.7 per cent. over 1830. Absolutely, however, the gain was very large, and was reflected not only in the extension of the settled area, but also in the thickening of population in the older part of the country; indeed, the decade from 1820 to 1830 was notable for the growth of population within the previously settled

[1] *United States Stats. at Large*, V., 34.
[2] Twelfth Census (1900), *Statistical Atlas*, 25. The figures that follow are drawn from this work.

area rather than for any striking or general extension of the frontier.

Of the total area of 1,793,400 square miles in 1830, only 628,017 square miles were included within the settled area bounded by the Atlantic Ocean, the Gulf of Mexico, and a tortuous frontier-line about 5300 miles long. There were still large unsettled tracts in northern Maine, northern New York, and northwestern Pennsylvania, though in the latter two states they were rapidly dwindling, and at the end of another decade had nearly disappeared. The Indian occupancy in Georgia and Alabama barred the way to the settlement of some of the best lands of those states, though in each case there had been in ten years a marked gain in numbers.[1] Louisiana and Mississippi showed small gains in settled area, as did Missouri, except along the Missouri River as far as the Kansas; though each of these states showed large gains in total population. The larger part of the area of Michigan and Florida territories was still unoccupied, and the population of Arkansas was sparse. In the decade 1830–1840, westward expansion swelled the settled area to 807,292 square miles, or 900,658 square miles if certain tracts still unoccupied be included; while the frontier-line decreased to a length of 3300 miles.

Of the states, New York, with a population in

---

[1] See Turner, *Rise of the New West* (*Am. Nation*, XIV.), chap. xviii.

1830 of 1,918,608, was the largest; Pennsylvania and Virginia came next, each with over 1,200,000. The New England states showed small gains since 1820; Massachusetts, with a population of 610,000, being more than twice as populous as any of the others. The new western states of Ohio, Indiana, Illinois, and Missouri, on the other hand, were expanding by leaps and bounds. In Indiana the population rose during the latter period from 343,031 to 685,866, in Illinois from 157,445 to 476,183, in Ohio from 937,903 to 1,519,467. Of the southern states, Virginia, North Carolina, and South Carolina showed but modest gains during the preceding decade; but Georgia advanced from 340,985 to 516,823, Alabama from 127,901 to 309,527, Mississippi from 136,621 to 375,651, and Louisiana from 215,739 to 352,411. The decade 1830–1840 did not alter the relative positions of these five states; but Michigan, which as a territory in 1830 mustered 31,639 people, could boast, ten years later, of 212,267. It was clear that the west and the lower south were growing the fastest, and that the balance of political power could not long remain unaffected by the changing distribution of the population.

The United States was still a rural country. There were in 1830 but twenty-six places classed by the recent censuses as "urban"—that is, containing a population of 8000 or over; while the urban element represented but 6.7 per cent. of the total population. There were but forty-four such

communities in 1840, containing 8.5 per cent. of
the population.[1] New York, with a population of
202,589 in 1830, was the largest city; then came
Baltimore with 80,620, Philadelphia with 80,462,
Boston with 61,392, New Orleans with 46,082,
Charleston with 30,289, Cincinnati with 24,831,
Washington with 18,826, Richmond with 16,060.
With the exception of Richmond and Norfolk (Vir-
ginia), Nashville (Tennessee), and Lexington and
Louisville (Kentucky), no community in any south-
ern state numbered so many as 5000 inhabitants.[2]
The largest town in Ohio, next to Cincinnati, was
Zanesville, with a population of 3094. St. Louis
County, with a population of 14,907, was the largest
centre in Missouri.[3]

In the country, as a whole, the predominant race
element was English. Until the census of 1850,
detailed information regarding the sources of the
population is lacking; but prior to 1845, when
famine and economic distress in Great Britain and
Ireland led to a great migration to America, the
addition of non-English elements was comparatively
small. Absolutely, however, the figures of foreign
immigration show a decided increase during Jackson's administrations, rising from 27,382 in 1828
to about 50,000 in 1832, and 79,340 in 1837.[4] The

---

[1] Twelfth Census (1900), *Statistical Atlas*, 40.
[2] Twelfth Census (1900), *Population*, I., 430, 431.
[3] Fifth Census (1830), 135, 151.
[4] United States Industrial Commission, *Report* (1901), XV., 268.

distribution of the foreign-born cannot at this period be followed with exactness, but comparatively few emigrants, except the Irish, remained in New England, and none of any nationality went to the slave states. Probably far the larger number eventually made their way, sometimes by successive removals, to the west, where land was cheap and good, taxes low, and political privileges liberal.

Of greater significance was the westward migration from the older eastern states. Ever since the "Ohio fever" which followed the War of 1812, a steady stream of population had flowed through the gaps of the Appalachian Mountains into Ohio and Tennessee, and thence on into Indiana, Illinois, Michigan, Kentucky, and Missouri. Many New England towns have never recovered from the blow which this loss of population gave them. The men who, in the thirties, made the central west a political and social power were not alien emigrants from Europe, nor yet the restless element for whom the settled communities of the east were too confined: they were the choicest and most vigorous men of New England, New York, and Pennsylvania, poor or of moderate means, to be sure, but industrious, intelligent, brave, resourceful, seeking in the new lands a freer political life and wider industrial opportunity. To a considerable extent this emigration followed parallel lines, the two great streams from north and south touching in southern Ohio, Indiana, and Illinois, and marking with a somewhat composite character the institutions of local government there.[1]

The facilities for travel, though just on the verge of a great revolution, were still primitive. The Baltimore and Ohio Railway, the first in the country built for the transportation of passengers and freight, did not open its fourteen miles of track until the late summer of 1830. Railway building, however, was in the air, and numerous railroads had been chartered or projected; but for a time the progress was slow. Travellers in the interior, except by river, had still to rely upon the stage-coach, the post-chaise, or private conveyance. In New England and parts of the middle and southern states the construction of turnpikes had facilitated travel, but in the country at large the roads were poor. It was no mere desire to spend an accumulated surplus, or to thrust upon the federal government local tasks, that led to the demand for internal improvements, but rather a general realization of the supreme importance of adequate means of communication if the Union was to be held together and its natural resources developed.

The opening of the Erie Canal in 1825 had not only assured the commercial supremacy of New York City, but had also greatly stimulated the economic development of the west, particularly of Ohio. The canal lowered the time and cost of transportation, offered a practicable route to the

[1] Bryce, *Am. Commonwealth* (3d ed.), I., 600.

seaboard for lumber, grain, and ore, encouraged emigration from the east, and increased the profitable openings for labor. It was not uncommon for fifty canal-boats to start westward from Albany daily.[1] Every western river, moreover, had its steamboats and other craft, carrying the corn, bacon, and mules of the central west to New Orleans and other southern points, and building up a trade which tended more and more to bind the two regions in political sympathy. No considerable area of the west was cut off from a market, by way of the Mississippi to the Gulf or the lower south, or else by way of the Great Lakes to Buffalo and thence by the Erie Canal to New York and the Atlantic seaboard.

The changes wrought in state and local government by the rise of the new democracy will be dealt with in a later chapter. It will be sufficient to point out here that the constitution - making of the period after 1815 shows, among its prominent characteristics, a desire for greater political equality, a willingness to give the legislature a freer hand than it had before 1800 at some points, while further restraining it in others, a distrust of the executive power, and an expanding confidence in popular virtue. The abolition of property or religious tests for voting or holding office, the attempt to base representation solely upon numbers, the enlargement of the legislative powers of the upper houses of assembly, the

[1] McMaster, *United States*, V., 135.

restriction of the governor's authority, the popular
election of judges, the encouragement of education,
and the permission, expressed or implied, to the
legislature to use the credit of the state for the encouragement of banks, canals, roads, and similar
enterprises, are illustrations in point. In no country in the world was there greater legal and political
freedom for the individual, or less conscious control
of individual action by government, than in the
United States between 1830 and 1840.

In local government there was less change. In
the older states, local institutions hardly changed
at all, save as here and there a populous town took
on the style and manner of a city. In the west, local
government savored of the region from which the
bulk of the population came, tempered, however,
by the conditions of life in a new and thinly settled
country, and showing a preference for the county
rather than the town as the local unit.

Intellectually, the United States was just passing
from youth into young manhood. Of the group of
writers who made the middle of the nineteenth
century famous in American literature, only Bry-
ant, Cooper, and Simms had as yet attracted wide
attention. The time was still, in the older states,
one of letter-writing, of leisurely reading of scholarly
books, and of instinctive popular respect for min-
isters, lawyers, and college professors. Of material
well-being there was everywhere a generous share.
There was little poverty, still less of leisured idle-

ness, and no excess of crime. But there were signs of change. In New England, highly respectable foreign trade had begun to give place to less respectable manufacturing. Men obviously cared less for form and dignity than did their predecessors of even a decade ago. In the west, manners were as rude as were the conditions of life, and culture of any sort seemed indeed remote. Beyond the Appalachians, however, the children of the east were subduing a continent; and it was from this struggle for mastery that a new democracy, unlike anything yet seen in America, emerged.

CHAPTER II

EARLY PUBLIC LIFE OF JACKSON
(1767–1823)

IT is not without significance that the man who, more than any other, typified the democratic revolution of the thirties should have been of obscure origin, and that the place of his birth should have been long a matter of dispute. The Jackson family, of Scotch or Scotch-Irish race, emigrated to America in 1765, and settled at Waxhaw, Mecklenburg County, North Carolina, near to the southern boundary of the colony.[1] Andrew Jackson was born March 15, 1767. Of his early life little is known, save that it probably did not differ from that of the life of the ordinary poor family on the frontier in his day. Experience of the hardships of the Revolution, during which he and his brother suffered a short imprisonment by the British at Camden, gave him an early bias against England which later, as president, he was able successfully to overcome.

In 1788, Jackson was admitted to the bar, and

[1] Sumner, *Jackson* (rev. ed.), 2. Jackson appears to have believed that he was born in South Carolina.

shortly removed to Tennessee, where he became
United States district attorney, and later, in 1798,
a judge of the superior courts of the new state.
Neither the study nor the practice of the law, however, ever gave him much knowledge of law, or
developed in him a judicial habit of mind.   He
was a member of the constitutional convention of
1796, where he was appointed on the committee to
draught a constitution;[1] and he became the first
representative from Tennessee in Congress.   On
the expulsion of William Blount, one of the senators
from Tennessee, and formerly governor of the "Territory South of the Ohio," on charges of having
intrigued to secure a transfer of New Orleans to
Great Britain, Jackson succeeded him, but resigned
in April, 1798.   His congressional career was unimportant, save for his successful pressing of the
claims of Tennessee for the reimbursement of expenses incurred in an Indian war.[2]   Gallatin noted
Jackson's rough exterior,[3] and Jefferson later pict-
ured him as so choking with rage that he could not
speak.[4] The former may well have been the case,
but the latter accords ill with the courtly bearing for
which Jackson was later noted.

The schemes of Aaron Burr, whom Jackson had
met in Philadelphia, at first attracted him, and he

[1] Caldwell, *Tennessee*, 85.
[2] *United States Stats. at Large*, I., 509.
[3] Hildreth, *United States*, IV., 692.
[4] Webster, *Private Correspondence*, I., 371; Parton, *Jackson*,
I., 219, questions Webster's accuracy.

undertook to furnish boats for the expedition down the Ohio, but he refused to countenance any movement against the United States.[1] His sympathies, however, remained with Burr, and at the trial at Richmond, where he attended as a witness, he made a speech in which he defended Burr, and denounced Jefferson as a persecutor.[2]

On Jackson's share in the War of 1812 it is unnecessary to dwell. It was his great opportunity. He offered his services as soon as the declaration of war was known, and served with an energy and skill which showed him to be a master of frontier fighting. It was his successful operations against the Creek Indians, however, that first made Jackson the idol of the southwest; and the brilliant repulse of the British at New Orleans only spread, but did not originate, his fame. That he profited by the incapacity of his opponents, that the conditions did not call for military genius of a high order, and that a great victory in any quarter, least of all in the southwest, was totally unexpected by the public, does not lessen the credit due him. Good-fortune came to him, and he knew how to use it.[3]

The natural tendency of Jackson to take the law into his own hands was strengthened by the possession of supreme military power. In February,

[1] Channing, *Jeffersonian System* (*Am. Nation*, XII.), chap. xii.

[2] Parton, *Jackson*, I., 333.

[3] Babcock, *Rise of American Nationality* (*Am. Nation*, XIII.), chap. viii.

1815, six soldiers who had been guilty of gross insubordination were tried by court-martial, and executed at Mobile by Jackson's orders—a proceeding for which Jackson later disclaimed responsibility.[1] After the repulse of the British at New Orleans, Jackson remained in control of the city, proclaimed martial law, and refused to credit a report of peace which reached him through English sources. One Louaillier, a member of the state legislature, who had criticised in print a recent order of Jackson directed against the French inhabitants of the city, was arrested and tried by court-martial. Judge Hall, of the United States district court, issued a writ of habeas corpus for him, whereupon he was arrested by military order, as was Dick, the United States district attorney, who obtained a writ of habeas corpus in Hall's favor from a state court. All three, however, were shortly released. An order from the United States court commanding Jackson to show cause why he should not be punished for contempt of court was met by a general defence, which the court refused to accept, and a fine of one thousand dollars was imposed.[2] An explanation of the affair was requested in April, 1815, by the secretary of war, but no further action

[1] On the "coffin handbill" controversy, Jackson to Lewis (1827), in Sumner, *Jackson* (rev. ed.), 52; Parton, *Jackson*, II., 277–300; Report to House of Representatives (1828), in *Niles' Register*, XXXIV., 55–75.

[2] Documents in Parton, *Jackson*, II., 309–311; *Niles' Register*, VIII., 246–252.

was taken.[1] In 1844, Congress refunded the amount of the fine with interest.[2]

In 1814, Jackson had been made a major-general in the United States army. In April, 1817, being still in command of the division of the south, he issued at Nashville an order "forbidding obedience to any order from the war department not issued through him as commanding-general." A private criticism of the order by General Scott, "as mutinous in its character and tendency" and disrespectful to the president, was communicated to Jackson, and led to a heated correspondence between the two. In the end, Jackson challenged his superior officer to a duel, which Scott declined. Calhoun, who became secretary of war in October, conceded Jackson's contention, and later wrote a private letter explaining his views.[3]

Ever since the outbreak of the War of 1812 there had been trouble on the Florida border, where the Indians, reinforced by refugee Creeks and negroes from Georgia, and guided during the war by English officers, were a perpetual menace. A fort on the Appalachicola, containing large supplies of arms and ammunition, seized by the negroes at the close of the war, was attacked and destroyed by a force under General Gaines, sent to maintain peace

[1] Parton, *Jackson*, II., 320.
[2] *United States Stats. at Large*, V., 651.
[3] On this controversy, Parton, *Jackson*, II., 373–376; Calhoun *Corresp.* (Jameson's ed.), 152–155.

on the border, in July, 1816. In November the
principal town of the Creeks was burned. Both of
these posts were within Spanish territory, but Spain
either could not or would not keep the Indians and
negroes in check, while the latter replied by spread-
ing their forays along the frontier, and attacking
the boats ascending the Appalachicola. There was
a strong feeling in the United States in favor of the
annexation of Florida, but Spain as yet refused to
treat.

January 6, 1818, Jackson, who had just been
ordered to command in Georgia, wrote to President
Monroe, urging that not only must the Indians be
chastised, if need be on Spanish territory, as authorized by Gaines's orders, but also "that the arms of
the United States must be carried to any point
within the limits of East Florida where an enemy
is permitted and protected, or disgrace attends";
adding, "Let it be signified to me through any
channel (say Mr. J. Rhea) that the possession of
the Floridas would be desirable to the United States,
and in sixty days it will be accomplished." [1] No
reply was made to this letter, and Monroe did not
read it for a year; but Jackson interpreted the silence
as acquiescence, and read his orders from the secretary of war in the light of his own purposes. He
reached the Florida border in March, burned a
number of Indian villages near what is now Talla-

[1] Parton, *Jackson*, II., 433; Benton, *Thirty Years' View*, I.,
169.

hassee, and took St. Mark's, the only Spanish fort in that part of Florida.

If it occurred to Jackson to justify an invasion, without orders, of the territory of a nation with which the United States was at peace, he doubtless found excuse in the supposed aid given to the Indians by agents of England, and in the evident inability of the Spanish authorities to maintain order. Robert Arbuthnot, a Scotch trader, attempting to escape, was seized and confined; and two Creek chiefs, enticed on board an American vessel in the harbor, were summarily hanged. Jackson then pushed on to a Seminole village on the Suwanee, and burned it, but a letter of warning sent by Arbuthnot to his son enabled the Indians to remove most of their property. An Englishman, Robert Ambrister, found in the neighborhood, was made prisoner. Returning to St. Mark's, a court-martial was convened, and Arbuthnot and Ambrister put on trial. The charges against Arbuthnot were that he had stirred up the Creeks to make war upon the United States, and had further acted as a spy. On the latter charge he was acquitted, but on the former he was found guilty and sentenced to be hanged. Ambrister was convicted of inciting and aiding the enemy, and sentenced to death; but the sentence was modified to fifty lashes on the bare back and twelve months' confinement at hard labor. Jackson disapproved the finding of the court in the case of Ambrister, and restored the original sentence.

On April 29, 1818, the two men were executed. There was not sufficient evidence to sustain any of the charges against either of them.[1]

In May, Jackson took Pensacola. A force of Georgia militia having attacked and destroyed a village of friendly Creeks, most of whose men were serving in Jackson's army, Jackson opened a heated correspondence with Governor Rabun, denied the right of the governor to engage in military operations when a federal force was in the field, and had Wright, the Georgia officer concerned, arrested. Wright was released on habeas corpus, placed on parole, and shortly fled the region. The legislature of Georgia approved the conduct of the governor, and the United States paid an indemnity to the Creeks.[2]

The news of Jackson's invasion of Florida called forth a prompt protest from Onis, the Spanish minister. Great Britain, on the other hand, contented itself with an investigation.[3] Monroe and his cabinet, with the exception of John Quincy Adams, the secretary of state, were of the opinion that Jackson's acts should be disavowed and suitable reparation made; and Calhoun, the secretary of war, thought that Jackson should also be censured for

---

[1] On Arbuthnot and Ambrister, see Babcock, *Rise of American Nationality* (*Am. Nation*, XIII.), chap. xvii.; Parton, *Jackson*, II., 463–488; report of the trial, *Niles' Register*, XV., 270–281.

[2] On this controversy, *Am. State Papers, Military*, I., 774–778; Hildreth, *United States*, III., 645.

[3] Rush, *Court of London*, 364–366, 473–489.

insubordination—a contention from which were later
to flow important consequences. Adams, however,
awake to the diplomatic advantages which the incident afforded, was willing to attempt a justification of Jackson's course, while agreeing to the restoration of St. Mark's and Pensacola, a view in which
the president and cabinet concurred.[1] Calhoun communicated official congratulations to Jackson, and
Monroe took the trouble to argue with him the
propriety of restoring the captured forts,[2] and later
sought his opinion regarding the pending Florida
treaty. The House of Representatives, by a vote
of 54 to 90, refused to pass a resolution disapproving
Jackson's course, and the adverse report of a Senate
committee, February 24, 1819, led to no action.[3]

But for the extraordinary prominence given to
this affair in the political struggles of later years,
the arbitrary and unwarranted conduct of Jackson
might have taken its place with the innumerable
similar violations of justice and humanity by other
military commanders who possess political influence.
The secret of the first opinion of the cabinet was
well kept, and Jackson's course was officially approved. For more than ten years Jackson rested
in the belief that Calhoun was his friend, and that
his real enemies were Crawford, of Georgia, the sec-

---

[1] Gallatin, *Writings*, II., 117.
[2] Parton, *Jackson*, II., 518–528.
[3] *Am. State Papers, Military*, I., 735–743; *ibid.*, *Misc.*, II.,
799–913.

retary of the treasury, and a pronounced political opponent of Calhoun, and Clay, who was in factious opposition to Monroe because of failure to obtain the coveted office of secretary of state, and who, with Crawford, headed the attack on Jackson's conduct in Florida in the session of 1818–1819. It is interesting to note that Adams, between whom and Jackson there was soon to develop bitter enmity, appears as the official defender of Jackson's course, and in his communication to Onis adduced arguments which were essentially those of Jackson himself.[1]

The treaty of 1819 with Spain for the purchase of the Floridas was ratified February 22, 1821, although the actual transfer did not take place until five months later. In March, Jackson was appointed governor of the new acquisition.[2] The position was a delicate one, not only because of Jackson's prejudice against the Spanish authorities, but also because the laws of the United States had not yet been extended to the territory. Jackson's course was as high-handed as at New Orleans and St. Mark's. A refusal by Callava, the ex-governor, to deliver certain papers relating to a land controversy was followed by his summary arrest and imprisonment, and a quarrel with the judges who had issued a writ of habeas corpus for Callava.[3]

---

[1] *Am. State Papers, Foreign*, IV., 497–499.

[2] *Niles' Register*, XXII., Suppl., 148.

[3] Documents in *ibid.*, XXI., 73–75, 86–89, 149–152; cf. Turner, *Rise of the New West* (*Am. Nation*, XIV.), chap. x.

Some friends of the ex-governor, who ventured to defend him in print, were ordered out of the territory. In October, Jackson resigned, having already retired from the army. Monroe's offer of the Mexican mission in 1823 was declined. Shortly after he was elected to the Senate from Tennessee.

The briefest survey of Jackson's public career down to the time when he became a presidential candidate is sufficient to show the essential traits of his character. All but an insignificant portion of his fifty-seven years had been passed either on the frontier, or in communities whose frontier characteristics were still predominant. His education was of the slightest, and there is no evidence that he ever sought to make good his deficiencies in this respect; but he was not illiterate; he could express himself in clear and vigorous English, and his ideas were his own. A strong common-sense, instinctive sympathy with the opinions of the lower classes, a large capacity for vigorous and aggressive leadership, and an open contempt for forms and theories had brought him to the front and given him an enthusiastic following. His judgments were quick and erratic, his opinions the result of impulse and temper rather than of observation and reflection. No one ever illustrated more perfectly the dictum of a certain sect of Greek philosophers, that truth was that which was most vividly apprehended. All of Jackson's notions were vivid; they admitted of no controversy; all who were not for him were against him. Again and again his hasty temper and arbitrary methods had involved him and others in needless and fruitless entanglements from which a modicum of self-control and regard for the rights or feelings of others might have saved him; yet no one could have profited more than he by sheer good luck. Of all the men whom the winds and currents of American life had thus far thrown to the surface, none had less respect for the past, less breadth of culture or personal experience, less self - restraint than Andrew Jackson. It is a matter of profound significance that the leadership of the new democracy, which was to work a revolution "in head and members" of American political methods and ideals, should have been devolved enthusiastically upon a man apparently so dangerous.

CHAPTER III

ELECTION OF 1828

(1824–1829)

THAT Jackson should become a candidate for
the presidency was, in view of his public career
and of the conditions which had determined the
selection of the first five presidents, not only natural,
but inevitable. He stood high in the esteem of the
people of Tennessee, had held important local offices,
and had served acceptably, if not with prominence,
in the Senate and House of Representatives. In
the rough and ready life of the frontier he had
proved himself a born leader of men. His education was crude, his tastes uncultivated, his temper
violent and ill-governed; but he had somehow acquired dignity of manner, his sincerity and honesty
were undoubted, and his private morals were singu-
larly pure. His military reputation exceeded that
of any living American; and a soldier candidate has
always been popular in the United States. Further,
as a product of the new west, he understood, better
than any man of his time, the temper of the section
whose idol he was soon to become and whose political creed he was to formulate and enforce. He had

shown no desire for political life, and had kept himself free from political entanglements. Not the least element of his strength was his entire independence of the political hierarchy which had controlled the federal government since the accession of Jefferson, and which was not yet disposed to relinquish its power.

There was early recognition of Jackson's availability. November 20, 1815, Aaron Burr wrote to his son-in-law, Joseph Alston, governor of South Carolina, a long letter denouncing Monroe and the caucus system, and urging the nomination of Jackson.[1] Adams notes in his diary in December, 1818, the disposition of "a considerable party" to bring Jackson forward as a candidate, though himself confident that Jackson's recent course in the Florida war had alienated support.[2] Jackson himself made light of the suggestion even as late as 1821. That his cause was skilfully urged, however, notwithstanding his disclaimer of fitness, was largely due to his friend, William B. Lewis, who devoted his consummate political abilities to paving the way for an announcement of the candidacy. In July, 1822, Jackson was nominated for president by the legislature of Tennessee, and the six years' campaign began.

In 1824, though Jackson's political opinions were unknown, he was endorsed by numerous local conventions in all parts of the country. In Penn-

[1] Parton, *Jackson*, II., 351.   [2] Adams, *Memoirs*, IV., 197.

sylvania the Calhoun and Jackson forces united;
Jackson received the nomination of a Federalist
convention for first place, and later of a Democratic
convention also, while Calhoun, whose weakness in
comparison with Crawford had caused his withdrawal, was generally supported, save in Pennsylvania, for second place, with the understanding
that he was to succeed Jackson when the latter had
served one term. It will be remembered that Jackson at this time was a friend of Calhoun, and had no
personal hostility to Adams; but he was an opponent
of Clay and Crawford, in each case on personal
grounds. Of the four candidates, Jackson received
99 electoral votes, Adams 84, Crawford 41, and
Clay 37. The popular vote, to which Jackson and
his supporters later attached great importance as
an indication of the "will of the people," is at that
point without significance. With the exception of
Pennsylvania, which gave 36,000 votes for Jackson
against 10,337 for the combined opposition; Alabama and Mississippi, whose votes showed large
majorities for Jackson; and Tennessee, where 20,197
votes were cast for Jackson, as against 528 for Adams
and Crawford, there is nothing in the popular vote
to show that in 1824 Jackson was the popular choice.[1]
Adams was chosen by the House of Representatives.

When, in January, 1825, Clay and Adams were
accused of a "corrupt bargain," Jackson, who up

---

[1] See the figures in Stanwood, *Hist. of the Presidency*, 136; cf.
Turner, *Rise of the New West* (*Am. Nation*, XIV.), chap. xv.

to that time had maintained friendly relations with Adams, took up the charge and spread it on his way home to Tennessee from Washington; and upon him must be placed the chief responsibility of disseminating it and keeping it alive.   There is no reason to believe that Clay was seriously hurt by the charge, though naturally he was industrious in repelling it. The charge came, no doubt, to be widely believed, but the masses who repeated it would have taken up any charge against Clay or anybody else, had it been uttered with the same Jacksonian accent of sincerity.[1]

The opposition to Adams, and the success of Jackson as titular leader of it, were mainly the result of two causes.   The first was Adams himself.   Adams was the choice of a minority and of a section, rather than of the country.   He was a skilful diplomatist and trained administrator, but he was not built of presidential timber.   His political views and suggestions, as set forth in his messages, are those of a far-seeing man, but he never showed large capacity for leadership.   He lacked the power of arousing enthusiasm or winning friends.   It is true that the personal and political opposition which he encountered, in Congress and out, was of a meaner and more despicable sort than has fallen to the lot of any other president; but it is also clear that he did not command respect.   It is to his lasting credit that he

[1] Cf. Turner, *Rise of the New West* (*Am. Nation*, **XIV.**), chap. xvi.

refused to employ either money or the federal
patronage to strengthen his position, but the very
loftiness of his ideals alienated more support than
it won. He was a weigher of scruples and values in
a time of transition, a representative of old-school
politics on the threshold of triumphant democracy.
The people did not understand him, but they felt
instinctively that he was not one of themselves; and,
therefore, they cast him out.

The second and greater cause was the wide-spread
popular revolt against the existing political order.
When Benton declares [1] that "the election of Mr.
Adams was perfectly constitutional, and as such
fully submitted to by the people; but it was also a
violation of the *demos krateo* principle, and that violation was signally rebuked," he exposes the root
of the matter. It was not against the election of
Adams, as such, that either Jackson or the people
at heart protested, and least of all against a "corrupt bargain," but against a political system which
made such an election and such a bargain possible.
The doctrine of the "will of the people," of which
Benton became the chief advocate and Jackson the
principal beneficiary, was revived, and urged with
a vigor which caused most people to believe it something new. The notion that Jackson, who had no
connection with the caucus machine, was, nevertheless, the real choice of the people, took firm hold of
the popular mind, particularly in the south and

[1] Benton, *Thirty Years' View*, I., 47.

west, and was sedulously cultivated by Jackson and his friends. That Jackson himself sincerely believed it, and that he did not desire the presidency until after his defeat in 1824, seems reasonably clear.

The obvious remedy for the ills complained of lay in such amendment of the Constitution as would provide for the popular election of president and vice-president. The subject had, indeed, often come before Congress, but not until now had there been any wide popular interest in it. McDuffie and Benton had each proposed amendments in Congress, in 1824, providing for the choice of presidential electors by districts.[1] Calhoun declared, in June, 1825, that an amendment was indispensable: "Let the people have the power directly; let the votes be by districts; and, if there be no choice, let the two highest candidates be sent back to the people, and all will be well." [2] A plan embodying this suggestion was reported, in the session of 1825–1826, by a Senate select committee of which Benton was chairman, but failed to secure the necessary two-thirds vote, as did a similar proposition reported in the House.[3] Jackson later advocated a similar change in each of his eight annual messages, but without securing for it favorable consideration.

The political elements from which Jackson derived support were numerous and discordant. At

[1] Benton, *Thirty Years' View*, I., 37.
[2] Calhoun, *Corresp.* (Jameson's ed.), 230.
[3] Benton, *Thirty Years' View*, I., 78.

the bottom were a large number of men, "products of the continually advancing political activity among the less educated classes," [1] who had entered political life during Monroe's second term, and who, having no claim to recognition from Adams, went into opposition. It was to these men that the antagonism to Adams in Congress was mainly due. The supporters of Crawford, in 1824, generally declared for Jackson after the election. Calhoun, sure that "the people" would triumph, was for him,[2] as was also Van Buren, the shrewdest politician of them all. It was Van Buren, more than any one else, who applied to national politics the principles of organization and of the distribution of spoils which had been developed in New York by the Albany Regency. It is clear that the new Democratic party thus formed was not the lineal descendant of the old Democratic-Republican party, and that its principles were not identical with those of Jefferson. Its composition was heterogeneous, and its principles, until after 1830, were summed up in opposition to Adams and advocacy of Jackson. The solidification of the new party was practically completed by 1826, though it was not until some years later that the name of "Jackson men" was generally relinquished in favor of "Democrats."

The Clay and Adams factions united under the name of National Republicans, a name which was later

---

[1] Sumner, *Jackson* (rev. ed.), 130.
[2] Calhoun to Jackson, June 4, 1826, *Jackson MSS.*

exchanged for that of Whigs. In so far as the reorganized Democrats, who still often called themselves Republicans, formed a strict-constructionist party, the National Republicans championed loose or broad construction of the Constitution; but the chief article of their creed was advocacy of the "American system" of a protective tariff and internal improvements.

Adams, meantime, though assumed to be the anti-Jackson candidate in 1828, did nothing to form an administration party, nor, for that matter, to strengthen himself with Congress or the country. In a time when every man's hand was against him, he acted as if every man was as unselfish and high-minded as himself. He refused to remove officials, even in his cabinet, who were intriguing against him, to answer attacks upon himself, or to make speeches. He elaborated policies in his messages, only to give his enemies additional weapons with which to attack him. Calhoun, though early declaring that his own policy had never depended on his position, "but on principles and truth," wrote, June 24, 1825, that his position afforded him "an opportunity, which will not be neglected, of proving" his "devotion to the power of the people, as against that of political leaders";[1] and he did not hesitate, as vice-president, to appoint committees hostile to Adams, until, in the session of 1825–1826, his power of appointment was taken away.[2]

---

[1] Calhoun, *Corresp.* (Jameson's ed.), 232.
[2] Sumner, *Jackson* (rev. ed.), 140.

Aside from the discussion of the proposed Panama mission, the advocacy of which was used to discredit Clay,[1] and the passage of the tariff of 1828, the political aspects of which will be dealt with later, the principal business before Congress was the making of political capital for use in the coming election. There was a working administration majority in the Senate, and a narrow majority of five in the House, in the session of 1825–1827; after that both branches of Congress were in the control of the opposition. A report, May 4, 1826, of a select committee on executive patronage, of which both Benton and Van Buren were members, inveighed against the system which vested so great appointing power in the hands of the president, and recommended a constitutional amendment prohibiting the appointment to office of senators and representatives during the period for which they were elected. Six bills were also reported, five of them relating to appointments and the tenure of offices.[2]   No action on any of these propositions was seriously expected or desired, and none was taken.

No election had ever been so carefully planned. In October, 1825, Jackson was nominated for president by the legislature of Tennessee, and resigned from the Senate.[3] For the next three years he was "the central figure in an extraordinary num-

---

[1] Turner, *Rise of the New West* (*Am. Nation*, XIV.).

[2] Fish, *Civil Service*, 73–75; Benton, *Thirty Years' View*, I., 80–87.   [3] *Niles' Register*, XXIX., 156.

ber of receptions and public dinners." [1]   Friends in
Washington and elsewhere, among them Lewis,
Benton, Buchanan, Swartwout, Henry Lee, Overton, Van Buren, and Eaton, managed his canvass.
The *United States Telegraph*, a Jackson organ, was
established at Washington in 1826, under the edi-
torship of Duff Green, of Missouri.   The New York
Courier and Inquirer was for Jackson.   The newspapers throughout the country were filled with
partisan writing, and a considerable crop of pam-
phlets, hand-bills, and cartoons appeared. [2]   Local
Jackson committees were organized, and the mar-
shalling of the voters carefully looked after.   In
1824, New York adopted the district system of
choosing presidential electors, though the effect of
this change was to divide the vote.   Vermont,
Georgia, and Louisiana made a similar change.   The
Adams men, on their part, professed confidence in
the election of their candidate.   A party organ,
*Truth's Advocate and Monthly Anti-Jackson Expos-
itor*, was established in 1828.   Pennsylvania, notwithstanding its overwhelming majority for Jackson
in 1824, and its choice of Democratic congressmen
in 1826, was counted a doubtful state.   Much reliance was placed in the large Clay vote, in 1824, in
Missouri, Ohio, Indiana, Illinois, and Kentucky, although Illinois and all the southern states except
Louisiana had elected Democratic representatives
in 1826.

[1] *Niles' Register*, III., 99.   [2] Sumner, *Jackson* (rev. ed.), 145.

The formal issues of the campaign were subordinate to "Hurrah for Jackson!" The defeat of Adams and Clay, the rebuke of the "corrupt bargain," and the vindication of Jackson's claim to have been the popular choice in 1824, were the main contentions. Jackson's military record, particularly at New Orleans, was spread before the voters, the brilliancy of his successes being little, if at all, dimmed by attacks on his conduct in Florida. His congressional career was ransacked to show that he was a radical Jeffersonian Democrat in 1796, when he voted with Edward Livingston and others against the address to Washington in the House; that he had voted at the same session in favor of taxing slaves, as did most of the southern members; in favor of completing three frigates already under construction; against the further purchase of peace with Algiers; and against an appropriation for furniture for the new executive mansion at Washington. In the Senate, in 1823–1825, he had voted in favor of several bills for internal improvements; against various bills lowering or removing the import duties on iron, wool, cotton and woollen goods, and cotton bagging, and in favor of bills lowering the duty on blankets and removing that on frying-pans.[1] While the tariff of 1824, which he supported, was pending, Jackson wrote a letter to Dr. L. H. Colman, a member of the Virginia legislature, declaring himself in favor of a "careful" and "judicious" tariff, and also

[1] Parton, *Jackson*, II., 212, 215; III., 33.

"of a judicious examination and revision of it."
The letter was quite evidently revised, perhaps by
Lewis, and intended for public consumption.[1]

The antimasonic excitement was also a factor
in the campaign, particularly in New York. The
mysterious disappearance of William Morgan, of
Batavia, New York, in 1826, following the discovery that he had written a book purporting to
reveal the secrets of freemasonry, led to the plausi-
ble charge that he had been murdered by the
masons or at their instigation. A wave of popular
excitement and indignation swept over the rural
communities of western New York, and before long
extended to other states, especially Massachusetts,
Connecticut, Vermont, Pennsylvania, and Ohio.[2]
Jackson was a mason, as was Clinton, who supported
him. The Clintonians divided, however, the anti-
masonic wing supporting Adams in 1828. The Jackson men charged that Adams was a mason, which
he was not.[3]

Various false and scurrilous attacks upon Adams,
and imputations upon Jackson on account of his
ambiguous marriage, need not be repeated here.
They were the dirty scum on the surface of a churn-
ing political sea, and had no real effect upon the
election. Calhoun could refuse to maintain order

---

[1] Parton, *Jackson*, III., 35, for the letter.
[2] McCarthy, *Anti-Masonic Party*, 371–374 (Am. Hist. Assoc., *Reports*, 1902, I.).
[3] Morse, *John Quincy Adams* (rev. ed.), 209.

in the Senate; Randolph could rave in "besotted violence" against the "puritanic-diplomatic-black-legged administration,"[1] and fight a duel with Clay in consequence, without losing or gaining a vote for either candidate. The question at issue was not the fitness of the candidates, but their "availability."

For the vice-presidency, it was understood that Calhoun would have the support of the Jackson men, but his treatment of Adams would of itself have made impossible any other connection. As Calhoun could hardly expect to serve more than two terms, the question of his probable position in 1832 was an important one. Clay thought of the place, and even spoke to Adams about it. The names of Barbour, the secretary of war, William Henry Harrison, and Crawford were also suggested. Richard Rush, of Pennsylvania, who was eventually nominated by the administration convention at Harrisburg, had voted against Adams.

Of the twenty-four states that took part in the election of 1828, eighteen voted by general ticket, while only two, Delaware and South Carolina, adhered to the older method of election by the legislature. Maryland and Tennessee voted by electoral districts. In Maine and New York the election was by congressional districts, the members so chosen selecting the two electors at large. Jackson received 178 electoral votes against 83 for Adams.

[1] Benton, *Thirty Years' View*, I., 72.

Calhoun, the candidate for vice-president, received 171 votes, seven of the nine votes of Georgia being given to William Smith, of South Carolina. New England voted for Adams, with the exception of one of the nine votes of Maine. In New York the antimason issue divided the vote, twenty of the thirty-six votes going to Jackson. The Maryland vote was also divided, Jackson receiving five of the eleven votes. In the other states there was no division of the electoral vote, and all except New Jersey and Delaware were carried by Jackson.[1] "Adams got not a single vote south of the Potomac or west of the Alleghanies."

The popular vote showed 647,276 for Jackson and 508,064 for Adams. All the New England states except New Hampshire gave Adams heavy majorities; and a similar preponderance was true of most of the states that voted for Jackson. In New York, on the other hand, Jackson received only 140,763 votes as compared with 135,413 given for Adams. Maryland gave 24,565 for Jackson and 25,527 for Adams; Louisiana, 4603 for Jackson and 4076 for Adams; Ohio, 67,597 for Jackson and 63,-396 for Adams. In Pennsylvania the Jackson majority was almost exactly as two to one, the votes for the two candidates being 101,652 and 50,848 respectively. There were still states in which the Adams or anti-Jackson following was strong; but a comparison of the total vote of the states in 1828

[1] Stanwood, *Hist. of the Presidency*, 148.

with the figures, so far as obtainable, of the vote in 1824 shows how thoroughly the country had become aroused and how sweeping was the victory.

Benton characterizes the election of 1828 as "a triumph of democratic principle, and an assertion of the people's right to govern themselves." [1] It was all this, and more. To personal vindication of Jackson was added emphatic popular endorsement of the social and political order with which he was identified. In the election of Jackson the people of the United States turned their backs on their early principles of statesmanship, and entrusted the conduct of the federal government to an untrained, self-willed, passionate frontier soldier. That he was not of the old school was, in the eyes of his supporters, a commendation. It was as idle then as it is now to bemoan the change. A great democracy will never be governed for long together by its best men, but by its average. To the average voter in 1828, Jackson was a great popular leader because they held him to be also a typical democrat. With him, democracy springs into the saddle. It had yet to show how well it could ride.

[1] Benton, *Thirty Years' View*, I., 111.

CHAPTER IV

THE BEGINNING OF PERSONAL POLITICS
(1829–1837)

THE election of Jackson was the signal for an outburst of popular enthusiasm such as had not been witnessed since the first election of Washington. The journey from the "Hermitage" to the capital, where Jackson arrived early in February, was a continuous ovation. A motley army of office-seekers, personal friends, and sight-seers flocked to Washington to cheer the "old hero." Webster wrote that there was "a monstrous crowd of people" in Washington on the day of the inauguration, some of whom had come five hundred miles to see Jackson. "They really seem to think," he added, "that the country is rescued from some dreadful danger." [1] Judge Story, of the supreme court, an Adams man, describes how the new president, going to the "palace," as he calls the executive mansion, after the inauguration, was visited "by immense crowds of all sorts of people, from the highest and most polished down to the most vulgar and gross in the nation. . . . The reign of King Mob seemed

[1] Webster, *Private Corresp.*, I., 470, 473.

triumphant." [1]   Parton, who preserves with cynical
impartiality the spectacular incidents of Jackson's
time, records how the crowd upset the pails of orange
punch, broke the glasses, and stood with muddy
boots on the "damask satin-covered chairs" in their
eagerness to see the president.

Jackson's inaugural address [2] set forth, in dignified
phrases and with commendable brevity, but with
varying degrees of definiteness, the principles by
which he proposed to be guided.   The address was
the joint production of Jackson, Lewis, and Henry
Lee, the latter being responsible for the literary
form. [3]   Jackson declared it to be his purpose, in
administering the laws of Congress, to "keep steadily in view the limitations as well as the extent of the
executive power."   In his conduct touching the
rights of the several states, he hoped "to be ani-
mated by a proper respect for those sovereign members of our Union, taking care not to confound the
powers they have reserved to themselves with those
they have granted to the Confederacy."   "A strict
and faithful economy," with special reference to
the extinguishment of the public debt, was promised.   On the subject of the tariff the expressions
were vague: "the spirit of equity, caution, and compromise in which the Constitution was formed re-
quires that the great interests of agriculture, com-

[1] Story, *Story*, I., 563.
[2] Richardson, *Messages and Papers*, II., 436–438.
[3] Parton, *Jackson*, III., 164, 172.

merce, and manufactures should be equally favored, and that perhaps the only exception to this rule should consist in the peculiar encouragement of any products of either of them that may be found essential to our national independence." The promotion, so far as consistent with the Constitution, of "internal improvements and the diffusion of knowledge," was characterized as "of high importance." For those who had dreaded the election of a military hero as president, there was the assurance that no increase of the army would be sought, and that friendly relations with foreign nations would be cultivated. A "just and liberal policy" towards the Indians was also promised.

The declaration regarding the civil service, on the other hand, was well calculated to "make half the office-holders in the country quake in their slippers." [1] "The recent demonstration of public sentiment inscribes on the list of executive duties, in characters too legible to be overlooked, the task of *reform*, which will require particularly the correction of those abuses that have brought the patronage of the federal government into conflict with the freedom of elections, and the counteraction of those causes which have disturbed the rightful course of appointment and have placed or continued power in unfaithful or incompetent hands." The phraseology was cumbrous, but the meaning was soon made clear.

[1] Parton, *Jackson*, III., 172.

Rarely have the chief questions which were to engage the attention of an administration been more accurately foreshadowed. Benton calls the inaugural "a general chart of democratic principles." [1] That it "straddled" two of the most important issues was inevitable, in view of the fact that Jackson, who was on record as having favored both protection and internal improvements, was now the leader of a party bound eventually to oppose both those policies. The absence of any allusion to the Bank of the United States would seem to indicate that Jackson had not yet come to regard that institution as a national menace.

The breach with Adams was complete. Jackson refused to call upon the retiring president, and the two were never reconciled. Adams, on his part, while "complaining not at all of the measure meted out to him," [2] confided to his diary his expressions of ill-humor and chagrin. With Calhoun the relations of Jackson continued friendly. The secret of the cabinet appointments was well kept. Webster wrote on January 17 that Jackson answered no letters, and that the membership of the cabinet was as well known in Boston as at Washington—that is, not at all. A month later he notes that "the typographical crowd" — Hill of New Hampshire, Kendall of Kentucky, and others—"is assembled in great force," and that Van Buren will probably be

---

[1] Benton, *Thirty Years' View*, I., 119.
[2] Webster, *Private Corresp.*, I., 467.

secretary of state; beyond that, "nothing is yet determined." As to the policy of the new administration, the public were equally in the dark, though Webster doubtless expressed the general opinion when he wrote that Jackson would "bring a breeze with him," but that no one could tell which way it would blow.[1]

The cabinet appointments were announced in the *Telegraph* February 26.[2] The leading portfolio, that of secretary of state, was given to Martin Van Buren. Van Buren had been in the Senate from 1821 to 1828, resigning to become governor of New York, which position he held only from January 1 to March 12, 1829. He had been the leading spirit in the Albany Regency, and, after the defeat of Crawford, one of the most prominent supporters of Jackson. A tour in the south in the spring of 1827 had done something to insure the adherence of Crawford to Jackson's standard. Van Buren's skill in manipulating politics had already earned him the sobriquet of "the little magician," while Adams found in him "much resemblance" to Burr. He did not take up the duties of his new office until April 4, the business of the department being conducted in the interim by James A. Hamilton, a son of Alexander Hamilton and a strong Jackson supporter.

Calhoun had written in January that he hoped

[1] Webster, *Private Corresp.*, I., 467, 470.
[2] Parton, *Jackson*, III., 174. Webster knew of the list February 23; *Letters* (Van Tyne's ed.), 141.

for "an able, sound man" at the head of the treasury department, as an important step in the direction of tariff revision. The new secretary, Samuel
D. Ingham, of Pennsylvania, had been a member
of the House of Representatives most of the time
since 1813. He was a friend of Calhoun, an active
disseminator of the "corrupt bargain" charge, and
a capable man of business. He was said to have
been urged by the entire Pennsylvania delegation
in Congress, after that state had failed to receive
the first place.[1] The secretary of war was John H.
Eaton, of Kentucky, a senator from that state since
1818, a warm personal friend of Jackson, and broth-
er-in-law of Lewis. There was particular opposition
to his name when the list was announced, and it was
reported that McLean would be substituted. John
Branch, the secretary of the navy, had been govern-
or of North Carolina, and twice senator. He was
a friend of Calhoun, and had voted against the confirmation of Clay as secretary of state. John M.
Berrien, of Georgia, the attorney-general, had been
in the Senate since 1824. It had been expected that
John McLean, postmaster - general, who had held
office since 1823, would continue under Jackson;
but he refused to approve the policy of a "clean
sweep" in his department, and was made an associate
justice of the supreme court, succeeding Judge

---

[1] Calhoun, *Corresp.* (Jameson's ed.), 270; Parton, *Jackson*,
III., 175. South Carolina would have preferred Cheves; Hayne
to Van Buren, February 14, 1829, *Van Buren MSS.*

Trimble, of Kentucky.[1] John Pope, of Kentucky, who had wanted to be attorney-general, was also an applicant for Trimble's place.[2] William T. Barry, of Kentucky, who had been "slated" for the justiceship, accepted the postmaster-general's place.

The Senate met in executive session immediately after the inauguration, and sat until March 17. On the 6th the executive nominations made during the previous session, and which had not been acted on, were withdrawn.[3] The members of the cabinet, all of whom were at the time, or had lately been, members of Congress, were confirmed. With the exception of Van Buren, the cabinet was a weak one, and its members had not been accustomed to working together. Jackson, on the other hand, declared it to be "one of the strongest, as I believe, that ever has been in the United States."[4] A ruling principle in selection was opposition to Clay. Branch, Berrien, Eaton, Ingham, and Barry were avowed anti-Clay men. Calhoun, who was expected to stand high in the executive councils, was understood to be represented by Ingham, Branch, and Berrien, though neither of these was his first choice. As regards geographical representation, the north and the south had each two members, and Kentucky

[1] Webster, *Letters* (Van Tyne's ed.), 142; Louis McLane to Van Buren, February 19, 1829, *Van Buren MSS.*
[2] Pope to Jackson, February 19, 1829, *Jackson MSS.*
[3] Richardson, *Messages and Papers*, II., 439.
[4] Letter of April 26, 1829, *Jackson MSS.*

two, while New England, the central west, and the lower south had none.[1]

Jackson's theory of the proper relation between the president and his cabinet will be referred to more than once in the course of this narrative, and particularly in the discussion of the removal of the deposits. It has been charged that, in choosing his cabinet, Jackson had no intention of surrounding himself with a body of constitutional advisers, whose views he would be under special obligation to consult. There is reason for thinking that this was not originally his conception of the cabinet. An undated "Memorandum of points to be considered in the administration of the government," in Jackson's handwriting, contains as its second head: "A genuine old-fashioned cabinet to act together and form a councel consultative."[2]

If, however, this were really Jackson's opinion, he shortly surrendered it. In actual practice, a cabinet officer was to him not a member of "a councel consultative," but rather a chief clerk, a statutory head of an executive department, charged by law with the performance of certain duties, and removable at any time by the president, but not an official on whom the president was bound to lean. This view had been upheld as "the original theory of the

---

[1] Webster, *Letters* (Van Tyne's ed.), 145; Sumner, *Jackson* (rev. ed.), 183; Von Holst, *Calhoun* (rev. ed.), 65; Fish, *Civil Service*, 108.

[2] *Jackson MSS.* Filed with papers of October, 1828.

law." [1] Whether this was still the proper view or not, Jackson from the beginning acted upon it. The practice of holding cabinet meetings was shortly discontinued, and a small group of political friends became, so far as the nature of Jackson himself would admit, the real advisers of the president and directors of his policy.

The principal members of this "kitchen cabinet" were William B. Lewis, Amos Kendall, Duff Green, and Isaac Hill. Lewis, whose skilful devotion to Jackson's cause has already been noted, wished to return to his plantation in Tennessee after the inauguration, but was persuaded to remain, and was made second auditor of the treasury, preferring this office to that of fourth auditor because it demanded less work. [2] Amos Kendall, a native of Massachusetts, lately editor of a Jackson newspaper in Frankfort, Kentucky, and a bitter enemy of Clay, was a man of remarkable administrative ability and unusual literary power. Able, adroit, silent, untiring, he became before long the dominant personality in this unofficial group, and the man who, probably more than any other, influenced Jackson's thoughts and acts, both bad and good. He was made fourth auditor of the treasury, retaining the position until 1835, when he became postmaster - general. Duff Green was the editor of the *United States Telegraph*, the leading Jackson organ. Though an ardent par-

[1] Sumner, *Jackson* (rev. ed.), 181.
[2] Kendall, *Autobiography*, 308.

tisan of Jackson, he was also a Calhoun man. He had obtained, before the inauguration, a share of the public printing, and before long was prosperous.[1] Isaac Hill, of New Hampshire, editor of the *New Hampshire Patriot*, had championed Jackson's cause with untiring zeal, though he failed by nearly four thousand votes to carry New Hampshire for Jackson in 1828. Like Green, he favored the removal from office of all who had opposed Jackson. He was appointed second comptroller of the treasury, but was rejected by the Senate, and was out of office until 1831, when, with the help of the administration, he was elected senator from New Hampshire.[2]

Besides these four, Jackson relied much upon his nephew and private secretary, Andrew J. Donelson. Inasmuch as Jackson's wife died in December, 1828, Mrs. Donelson presided over the White House. Jackson also consulted James Watson Webb, editor of the New York *Courier and Inquirer*, who was intimate with both Van Buren and Calhoun, and remained attached to the latter, notwithstanding the breach with Jackson; and General Call, delegate from Florida territory, and earlier a military aide. No member of the official cabinet except Eaton seems to have belonged to this secret, intriguing group; but Van Buren did not oppose it, and Barry was subservient to it.[3]

---

[1] Parton, *Jackson*, III., 181.
[2] A result foreseen by Webster, *Letters* (Van Tyne's ed.), 153.
[3] Sumner, *Jackson* (rev. ed.), 187.

The existence of the "kitchen cabinet," and the power which it came to exercise, were rendered possible less by the political conditions of the time than by certain prominent characteristics of Jackson himself. Notwithstanding violent prejudice, narrow outlook, and ill-controlled temper, Jackson was easily influenced by the opinion of those about him. "I am not a candidate for the presidency by my own volition, but by the selection of the people," wrote Jackson.[1] It was his firm conviction that he had a mandate from the people to reform the government and destroy abuses; but no one ever listened more carefully than he to the distant rumblings of public opinion, or foresaw more surely what the masses were likely to think. It was largely through the "kitchen cabinet," and particularly through Amos Kendall, that Jackson formed and directed and expressed popular thought, and organized the support which not only gave him a second term as president and sustained his vigorous treatment of nullification and the bank, but made him also that most dangerous influence in a democracy—a popular idol. Jackson's political opinions show, on the whole, less growth during his eight years of office than might have been expected; it is the people, and not the president, whose beliefs are formulated and developed; and the great task of interpreting the voters to themselves was the lot of the president's confidential advisers. To say that the phrase

[1] To R. M. Johnson, September, 1828, *Jackson MSS.*

"popular government" took on in the process a new meaning is only to say that the "kitchen cabinet" did its work with consummate success.

Jackson's inaugural laid special emphasis on the necessity of reform in the federal civil service. The right of the president to remove officials from office at his own discretion, without the consent of the Senate, had been settled in 1789, in connection with the establishment of a department of foreign affairs;[1] but the power thus conceded as constitutional had not yet been exercised in a spirit of offensive partisanship. Under Jefferson, indeed, the civil service had been reorganized, half of those who were in office in 1801 being out of office in 1805;[2] but few of the changes were for political reasons. So far as any theory of the matter had developed, it was that while new appointments were properly to be made chiefly from the members of the administration party, incumbents, especially of minor offices, were not to be removed merely on political grounds. Changes had been facilitated by the passage of the act of 1820,[3] limiting the terms of district attorneys, collectors of customs, receivers of public moneys for lands, and various other officers, to four years; but the act, intended in part, at least, to insure the accountability of financial officials, had not been followed by any serious change of personnel.

---

[1] Debate summarized in Salmon, *Appointing Power*, 16–23.

[2] Fish, *Civil Service*, 42.

[3] *United States Stats. at Large*, III., 582.

Of the six bills reported to the Senate by Benton, in 1826, one was to prohibit the appointment of members of Congress to office.[1] A report was submitted showing that since the inauguration of the government, 117 members of Congress had been appointed to office either during their term or within six months thereafter. Of the 117, 90—31 from the Senate and 59 from the House—had been in the department of state, 63 of these under Jefferson, Madison, and Monroe. Jackson, in his letter to the legislature of Tennessee resigning the senatorship, indorsed a proposition similar to Benton's, but with the period of ineligibility extended to two years after the end of the congressional term. He excepted judicial offices on the ground that changes were infrequent, and that "no barrier should be interposed in selecting for the bench men of the first talents and integrity."[2] Even before this, Jackson was on record as opposed to partisan appointments. In November, 1816, writing to President Monroe on behalf of William H. Drayton, whom he was urging strongly for secretary of war to succeed Crawford, he had said: "In every selection party and party feeling should be avoided. Now is the time to exterminate the *monster* called party spirit. By selecting characters most conspicuous for their probity, virtue, capacity, and firmness, without any regard to party, you will

---

[1] Benton, *Thirty Years' View*, I., 83.
[2] Parton, *Jackson*, III., 96.

go far to, if not entirely, eradicate those feelings which, on former occasions, threw so many obstacles in the way of government. . . . The chief magistrate of a great and powerful nation should never indulge in party feelings." [1]

Although Jackson was the acknowledged leader of a new régime, and a bitter enemy of Clay and Adams, and although the political methods of Van Buren and others were well known, there seems to have been no general expectation in official circles, prior to March 4, 1829, that radical changes were in contemplation. The "memorandum of points," already quoted, embraced "a high-minded, enlightened principle in the administration as to appointments and removals." Webster wrote in January that "great efforts are making to put him (Jackson) up to a general sweep, as to all offices; springing from great doubt whether he is disposed to go it." On March 2 he notes the general impression that no great number of changes will be made.[2] Thirty-eight nominations made by Adams were left without action by the Senate, in order that the choice might be made by Jackson.[3] The fact that Jackson was supposed not to contemplate a second term, and that office-holders at Washington and elsewhere were among his strongest supporters, may have strengthened official confidence. There was, how-

---

[1] Parton, *Jackson*, II., 361.
[2] Webster, *Private Corresp.*, I., 467, 472.
[3] Salmon, *Appointing Power*, 54.

ever, a feeling of uncertainty, strengthened, no
doubt, by the demands of Jackson's supporters for
the punishment of their opponents, and by newspaper predictions of extensive changes impending.[1]

Upon the adjournment of the Senate, March 17,
1829, a general proscription began. Writers have
vied with one another in depicting the terror that
prevailed, especially in Washington. Age, length
of service, satisfactory performance of duties, or
financial dependence were no protection. Men who
had grown old in the government service were dismissed at a moment's notice, and without recourse.
Clerks whose living depended on their official salaries,
and who had been rendered unfit, by reason of long
employment in a bureau, for other occupations
equally remunerative, were beggared. As a consequence, debts could not be collected or rents
paid. It was reported in July that thirty-three
houses which were to have been built in Washington during the year had been stopped because of
the wide-spread uncertainty and demoralization,
and that there were many cases of individual distress.[2]

What added to the excitement was the fact that
in most cases no reason for a removal was given,
save that some one else wanted the place. The
third item in Jackson's "memorandum of points"—
"no solicitors to be appointed"—was apparently
forgotten. Men who were in office one hour were

[1] Fish, *Civil Service*, 105.   [2] Parton, *Jackson*, III., 214.

out of it the next, yet without knowing why they were dismissed. Nor was the fitness of the candidate always considered; the chief test was loyalty to Jackson. All the executive departments were affected, as well as the post-offices, custom-houses, and other agencies throughout the country; and as the removal of the head of an office frequently carried with it numerous changes among subordinates, the "reform" became far-reaching.

Kendall, who received his commission as fourth auditor of the treasury March 21, wrote to a friend three days later that "the interest of the country" demanded that his office should be "filled with men of business, and not with babbling politicians. Partisan feelings shall not enter here, if I can keep them out. To others belong the whole business of electioneering." [1] No one, however, went at the business of removal more thoroughly than he; indeed, if Kendall did not himself suggest the policy of Jackson, he certainly showed himself to be in hearty sympathy with it, and an adept in carrying it out. A circular of instructions which he shortly drew up declared that "clerks in this office hold their offices at the will of the Auditor and the Secretary of the Treasury. Independent of that they will have no right to their places. When that will decides on their removal, their rights cease." That he had some compunctions at the distress which the removals occasioned, would appear from a letter of

[1] Parton, *Jackson*, III., 182.

June 1 to his wife, in which he says: "I turned out six clerks on Saturday. Several of them have families, and are poor. It was the most painful thing I ever did; but I could not well get along without it. Among them is a poor old man with a young wife and several children. I shall help to raise a contribution to get him back to Ohio, where he came from, and intend to give him fifty dollars myself." [1]

In the post-office department there were 491 removals of postmasters and deputies, besides subordinates. [2] The largest number, 131, was in New York; then came New Hampshire — Isaac Hill's bailiwick — with 55, Ohio with 51, Pennsylvania with 35, Massachusetts with 28. In few cases had there been complaints of the service. The custom-houses at Portsmouth, Boston, New York, Philadelphia, and New Orleans were purged. Swartwout, who had been one of Jackson's trusted political correspondents, and who was now appointed collector at New York — though Van Buren wrote that the appointment was made against his "decided and earnest remonstrance" [3] — was "a chronic beggar for office," [4] and later a defaulter. Calhoun, however, was "gratified" at the confirmation, and felt "confident that he will not

---

[1] Kendall, *Autobiography*, 292, 317.
[2] *Niles' Register*, XXXVIII., 105.
[3] Van Buren to Cambreleng, April 23, 1829, *Van Buren MSS*.
[4] Salmon, *Appointing Power*, 57.

disappoint the expectations of his friends." [1]   It
was estimated that a thousand removals had been
made before the meeting of Congress in December,
and twice that number by the end of Jackson's first
year.   Most of the important offices were included
in the list.

There was not, however, a "clean sweep." [2]   Kendall, in his review of the condition of the government
during the first three years of Jackson's term, states
that only one-seventh of the officials at Washington,
one-sixteenth in the post-office department, and
one-eleventh in the country at large were replaced
during that period.   Benton, who regarded the removals as "indispensable," in view of the small
number of resignations, declares that judicial officers,
save one judge, were not disturbed; that only four
out of seventeen foreign representatives were recalled during the first year, and that in the departments at Washington a majority of the employés
remained opposed to Jackson throughout his administration. [3]   Certain it is, however, that there
were loud complaints of the number and the circumstances of removals, particularly of postmasters; that
the public service deteriorated, and that business men
and others who had to deal with federal agencies
were embarrassed and annoyed.   There was par-

---

[1] Calhoun, *Corresp.* (Jameson's ed.), 272.

[2] On the number of removals, *Debates of Congress*, VI., 392.

[3] Kendall, *Autobiography*, 301; Benton, *Thirty Years' View*,
I., 160.

ticular complaint of the appointment of Jackson
editors, fifty-five of whom received offices during
the first two years, many of them continuing their
editorial duties while holding office.[1]

In his first annual message, December, 1829,
Jackson urged the propriety of excluding members
of Congress "from all appointments in the gift of
the President in whose election they may have been
officially concerned." Judicial, diplomatic, and cabinet officers were excepted. The excepted officers
were obviously the ones of most importance, yet
Jackson himself had negatived his own recommendation in advance by appointing, within three
months of his inauguration, two collectors, an ap-
praiser, and a district attorney from members of
Congress. His appointments of this class in one
year were more numerous than those of any of his
predecessors in a term.[2] The message further recommended a general extension of the law which
limited certain classes of appointments to four years.
The reasons advanced in support of such a step were
as ridiculous as they were specious. Long continuance in office, Jackson declared, inevitably be-
gets indifference to the public interests, and opens
the way for incompetency and corruption. "The
duties of all public officers are, or at least admit of
being made, so plain and simple that men of in-

---

[1] Salmon, *Appointing Power*, 59.
[2] Young, *American Statesman*, 480; Sumner, *Jackson* (rev.
ed.), 191; *Debates of Congress*, VI., 242.

telligence may readily qualify themselves for their performance." Moreover, as no one has any more intrinsic right than another to an office, "no individual wrong" is done by removal, "although individual distress may be sometimes produced." "He who is removed has the same means of obtaining a living that are enjoyed by the millions who never held office." [1]

Two months elapsed before all the nominations made during the recess were sent in, and the subject was before the Senate for two months more. Frequent requests for a statement of the reasons for particular removals were made, and were availed of as occasions for debate. Webster doubted whether the Constitution vested in the president the power of removal without the consent of the Senate, holding it to be "only incident to the power of appointment." He asked Chancellor Kent for an opinion, and the great jurist, who had heard the question debated in 1789, was inclined to agree with Hamilton, in the *Federalist*,[2] that the consent of the Senate was needed. "The power to appoint and reappoint, when all else is silent, is the power to remove." At the same time, he regarded the action of the first Congress and the acquiescence of half a century as closing the constitutional question.[3]

[1] Richardson, *Messages and Papers*, II., 448.
[2] *Federalist*, No. 77.
[3] Webster, *Private Corresp.*, I., 483, 486, 487.

Against the expediency of such wholesale removals, with the resulting demoralization of the
public business, there was better ground for argument. Many of the nominations were eventually
rejected by the Senate. A few very objectionable
ones were withdrawn.[1] Webster wrote that the debate, of course in secret session, was "sometimes
pretty warm," and refers to "the importunities of
friends and the dragooning of party." "Were it
not for the fear of the out-door popularity of General Jackson," he adds, "the Senate would have
negatived more than half his nominations."[2] Kendall's nomination was confirmed only by the casting
vote of the vice-president, perhaps from fear lest
Kendall, if rejected, might establish a paper in opposition to the *Telegraph*.[3]

To just what extent Jackson's policy changed the
personnel of the civil service cannot be stated with
precision. If the statements of Kendall and Benton
be accepted—and there is no reason to doubt their
approximate correctness—only a minority of office-
holders were directly affected.[4] All the evidence
seems to show that it was the manner as much as
the number of removals that impressed public opinion, and that after the first year the excitement
largely subsided. We do not hear much of the

[1] See, *e.g.*, Richardson, *Messages and Papers*, II., 474, 477.

[2] Webster, *Private Corresp.*, I., 501.

[3] Sumner, *Jackson* (rev. ed.), 191, quoting an ambiguous
passage from Kendall, *Autobiography*, 371.

[4] Fish, *Civil Service*, 125-127.

subject after 1830, partly, perhaps, because those who remained in office had been terrorized, and partly because there were few more important offices to fill. There was occasional discussion of the constitutional issue in Congress, and in 1835 a bill, introduced by Calhoun, providing for a repeal of the act of 1820, and for the submission of the reasons for removals to the Senate, passed the Senate by aid of the combined opposition; but the House took no action.

The substantial victory, therefore, lay with Jackson. There is no evidence that he ever regretted the course he had pursued. Frequent reference in his letters to the corrupt use of executive patronage by Adams suggests probably the main reason why Jackson thought such wholesale reform necessary. He seems to have convinced himself, also, that there was dishonesty in the public service. He wrote to Van Buren that the late removals of comptrollers and auditors had been made in the interest of honesty, adding, characteristically: "The people expect reform—they shall not be disappointed; but it must be *judiciously* done, and upon principle."[1]   In September, 1829, he wrote again to Van Buren that there were no complaints against General Cass, governor of Michigan territory, and no intention of removing him, "unless, in the settlement of his accounts, he should prove a defaulter, and you know

[1] Undated memorandum in reply to letter of March 31, 1829, *Jackson MSS.*

the rule is, friend or foe, being a defaulter, must go."[1]

Jackson certainly never abated his claim to the possession of absolute power of removal. A resolution of the Senate, February 3, 1831, declared it inexpedient to appoint citizens of one state to offices in another "without some evident necessity." In March, 1833, Jackson informed the Senate that he should make no further attempt to fill certain offices in Mississippi, because of the rejection of previous nominations under this rule.[2] In a special message of February 10, 1835, he refused to lay before the Senate charges against Gideon Fitz, removed from the office of surveyor-general south of the state of Tennessee, declaring that the repetition of such requests imposed upon him, "as the representative and trustee of the American people, the painful but imperious duty of resisting to the utmost any further encroachment on the rights of the executive."[3]

Jackson was not in any sense the originator of the spoils system, but the responsibility of transplanting it from the states to the broader and more fertile field of national politics must rest with him and his advisers. The growth of an office-seeking class dates from his time. There is nothing to show that the mass of the people, whose will Jackson al-

[1] *Van Buren MSS.*
[2] Richardson, *Messages and Papers,* II., 636.
[3] *Ibid.*, III., 133.

ways claimed to interpret inerrantly, viewed the
new departure with anything but approbation. The
reign of the old statesmanship was ended, and the
people were coming into their own.

CHAPTER V

TARIFF AND NULLIFICATION

(1816–1829)

THE tariff of 1816, while not, as has sometimes
been said, the first protective tariff, nevertheless marks the point at which customs duties for
revenue, with incidental protection, begin to give
place to customs duties laid primarily to afford
protection to domestic manufactures. This demand
for protection, growing by that which it fed upon,
led to a general revision of the tariff in 1824, and to
further protection to wool, cotton, hemp, linens,
iron, and other articles. The debate on the bill
showed a significant change of sentiment in eight
years, while the vote in the House indicated a wide
sectional divergence and the predominance of local
interests over alleged national ones. But the duties
of 1824 failed to give either satisfaction or industrial peace, particularly to the woollen interests.
To meet the demand for further protection, Mallary,
of Vermont, introduced in the House, January 10,
1827, the "woolens bill," which left the existing duty
of thirty-three and one-third per cent. ad valorem
undisturbed, but proposed extraordinary changes in

the so-called "minimum" principle of valuation.[1]
It was at once objected that the low-priced fabrics
could not be imported, and that the revenue would
decline. The bill passed the House, but was laid
on the table in the Senate by the casting vote of
the vice-president, Calhoun, who lost favor in New
York and Pennsylvania in consequence.[2]

The defeat of the Mallary bill was the signal for a
general agitation in favor of higher duties, in which
political and economic interests were inseparably
mixed. The resulting tariff act of 1828 was accompanied in its passage by one of the most unprincipled
intrigues of which Congress has ever been the forum.
The tariff was likely to have far-reaching effects on
the presidential campaign already in progress. So
far as the three leading candidates—Adams, Clay, and
Jackson—were concerned, there was little to choose,
since all were on record as favoring protection. The
Jackson leaders, however, who were appealing to
protectionist Pennsylvania on the one hand and the
free-trade south on the other, were anxious that
the question should be left open and no bill passed.
It was accordingly planned to report a bill imposing
such high duties on iron, wool, hemp, etc., as particularly to threaten New England manufacturers,
and thus compel New England, it was supposed, to
join with the south, now openly opposed to pro-

[1] *Debates of Congress*, III., 732.
[2] Sumner, *Jackson* (rev. ed.), 239. **On Van Buren's vote,**
Debates of Congress, III., 388, 496.

tection of any sort, and so defeat the bill. The Adams-Clay combination would thus be discredited, while Jackson would be left free to deal with the tariff as he saw fit.

Both the expected and the unexpected happened. The bill as reported by the House Committee on Manufactures provided for duties so high as to bear heavily on many established industries in New England and Pennsylvania, and gave the greatest dissatisfaction to the woollen interests; but the strong protection sentiment in the north and west was sufficient to carry the bill through. New England was still divided, 23 of its 39 votes in the House being given against the bill; but Webster, in the Senate, yielding to the changing sentiment of his section, spoke and voted for it, although the Massachusetts members in the House were almost a unit in opposition. The middle states gave 57 votes in favor of the bill to 11 against it, and the west 17 in favor to 1 against. The total vote in the House was 105 to 94; in the Senate, 26 to 21.[1]

It has been customary to say that the vote on the tariff of 1828, like that on the tariff of 1824, was sectional rather than partisan, and sheds no special light on national public opinion. It must be remembered, however, that from 1820 to 1830 party lines were loosely drawn and party doctrines but vaguely formulated. The factions and personal

[1] See table in Dewey, *Financial History of the United States*, 180.

followings which together formed the so-called
"Jackson men" were not yet welded into a party,
while their opponents, who shared with them the
common name of Republicans, had even less co-
hesion. Four years of tariff agitation had not
brought order into the political field, or erected
standards around which both leaders and followers
could gather. There can be little question, on the
other hand, that, aside from the personal enthusiasm
for Jackson and the democratic spirit which he
represented, the issue of protection *versus* free-trade
was more influential than any other in determining
the new political alignments and shaping the new
political opinions.

There was obvious reason why this should be the
case. Protection, as it presented itself in the United
States after 1816, involved the two great questions
which have been at the bottom of all fundamental
party division in our history—namely, the question
of economic or social expediency and the question
of constitutionality. Whether or not a protective
tariff was a good thing for the United States was to
be made clear, on the whole, by statistical inquiry
extending over a period of some years. Under our
system of government, however, not all intrinsically
good things are capable of adoption by the federal
government, but only those which are permitted
by the Constitution. It was inevitable, therefore,
that the question of the constitutionality of protection should come to be looked upon as the main

question at issue, the test by which the system must stand or fall; and while the argument from expediency was elaborately developed, particularly in the discussion of the tariff of 1828, it was on the point of constitutionality that the decision ultimately turned.

In 1816 the tariff had been considered, on the whole, from a national point of view, and in the light of an economic situation too exigent, apparently, to admit of wide difference of opinion. The flooding of the American market with English manufactured goods, offered at a price which defied successful competition, seemed to threaten the very existence of American manufactures, and to render impossible the development of domestic industry. A provision of duties which would enable American manufactures to establish themselves would, it was urged, not only bring about in a few years a desirable competition between home and foreign producers, but would also enlarge the market for American products and increase the demand for labor; while the benefits of protection, though accruing in the first instance to the manufacturers, would ultimately be diffused throughout the country, and benefit capitalists, laborers, farmers, and merchants alike. In other words, the protective policy was urged as expedient because its fruits were national; and what was for the good of all could hardly be opposed to the spirit of the Constitution, even though not directly sanctioned by its letter.

The twelve years from 1816 to 1828 saw a marked change of opinion regarding the tariff. Industries which had been encouraged by the act of 1816 demanded, first, a continuance of protection, and then an increase of it. Capital which had been invested in foreign trade was gradually transferred to manufactures. New England became a manufacturing section. Ohio insisted upon protection for wool, Kentucky for hemp, Pennsylvania for iron. Webster, though opposing with unanswerable argument in his earlier career the protection policy, yielded to the changing opinion of New England; and, when the tariff of 1828 was brought forward, he supported it publicly, though writing privately that "it will be a poor and inefficient aid to wool and woolens," and would, in his opinion, "positively injure the manufacturer." [1]

Of most significance, however, was the attitude of the south. In 1816, when Calhoun and William Lowndes [2] were zealously advocating protection, it was not clear but that the south might hope to obtain from the tariff incidental advantages, in increased demand for its raw products, more than sufficient to offset the enhanced prices of manufactured goods. But before long public opinion changed. As a predominantly agricultural region in which the production of staples, particularly cotton, tobacco, and rice, by slave labor was the

[1] Webster, *Letters* (Van Tyne's ed.), 136.
[2] Ravenel, *Lowndes*, 154.

basis of the entire economic life, the south had no
share in the industrial development which was
taking place in the north. Though rich in natural
resources, it not only had no manufactures, but it
insisted that with slave labor — the continuance of
which was assumed to be necessary—it could not
have manufactures. The south realized, therefore,
that it was paying higher prices for many of the
things it was compelled to buy, at the same time
that the market for its staples had not been materially widened or the prices of its raw products
materially raised. The assumption that the south
could not develop manufactures, like the assumption
that slave labor was essential to its prosperity, was
unfounded; but that the south, under the operation
of the tariffs of 1824 and 1828, had a serious grievance cannot be questioned.

With protection firmly intrenched in the manufacturing states, and with the west and southwest
demanding and receiving protection for wool and
hemp, the prospect of a return to lower duties grew
dim. The main hope of relief for the south appeared
to lie in attacking the constitutionality of the tariff.
The constitutional argument against the tariff, as
set forth in the numerous resolutions and protests
of southern legislatures, was largely drawn from
Jefferson's opinion, in 1791, against the constitutionality of a national bank,[1] and the Kentucky and
Virginia resolutions of 1798–1799, while that in favor

[1] Jefferson, *Works* (ed. of 1854), VII., 555–561.

of protection owed its substance to Hamilton's opinion in favor of the constitutionality of a bank,[1] and the development of Hamilton's doctrine in the decisions of Chief-Justice Marshall. While the fuller discussion of the constitutional doctrine thus formulated belongs to a later chapter of this work, the substance of the opposing arguments may properly be outlined here.

Since the power to levy protective duties is nowhere expressly granted to Congress by the Constitution, the authority for them must be found, if anywhere, in reasonable implication from the grant of some other power. The clause most relied upon by the advocates of protection was that which gives to Congress the power to "lay and collect taxes, duties, imposts, and excises, to pay the debts and provide for the common defence and general welfare of the United States." [2] It was insisted that, under this grant of power, Congress was given entire freedom in the imposition of taxes and other burdens, so long as the purpose of such exactions was either the payment of the public debt or the promotion of the public safety and general welfare; and that since a protective system was a provision for the general welfare, and the proceeds of the duties were applied to public objects, protective tariff duties were constitutional. As to the degree of protection, that was a matter for the discretion

[1] Hamilton, *Works* (ed. of 1851), IV., 104–138.
[2] Constitution, art. I., § 8, par. 1.

of Congress. The constitutional question must always be, not whether a power may be exercised in this way or that, but whether the power is granted at all.

Besides the power to impose taxes and duties, Congress has also the power to regulate commerce with foreign nations.[1] As the grant of power in this case is without restriction, it must be held that no limitation was intended; and in the case of the embargo and non-intercourse acts of 1807 and 1809, the power had in fact been exercised to the utmost extent—that, namely, of prohibiting commerce altogether.[2] A protective tariff, under which commerce would be given new directions, and stimulated at one point while restrained at another, might certainly be regarded as a regulation of commerce, and as such within the purview of the Constitution, even though the particular method or degree of regulation were not named in that instrument.

The objection to this argument took the form partly of dissent from the interpretation of the Constitution, and partly of denial of the alleged facts. It was denied that the power to regulate commerce implied an unrestrained choice of means, or that the "general welfare" clause was to be so construed as to give to Congress the right of levying taxes and imposts for any purpose it might choose; for that

---

[1] Constitution, art. I, § 8, par. 3.
[2] Cooley, *Const. Law* (3d ed.), 70.

would make "its discretion, and not the Constitution, the measure of its powers." [1] The only objects, it was urged, for which money could constitutionally be raised by federal taxation were the payment of the debt, the provision of public safety, and the general welfare of the community. And it was denied that a protective tariff operated for the general welfare. It was pointed out that the operation of such a system was necessarily unequal, that it favored certain industries at the expense of others, and that it was not, and from the nature of the case could not be, uniform in weight or effect upon different parts of the country. What protection meant, in practice, was the taxation of agricultural states for the benefit of manufacturing states, of particular industries and classes for the benefit of others; so that, instead of conducing to the general welfare, it was, in fact and necessarily, partial, discriminating, and unjust. To uphold such a policy as a legitimate regulation of commerce, or as taxation for the general welfare, was to adopt an interpretation contrary to the whole spirit and intent of the Constitution and in conflict with the obvious purpose of its framers. Favoritism for a few could never work the good of the many.

The argument thus briefly outlined was, of course, only the old contention of "loose construction" versus "strict construction" applied to a protective

---

[1] Ky. Resolutions (1798), in MacDonald, Select Documents, ⸸49.

tariff. That controversy was as old as the Constitution, and the battle had been waged, with varying degrees of energy and bitterness, over most of the important propositions that had come before Congress since 1789. The conditions of the question, however, had undergone a change almost revolutionary in character. The advocates of strict construction in 1828 felt, though not all of them clearly perceived, that their opponents had shifted their ground; and that instead of seeking the authority for federal action in the words of the Constitution, or in reasonable implication therefrom, "loose construction" had come to mean the right of the federal government to do whatever was not forbidden by the Constitution, provided the act was deemed to be for the general good. If such a theory of constitutional construction were to prevail, and the original notion of the Constitution as a grant of powers, under which everything not granted was withheld, were to be replaced by the theory that everything not withheld was granted, the federal government would be admittedly supreme, and "the reserved rights of the States" would speedily become only a form of words.

To what extent the arguments pro and con represented the reasoned conviction of those who used them cannot, naturally, be determined with much accuracy. No more then than now were the mass of the voters trained constitutional lawyers or unbiassed judges. The generation which preceded the

Civil War was, however, especially in the south, pre-eminently interested in certain great problems of constitutional law and political speculation, and discussed with avidity, and with sincere appreciation of their seriousness, issues which, like this of protection, involved the nature, stability, and peace of the Union. To regard the discussion on either side as academic is to miss entirely the significance of one of the great episodes in American history. There was felt to be too much at stake to waste time in mere banter of words.

The position of Calhoun in this discussion is peculiarly important, not only because of the great personal influence which he exerted, but also because of the vigor and boldness with which South Carolina stood out against what it believed to be constitutional error of a most dangerous sort. As a member of the House of Representatives, Calhoun had occupied broad national ground. He had favored the embargo as a preparation for war, supported protection as a matter of "vital importance," advocated internal improvements, and reported a bill to incorporate a bank. In a speech on the "bonus bill," February 4, 1817, he had declared that he saw no reason why the expenditure of federal money should be restricted to the execution of the enumerated powers. "I am no advocate for refined arguments on the Constitution. . . . If the framers had intended to limit the use of the money to the powers afterward enumerated and defined, nothing could have been more easy than to have expressed it plainly." [1]

During the years from 1817 to 1829, when Calhoun was secretary of war and vice-president, his public utterances on political questions of the day were few, and the course of his opinions cannot be clearly traced. A letter of July 3, 1824, to Robert S. Garnett, a representative from Virginia, shows him to have been still a nationalist. He is silent about the tariff, but still believes in the bank and internal improvements, and defends himself against the charge of inconsistency.[2] A year later, at a public dinner, he reaffirmed his early position on the tariff, and deprecated sectionalism as "against the spirit of the Constitution." [3] Here, however, he began to waver. It was his casting vote as vice-president that defeated the Mallary "woolens bill." In August, 1827, he wrote that the power of encouraging domestic manufactures "is highly dangerous, and may be perverted to purposes most unjust and oppressive." "What perhaps is a great defect in our system" is "that the separate geographical interests are not sufficiently guarded." [4]

It seems evident that it was the discussion over the "woolens bill" of 1827 that first shook Calhoun's confidence in the constitutional soundness

---

[1] On Calhoun's successive views, Von Holst, *Calhoun* (rev. ed.), 21; Calhoun, *Works*, II., 104–110, 153–173, 186–196.

[2] Houston, *Nullification in South Carolina*, 143–148.

[3] *Ibid.*, 63.   [4] Calhoun, *Corresp.* (Jameson's ed.), 250.

of his position, and that the enactment of the
"tariff of abominations" in 1828 completed the
change. What Calhoun at this time dreaded more
than anything else was sectional divergence, and
the fact that protection inevitably bred such divergence led him to repudiate it. In the procession
of events, Calhoun's change of opinion followed,
rather than preceded, a corresponding change in
public opinion in his state.[1] If he later led South
Carolina, it was because at an earlier day South
Carolina had led him. That he distrusted the
ability, possibly the disposition, of Jackson, appealing as the latter was to protection in the north and
anti-tariff sentiment in the south, to stem the tide,
and that he was chagrined at his failure to obtain
the presidency in 1828 is probable; but neither of
these influences appears materially to have affected
his views. It annoyed him, too, that his opponents
could truthfully charge him with inconsistency, but
it may be admitted that at both periods of his life
he was sincere.

Calhoun's change of attitude is rendered the more
striking by the fact that the political surroundings
of his public life, down at least to 1824, had been
opposed to particularism. On all the great questions which, down to 1817, had divided Federalists
from Republicans, he had taken the national side.
South Carolina was a Federalist state. So far as
Calhoun's published writings and speeches go, the

[1] Houston, *Nullification in South Carolina*, 60.

acute and fine-drawn theories of government and constitutional law whose pronouncement caused him to be regarded by the south as a profound political thinker, were of comparatively late development, and were not matured until his policy of high protection had been rejected by South Carolina, and he found himself at variance with his constituency in matters of political faith.

The south, meantime, had not failed to protest, internal improvements and the tariff being frequently joined in the indictment. Governor Wilson of South Carolina, in his message of December, 1824, called the attention of the legislature to "the alarming extent to which the federal judiciary and Congress have gone toward establishing a great and consolidated government, subversive of the rights of the States and contravening the letter and spirit of the Constitution of the Union." The state Senate promptly voted both internal improvements and the tariff unconstitutional; but the House refused to concur, declaring "that the People have conferred no power upon their State Legislature to impugn the Acts of the Federal Government or the decisions of the Supreme Court of the United States." A year later the House, by a vote of 73 to 38, affirmed "the inalienable right" of remonstrance against federal encroachments, and declared that "to lay duties to protect domestic manufactures" was "an unconstitutional exercise of

power." [1] Protection and internal improvements
were now for the first time formally condemned by
a state legislature.

In March, 1826, the general assembly of Virginia
reaffirmed the resolutions of 1798, in which the
federal government was held to be the result of
a compact to which the states are parties, and
declared a protective tariff unconstitutional and
"highly oppressive and partial in its operation."
Resolutions of March, 1827, solemnly protested
against the tariff as "unconstitutional, unwise, unjust, unequal, and oppressive." A protectionist
convention at Harrisburg aroused great excitement,
especially in South Carolina. The legislature of the
latter state, December 19, 1827, denounced the
tariff laws as "violations of the Constitution in its
spirit," and directed the senators and representatives of the state in Congress "to continue to oppose every increase of the tariff, *with a view to protect domestic manufactures.*" Five days later the
legislature of Georgia adopted a report declaring
that "an increase of Tariff duties will and ought to
be RESISTED by all legal and constitutional
means." In January, 1828, the legislature of North
Carolina, while not denying the right of Congress to
lay protective duties, submitted that the exercise
of such a power, in the way contemplated by the
"woolens bill," was "a direct violation" of the

[1] South Carolina votes in Ames, *State Documents on Federal
Relations*, III., 5–8.

spirit of the Constitution. The legislature of Alabama denounced the Harrisburg convention, declared protective duties "a palpable usurpation of
a power not given by the Constitution," and branded
the "woolens bill" "as a species of oppression little
less than legalized pillage." [1]

There remained, however, a further question.
Even assuming the course of the federal government
to be unconstitutional, what was to be done in case
the protest of the states went unheeded? Was
there any constitutional method of preventing further obnoxious tariff legislation by Congress, or of
arresting the operation of a federal statute? A protest that cannot be translated into terms of active
resistance is usually, in practice, of little weight.
The federal government, if unrestrained, might coerce a state; had a state any weapon with which
to coerce the federal government?

The "tariff of abominations" became law May
28, 1828. The passage of the act was followed in
South Carolina by renewed activity on the part of
its opponents. Public opinion was divided as to
the proper course to pursue, and the wide-spread
discussion of the matter in public meetings throughout the state had not brought unanimity. Conservative leaders like William Smith, Joel R. Poinsett, Governor Taylor, and Hugh S. Legaré were
for moderation, and were "outspoken in their

[1] Texts of these state resolutions in Ames, *State Documents on
Federal Relations*, III., 11–19.

determination to oppose any project tending directly or indirectly to weaken the bonds of union." [1] On the other hand, men like Langdon Cheves, George McDuffie, William Harper, and A. P. Butler were for resistance; and behind resistance lurked disunion. A popular demand arose for an early meeting of the legislature, but to this Governor Taylor refused to accede. There was anxiety, too, about the attitude of Jackson and the effect of the agitation on the approaching election. September 3, 1828, Senator Robert Y. Hayne wrote to Jackson that, while he believed nineteen-twentieths of the people of South Carolina were convinced that protection would eventually destroy the south, and even the Union itself, and while they regretted that their views and those of Jackson on the question were not in harmony, the state would, nevertheless, give Jackson cordial support; that there was no desire to dissolve the Union, and that the tariff excitement had nothing to do with the presidential election.[2]

The legislature met in November. December 19 a set of eight resolutions was adopted, protesting against the tariff as unconstitutional, as an abuse of power, and as a menace to the economic life of the state.[3] Accompanying the resolutions was an elaborate report, originally draughted by Calhoun,

[1] Houston, *Nullification in South Carolina*, 68.
[2] *Jackson MSS*.
[3] MacDonald, *Select Documents*, 231–234.

and known as the "South Carolina Exposition," [1] a
vigorous arraignment of the tariff on economic and
constitutional grounds. The constitutional argument follows the general lines of the doctrine laid
down in the Virginia and Kentucky resolutions of
1798–1799: that the federal government is formed
by compact between sovereign states; that the activity of the federal government is limited to the
powers delegated by the Constitution; that it has
not the right of judging conclusively of the extent
of its own powers; but that the states, as parties
to the compact, have equally the right of determining whether the Constitution has been observed or
violated, and of the proper mode of redress.

The chief interest of the "Exposition," however,
was in its declaration regarding the means by which
a state might protect itself against federal usurpation. That remedy was "interposition," and the
proper body to apply it was a convention. On this
point the "Exposition" says: "When convened, it
will belong to the Convention itself to determine,
authoritatively, whether the acts of which we com-
plain be unconstitutional; and, if so, whether they
constitute a violation so deliberate, palpable, and
dangerous, as to justify the interposition of the
State to protect its rights. If this question be decided in the affirmative, the Convention will then
determine in what manner they ought to be declared null and void within the limits of the State;

[1] Calhoun, *Works*, VI., 1–59.

which solemn declaration, based on her rights as a member of the Union, would be obligatory, not only on her own citizens, but on the General Government itself; and thus place the violated rights of the State under the shield of the Constitution." [1]

To avoid precipitancy, however, it was recommended that the legislature, after presenting its views "in this solemn manner," "allow time for further consideration and reflection," in hope that "a returning sense of justice on the part of the majority" may lead to a repeal of the obnoxious acts, and that the incoming of Jackson "may be followed up, under his influence, with a complete restoration of the pure principles of our Government." [2]

The "Exposition" is Calhoun's first formal statement of the doctrine of nullification. Both its strength and its originality have been much overrated. Stripped of its literary qualities—for the "Exposition" is very readable—the constitutional argument is elementary and not very skilfully worked out, and offers nothing which the Virginia and Kentucky resolutions had not already made familiar. The doctrine of "interposition" was Jefferson's, not Calhoun's, and is here phrased as hazily as when it was first announced. As compared with Hayne's speeches in the "great debate," or with Calhoun's own writings, in 1831, on the

[1] Calhoun, *Works*, VI., 45.   [2] *Ibid.*, VI., 55, 56.

same subject,[1] it is a slight performance. What
gave weight to the "Exposition," apparently, was
the fact that it was adopted as the formal expression
of opinion by the legislature, and that it came at a
time when the public mind was ready to receive it.

The "Exposition" was immediately printed and
widely circulated. It should be remembered that
Calhoun's connection with the document was not
known at the time, and that as late as 1830 his approval of nullification was denied.[2] Calhoun's position as vice-president and prospective candidate for
the presidency in 1832 may well have made him
shrink from publicity in the matter, but he was
not above fashioning in secret a weapon which his
friends could use against the government of which
he was a high official. Had Jackson known the
authorship of the "Exposition," he might well have
felt that his enemies were, indeed, those of his own
household.

The protest of South Carolina was followed by
similar action in Georgia, Mississippi, and Virginia.
The legislature of Georgia recommended the other
states to protest against the recent tariff as unconstitutional and injurious, and to adopt a policy of
"self-preservation" by relying as far as possible on
its own resources; while the House proposed a con-

---

[1] "Address on the Relations of the States and the Federal
Government"; "Report on Federal Relations"; "Address to
the People of South Carolina"; all in Calhoun, *Works*, VI., 59–
144.   [2] Houston, *Nullification in South Carolina*, 179.

vention of delegates from the southern states, "in event of the failure of the present Congress to repeal or modify" the tariff, to concert measures of resistance.[1] The general assembly of Mississippi, February 5, 1829, declared the tariff "contrary to the spirit of the Constitution," and impolitic and oppressive. The general assembly of Virginia reasserted the right of each state to construe the federal compact for itself, and declared its solemn conviction that the tariff laws "are not authorized by the plain construction, true intent and meaning of the Constitution."

The inaugural address of Jackson spoke with almost ludicrous indefiniteness regarding the tariff. The secretary of the treasury was a protected manufacturer from Pennsylvania. But the triumph of the democratic principles for which Jackson stood, and the overwhelming defeat of the "corrupt alliance" of Adams and Clay, inspired general hope that the policy of high protection would soon be radically modified. Until the meeting of Congress, accordingly, the agitation slumbered.

[1] The resolutions in Ames, *State Documents on Federal Relations*, III., 22-25.

CHAPTER VI

THE GREAT DEBATE ON THE CONSTITUTION
(1829–1830)

THE first session of the twenty-first Congress met on Monday, December 7, 1829. The roll of members contained many distinguished names. Among the senators were John Holmes, of Maine; Levi Woodbury, of New Hampshire, later secretary of the navy; Daniel Webster, of Massachusetts; Horatio Seymour, of Vermont; Theodore Frelinghuysen and Mahlon Dickerson, of New Jersey; John M. Clayton, of Delaware; John Tyler, of Virginia; William Smith and Robert Y. Hayne, of South Carolina; John Forsyth, of Georgia, later secretary of state; Hugh L. White and Felix Grundy, of Tennessee; Edward Livingston, of Louisiana, later secretary of state; John McLane, of Illinois; William R. King, of Alabama; and Thomas H. Benton, of Missouri.

Prominent among the three hundred and thirteen members of the House of Representatives were Edward Everett, of Massachusetts; C. C. Cambreleng and Gulian C. Verplanck, of New York; James Buchanan, of Pennsylvania; William S. Archer,

John S. Barbour, and Andrew Stevenson, of Virginia; William Drayton and George McDuffie, of South Carolina; R. M. Johnson, of Kentucky; John Bell and James K. Polk, of Tennessee; James Findlay, of Ohio; W. H. Overton, of Louisiana; and C. C. Clay, of Alabama. Andrew Stevenson was reelected speaker.

Jackson's first annual message [1] congratulated Congress on the continuance of peace at home and abroad, and on "the most cheering evidence of general welfare and progressive improvement." Chief among matters of domestic concern requiring attention was the method of electing the president and vice-president. The principles to be followed in the matter of appointments and removals were briefly stated, and the operations of the several executive departments passed in review. The debt was to be paid; the large amounts due the government by individuals to be collected; federal support for the Indians in Georgia and Alabama, in their controversy with those states, to be withdrawn; the United States circuit courts to be extended throughout the country; and naval construction to be stopped. Two brief paragraphs at the close of the message called attention to the expiration in 1836 of the charter of the Bank of the United States, and to the desirability of replacing the existing bank by a national one "founded upon the credit of the government and its revenues."

[1] Richardson, *Messages and Papers*, II., 442–462.

On the engrossing subject of the tariff, the message was vague, and its specific recommendations
unimportant. While the operation of the tariff, it
was stated, had not been as injurious to agriculture
and commerce, or as beneficial to manufactures, as
had been anticipated, the continuance of undiminished importations of foreign goods, joined to increased domestic consumption, had produced "low
prices, temporary embarrassment, and partial loss."
In the opinion of the president, some of the provisions of the tariff required modification; but beyond urging that revision be undertaken in a broad,
national spirit, and with regard to the paramount
interests of agriculture, the message offered no specific suggestion save that of a "gradual and certain" reduction of the duties on tea and coffee. A
revision of the customs administrative laws was,
however, recommended, especially with a view to reducing the long credit for duties on goods imported
from beyond the Cape of Good Hope. On the other
hand, the indefinite continuance of a high tariff was
virtually foreshadowed in the statement that, "after
the extinction of the public debt, it is not probable
that any adjustment of the tariff, upon principles
satisfactory to the People of the Union, will, until
a remote period, if ever, leave the Government without a considerable surplus in the treasury." The
"most safe, just, and federal disposition" of the
surplus would be "its apportionment among the
several States according to their ratio of representa-

tion," the authority for such distribution to be sought, if necessary, in an amendment to the Constitution.

The expressions regarding the tariff were obviously capable of any interpretation that any individual or section chose to put upon them, save that they did not indicate pronounced antagonism to the protective system. If Jackson had at this time any positive opinion on the tariff question, or any appreciation of the depth of feeling on the subject in the south, the fact does not appear from the generalizations of his first annual message.

December 29, Senator Samuel A. Foot, of Connecticut, offered the following resolution:

"*Resolved*, That the Committee on Public Lands be instructed to inquire into the expediency of limiting for a certain period the sales of the public lands to such lands only as have heretofore been offered for sale, and are subject to entry at the minimum price. And also, whether the office of Surveyor General may not be abolished without detriment to the public interest." [1]

As explained by Foot, the reasons for offering the resolution were to be found in certain statements in recent reports of the commissioner of the land office, to the effect that the quantity of land which remained unsold, at the minimum price of $1.25 per acre, exceeded seventy-two million acres; while the annual demand for land was estimated at about one

[1] *Debates of Congress*, VI., 3, 4.

million acres, subject to increase with the progress
of population and improvement. The distribution
of the sales, however, seemed to be very unequal:
for example, in one district of Ohio, where not more
than three or four hundred thousand acres, and
those inferior, were for sale, the cash sales amounted
to thirty-five thousand dollars, while in other places,
where immense quantities of superior land were
available, the sales, during 1828, amounted to only
two thousand dollars. Inasmuch as the lands were
the common property of the United States, and
every state was deeply interested in the disposition
made of them, he thought it legitimate to inquire
whether the indiscriminate sale of the public lands
should not be stopped for a time, or perhaps confined to the lands already on the market.[1]

The resolution was immediately attacked by Benton as an indication of hostility to the west, and of
a desire on the part of the east to check immigration; and he insisted on ample time for the discussion
of the whole subject. The debate began on January 13, and at once became general. Benton made
an elaborate speech,[2] in which the attitude of the
east towards the west was exhibited in a hostile
light, and the "copious and bitter draughts" which
the new states "have had to swallow" treated with
bitter invective. Not only the prosperity, but also
the political security, of the west, Benton declared,
depended upon the speedy and unimpeded settle-

[1] *Debates of Congress*, VI., 4.   [2] *Ibid.*, VI., 22–27.

ment of the country; and the east, which as yet held control in Congress, had no right to force upon the west a change of system which would check immigration by withdrawing the lands from the market.

Hayne, of South Carolina, followed, January 19, 1830, with a speech [1] in which he skilfully invoked the doctrine of strict construction and state rights. Interference with the free development of the west, either by limiting the land sales or by materially altering the conditions of sale, would add immensely to the power of the federal government, and strengthen that tendency to "consolidation" than which he believed there was "no evil more to be deprecated." He declared himself "opposed, in any shape, to all unnecessary extension of the powers or the influence of the Legislature or Executive of the Union over the States, or the people of the States"; and, most of all, "to those partial distributions of favors, whether by legislation or appropriation, which has [*sic*] a direct and powerful tendency to spread corruption through the land; to create an abject spirit of dependence; to sow the seeds of dissolution; to produce jealousy among the different portions of the Union, and finally to sap the very foundations of the Government itself." Further, interference with land sales, by checking the growth of the agricultural states, would contribute to the upbuilding of manufactures, and thus perpetuate the system of protection; and the people of the

[1] *Debates of Congress*, VI., 31-35.

United States were, and for a century ought to remain, "essentially an agricultural people."

Hayne's speech marked a turning-point in the
debate. Foot's resolution, indeed, remained before
the Senate, and was nominally the theme of discussion; but thenceforward it was the opposing interests
of the different sections of the Union, and not the
public-land system, that were debated. A modification of the resolution, adding to it a clause in-
structing the committee on public lands "to inquire
and report the quantity of the public lands remaining unsold within each State and Territory," and
raising the alternative question "whether it be expedient to adopt measures to hasten the sales, and
extend more rapidly the surveys," [1] did not change
the character of the discussion.

January 20, Webster first took part in the debate.
His theme was the defence of the east, particularly
New England and Massachusetts, against the charge
of hostility to the west and desire to hinder its
growth. In a brilliant and impressive speech [2] he
showed the groundlessness of Hayne's aspersions,
pointed to the influence of New England in securing
the adoption of the ordinance of 1787, and declared
that "from the day of the cession of the territories
by the States to Congress, no portion of the country
has acted either with more liberality or more intelligence, on the subject of the western lands in the
new States, than New England." What was consoli-

[1] *Debates of Congress*, VI., 35.   [2] *Ibid.*, VI., 35-41.

dation—"that perpetual cry both of terror and de-
lusion"—but the strengthening of the Union? He
regretted the disposition of some in the south to
"habitually speak of the Union in terms of indifference, or even of disparagement"; and while he trusted that Hayne was not one of those, he deprecated
ideas which tended to bring the Union into discussion "as a mere question of present and temporary
expediency."

Hayne replied at once in a speech [1] occupying
parts of January 21 and 25. "He would not deny,"
he said, "that some things had fallen from that
gentleman which rankled here (touching his breast),
from which he would desire, at once, to relieve himself. The gentleman had discharged his fire in the
face of the Senate. He hoped he would now afford
him an opportunity of returning the shot." Webster, who had business elsewhere, and had not expected to attend on that day, at once replied: "I
am ready to receive it. Let the discussion proceed."

In his speech, the so-called "Hayne's first reply,"
the South Carolinian, while disclaiming unfriendli-
ness to New England or its people, or any disposition
to attack them, denounced the conduct of the New
England Federalists, dwelt on their repeated opposition to the government, and held up to reproba-
tion and scorn the pretensions of the National Republicans. What was the "tariff of abominations"

[1] *Debates of Congress*, VI., 41–58.

but an illustration of the "consolidation" which
Webster had upheld? The people of New England
stood with the people of the south and west in the
great struggle for popular rights; but the maintenance of popular rights was to be found in a federal,
not a national, union, in a government whose powers
were confined strictly within the limits of the Constitution. Webster had ridiculed the notion that
a state had any recourse in case of "a gross, palpable, and deliberate violation of the Constitution"
by the federal government; and had added that, if
it might intervene by an exercise of its sovereign
authority, then the Union was "a mere rope of
sand." To the authority of Webster, Hayne would
oppose, without further argument of his own, the
"South Carolina Exposition" and the Virginia and
Kentucky resolutions. The South Carolina doctrine
was, he insisted, the historical republican doctrine,
"first promulgated by the fathers of the faith,"
"maintained by Virginia and Kentucky in the worst
of times," and embracing the very principles the
triumph of which, in 1798–1801, "saved the Constitution at its last gasp." South Carolina "has kept
steadily in view the preservation of the Union," but
the principle on which she acts is that of "resistance
to unauthorized taxation."

In citing the "Exposition" and the resolutions of
1798–1799, Hayne had taken his stand in favor of
nullification, but he had refrained from elaborat-
ing his own views on the subject. His speech **was**

Webster's opportunity. The "reply to Hayne"[1] which followed is justly regarded as the greatest piece of forensic eloquence which this country has produced; but it is its argument rather than its rhetoric which have given it permanent significance. What Webster sought was to force from Hayne or his supporters a full, frank, clear-cut statement of what nullification meant; and then, by opposing to this doctrine the Constitution as he understood it, to show its utter inadequacy and fallaciousness either as constitutional law or as a practical working scheme. No one was so well fitted for the task as Webster. He was the foremost New England states-man, the ablest American constitutional lawyer, and incomparably the greatest American orator that the country had yet produced; and he now, with little direct preparation,[2] summoned all his magnificent powers to expound, once for all, the nature of the Union he loved. Never, he wrote, had he spoken to an audience "so excited, so eager, and so sympathetic" as that which filled the Senate chamber on January 26 and 27, 1830.

An extended introduction, in which he once more defended New England and himself against the keen thrusts and irritating strictures of Hayne, ending with a splendid eulogy of Massachusetts, brought him to the main question. The doctrine cham-pioned by Hayne affirmed the constitutional right

[1] *Debates of Congress*, VI., 58-80.
[2] Webster, *Private Corresp.*, I., 488.

of a state government to interfere, whenever the
federal government transcended its constitutional
limits, and to arrest the operation of the federal
laws; since "the ultimate power of judging of the
constitutional extent of its own authority is not
lodged exclusively in the general government, or
any branch of it"; but, on the contrary, "the States
may lawfully decide for themselves, and each State
for itself, whether, in a given case, the act of the
General Government transcends its power."

To such a doctrine Webster opposed a flat denial.
Doubtless, he said, there is in every people a right
of revolution, beyond and higher than the Constitution; but "between submission to the laws, when
regularly pronounced constitutional, on the one
hand, and open resistance, which is revolution or
rebellion, on the other," there is no middle course.
On what ground, then, is such a doctrine upheld?
The error lies in a total misconception of the nature
of the federal government. According to Hayne,
the federal government is not only the creature of
the states, but of each of the states severally, "so
that each may assert the power, for itself, of determining whether it acts within the limits of its
authority. It is the servant of four and twenty
masters, of different wills and different purposes,
and yet bound to obey all." But the general government and the Constitution are the people's government and Constitution, "made for the people,
made by the people, and answerable to the people."

The states are unquestionably sovereign "so far as their sovereignty is not affected by this supreme law"; but the state legislatures are not sovereign over the people. On the contrary, the people, in framing the Constitution, chose to impose certain restrictions on state sovereignty; and whatever the wisdom of such restraints, they exist, and are binding upon every state.

To apply the South Carolina doctrine Webster held to be impossible. "In Carolina, the tariff is a palpable, deliberate usurpation; Carolina, therefore, may nullify it, and refuse to pay the duties. In Pennsylvania, it is both clearly constitutional and highly expedient; and there the duties are to be paid. . . . Does not this approach absurdity?" New England, in the days of its bitterest opposition to the embargo, never for a moment thought of adopting such a course as South Carolina now soberly recommends; and the embargo, Webster insisted, was a greater grievance even than the tariff.

Further, the people have not only established the federal government, but they have also provided, in the Constitution itself, "a proper, suitable mode and tribunal for settling questions of constitutional law." The Constitution declares that "the Constitution, and the laws of the United States which shall be made in pursuance thereof . . . , shall be the supreme law of the land; and the judges in every State shall be bound thereby, anything in the constitution or laws of any State to the contrary not-

withstanding." The judicial power of the United
States is, further, declared to extend to all cases in
law and equity arising under the Constitution and
laws of the United States. To give effect to these
provisions, a system of federal courts has been established, with a right of appeal on all questions of
constitutional power to the supreme court. With
the decisions of the courts the Constitution gives
the states no right to interfere. Should the Constitution, or the interpretation of it, be unacceptable
to the people, they may amend the Constitution at
their pleasure; but the only result of such attempt
at amendment as the South Carolina doctrine con-
templates must be "direct collision . . . between
force and force," which is treason. "It is rather
an awkward business," Webster remarked, grimly,
"this dying without touching the ground. After
all, that is a sort of hemp tax worse than any part
of the tariff."

The splendid peroration—incomparably the grand-
est flight of American eloquence — was argument,
too. Webster had attacked Hayne's position as
unconstitutional, incapable of practical application,
and revolutionary. He now stung his adversary
to the quick by exposing the covert trend to disunion. For himself, at least, there should be "no
cool weighing of the chances of preserving liberty, when the bonds that unite us together shall be
broken asunder"; no accustomed hanging over "the
precipice of disunion" in the effort "to fathom the

depths of the abyss below"; no reliance upon coun-
sellors "whose thoughts should be bent on consider-
ing, not how the Union should be best preserved,
but how tolerable might be the condition of the
people when it shall be broken up and destroyed."
That for which he lived should be "liberty *and*
union, now and forever, one and inseparable"; and
it was that motto that he could wish last to look
upon when he came to die.

Webster had accomplished his purpose. Hayne,
in his second reply, January 27,[1] furnished the
explicit statements which Webster had aimed to
draw out. The basis of his argument—far superior,
in arrangement and force, to that which he had
previously offered—is the assertion that, prior to
the adoption of the Constitution, each state "was
an independent sovereignty, possessing all the rights
and powers appertaining to independent nations";
and that after the Constitution was formed the
states remained "equally sovereign and independent as to all powers not expressly delegated to the
Federal Government." The Union, therefore, is a
compact between sovereign states; and since there
is no common superior, each party to the compact
is the rightful judge of violations of its provisions.
The claim that the Constitution gives to the federal
government the right of judging conclusively of the
extent of its authority was emphatically denied.
Questions of sovereignty "are not the proper sub-

[1] *Debates of Congress*, VI., 82–92.

jects of judicial investigation," and in any case are
not within the constitutional jurisdiction of the
supreme court.

The right of interposition, accordingly, is "as
full and complete as it was before the Constitution
was formed." The exercise of the right does not,
as Webster had contended, necessarily involve war,
since the central government is bound to respect the
decision of the "creating power"—namely, three-
fourths of the states. The burden of securing an
amendment of the Constitution, however, ought not
to be devolved upon a state, if for no other reason
than the small likelihood of obtaining a two-thirds
vote of Congress or a three-fourths vote of the states
against a proposition to which Congress was strongly
committed. It was, rather, the duty of the federal
government "to acquiesce in the solemn decision of
a State," to the extent of appealing to the people
for an amendment to the Constitution, and of refraining, in the mean time, from coercion. Interposition, in short, was a peaceful remedy as well as
a constitutional one.

Webster, in his "second reply to Hayne," [1] made
short work of Hayne's constitutional argument. If
the federal government is the result of a compact
between states, it cannot be also one of the parties
to the compact, as Hayne had implied. But even
conceding that the federal government is the result of a compact, one of the powers, nevertheless,

[1] *Debates of Congress*, VI., 92.

given to it by that compact is that of interpreting finally the Constitution. In the provision that the Constitution and the laws of Congress shall be the supreme law of the land, and that the judicial power of the United States shall extend to every case arising under that supreme law, the federal government is given, in express terms, the right of final judgment on its own acts. And even were the right of interpretation reserved to the states, it would still be necessary that they agree as to the manner of exercising it. One state alone could not construe or alter either Constitution or law.

But the Constitution is not a compact. The instrument itself declares that it was ordained and established by the people of the United States. Hayne had objected that "the people of the United States" meant no more than the people of the several states, taken collectively. The reply was that "it is in this their collective capacity, it is as all the people of the United States, that they establish the Constitution." Hayne's contention applied to the Articles of Confederation, which was a compact between states; "he speaks as if he were in Congress before 1789." But the government established by the Constitution, expressly designed to correct the defects of the Confederation, is "a popular government, founded in popular election, directly responsible to the people themselves." When the people become dissatisfied with the distribution of powers, they can alter it; "but until they shall alter it, it must stand as their will, and is equally binding on the General Government and on the States."

With the speeches of Webster and Hayne the "great debate" reached its climax. Foot's resolution remained before the Senate, indeed, for nearly four months, and most of the members spoke upon it; but although the discussion took a wide range, no one contributed anything further to the controversy in which alone the Senate and the country were interested. May 21 the resolution was laid upon the table.[1]

It will be convenient to consider at this point, once for all, the merits of the constitutional argument which this debate over nullification called forth. In resting his contention, as he did, upon the theory that the federal government was the result of a compact between the states, Hayne undoubtedly believed that he was stating, not only the true historical theory of the Constitution, but the sound legal and constitutional theory as well. He was, indeed, curiously illogical in making the federal government a party to the compact. Calhoun, in his "Address on the relations which the States and General Government bear to each other," dated July, 1831, expressly rejected this as an "error," and made a much better statement of the case when he asserted that the federal government "partook, in its nature and object, of the character of a joint commission, appointed to superintend

[1] *Senate Journal*, 21 Cong., 1 Sess., 316.

and administer the interests in which all are jointly concerned." [1]

It would be difficult to maintain that the compact theory was not at least as much an original theory of the Constitution as any other. While the Constitution unquestionably provided for "a more perfect union" than that of the Confederation, there is no evidence that any large proportion of those who debated the matter in 1787-1788 looked upon the new union, so far as the theory of a compact between the states was concerned, as radically different from the old. To have thought otherwise would have been unnatural. The Constitution was not yet in operation. Constitutional law there was none. The particular course of national development could not be predicted. What was sought was a practical working scheme, a remedy for obvious ills, and not theoretical perfection. If it were true that nearly every provision of the Constitution rested upon some precedent in the practice of the states,[2] it was also true that nearly every important provision was the result of compromise.

In the debates on the Constitution in the state conventions, a common objection was, indeed, the "consolidated government" which it was feared the new scheme would bring about; but the con-

[1] Calhoun, *Works*, VI., 59-94.
[2] Robinson, *Original and Derived Features of the Constitution* (Am. Acad. of Polit. and Social Science, *Annals*, I., 203-243); Stevens, *Sources of the Constitution*.

solidation referred to was that which would subordinate the states, or even reduce them to mere
administrative subdivisions, and not that transfer
of certain governmental powers from the states to
the nation which was involved in any federal organization.[1] And it was this fear of state subor-
dination that the friends of the Constitution sought
particularly to allay. Hamilton wrote in an early
number of the *Federalist:* "The proposed Constitution, so far from implying an abolition of the State
Governments, makes them constituent parts of the
National Sovereignty, by allowing them a direct
representation in the Senate, and leaves in their
possession certain exclusive and very important
portions of Sovereign power. This fully corre-
sponds, in every national import of the terms, with
the idea of a Federal Government." [2] Had it been
generally understood that the federal government,
once established, would be beyond the control of
the states save by the prescribed process of amendment to the Constitution, or that the federal judiciary
was to be the final interpreter of the Constitution in
all cases whatsoever, it may well be doubted whether
the "new roof" would have been accepted at all.

It was the development of the doctrine of "implied powers" that showed the direction in which
the federal government was tending. This doctrine, formulated in all essential particulars by

[1] Cf. the debates in New York; Elliott, *Debates* (ed. of 1896),
II., 205–414.   [2] *Federalist* (Dawson's ed.), No. 9, p. 54.

Hamilton in his opinion on the constitutionality of a national bank,[1] elaborated by Webster in his great constitutional arguments before the supreme court, and stated with consummate clearness by Marshall in a long series of decisions, had given the federal authority a scope far beyond anything that could have been dreamed of by those who saw the national government inaugurated. "Implied powers" had chartered a national bank, enacted the alien and sedition laws, decreed an embargo, voted money for internal improvements, and established a protective tariff. If progress were to continue in this direction, the authority of the nation would soon be everywhere supreme, and the "sovereignty of the States" would become, ere long, only a memory and a name.

It was against this trend towards nationalism that the nullification doctrine protested. Hayne invoked the ancient theory of the Constitution, as he conceived it: a union of sovereign states, creating a federal government of delegated powers, and answerable to the states for its conduct within the limitations imposed upon it. From such a theory the right of protest by a state, and of refusal to obey an obnoxious statute if the protest went unheeded, followed naturally.

To the theory of nullification, as thus propounded, Webster opposed the theory of "the people." The doctrine of "the people," formulated by Marshall

[1] Hamilton, *Works* (Hamilton's ed.), IV., 104–138.

in his opinion in McCulloch *vs.* Maryland,[1] in 1819,
and his most distinctive contribution to the theory
of American constitutional law, was given classical
expression by Webster in the "great debate." Yet
no theory could have had a slighter historical foundation. From the beginning of the ratification of
the Constitution to the end, there never was a
moment when "the people of the whole United
States" acted in "their collective capacity," or in
any other manner than as "the people of the several States." "The ratification of the conventions
of nine States shall be sufficient for the establishment of this Constitution between the States so
ratifying the same," is the declaration of the Constitution. If anything is clear beyond peradvent-
ure in the history of the United States, it is that
the Constitution was established by the states, acting through conventions authorized by the legislatures thereof, and not by "the people of the United
States" in any such sense as Webster gives to that
phrase. In so far as the Constitution was ratified
by popular conventions instead of by the state
legislatures it is, in truth, "the people's Constitution," and not the creation of the state governments; but outside the geographical limits of the
several states and the directions and conditions
imposed by state constitutions and laws, the people
of the United States have never yet had a voice in
the establishment of their fundamental law. For

[1] 4 Wheaton, 316–437.

the purpose of opposing Hayne's theory of the right
of state interposition, Webster voiced a theory not
only at variance with the facts, but so contrived also
as to miss the only vulnerable point of his opponent's position.   It was a glorious fiction, and it has
entered into the warp and woof of our constitutional
creed; but it was fiction, nevertheless.

For what was the essential fallacy of nullification?
It was the failure to recognize the inevitable supremacy of the central government, the inevitable sub-
ordination of the states in all matters over which
the central authority had control, wherever such
ascendency was not directly restrained by the letter of the Constitution.   Whatever the original
theory, whatever the apparent implication of the
Constitution, the claim by a state of a right to refuse obedience to a federal law could not, in practice, be conceded.   By whatever name it was called,
whether nullification, interposition, or any other,
such refusal was rebellion; and to admit the constitutional right of rebellion is to admit the right
of the states to destroy the Union.   Self-preservation and the nature of things, accordingly, if nothing else, will lead the central government to resort
to force to uphold its authority.   The remedy for
alleged usurpation, as Webster pointed out, is either
the political reconstruction of the governing body
by means of elections, or the reconstruction of the
Constitution by amendment.   Failing in these, a
state has no alternative but submission.

In other words, Hayne argued for a theory which, however once widely held, had been outgrown, and which could not under any circumstances be made to work in practice. Webster argued for a theory which, though unhistorical in the form in which he presented it, nevertheless gave the federal government ground on which to stand. The one pleaded for the states, the other for the nation. One looked to the past, the other to the present and future. One spoke as he who would bring back the ship of state to its former moorings; the other as a lawyer who, however great the actual change of conditions, would somehow make past and present seem to hang together. Both were statesmen, both loved their country; but Hayne would call a halt, while Webster would march on.

Finally, it is to be observed that the economic arguments of Hayne were, for the most part, passed over by Webster. The "abominations" of the tariff of 1828, the discrimination against the agricultural interests of the south, and the favoritism and sectionalism of the protective system as a whole, constituted a grievance of the utmost seriousness. Here, at least, Hayne was strong. The constitutional arguments of Webster prevailed, while those of Hayne were torn to shreds; but the economic indictment of the federal government remained the unshaken foundation of nullification, and the justification of the yet more startling protest of 1832.

CHAPTER VII

THE BANK OF THE UNITED STATES

(1823–1832)

THE first annual message of Jackson foreshadowed also another great controversy in which
the administration was to engage — that with
the Bank of the United States. In two brief paragraphs at the end of the message, Jackson called
the attention of Congress to the fact that the charter of the bank would expire in 1836, and that,
as the bank would undoubtedly apply for a renewal
of its charter, the matter could not too early receive
the attention of Congress. "Both the constitutionality and the expediency of the law creating this
bank are well questioned by a large portion of our
fellow-citizens; and it must be admitted by all, that
it has failed in the great end of establishing a uniform and sound currency." If such an institution
were thought essential to the fiscal operations of the
government, it was submitted "whether a national one, founded upon the credit of the government
and its revenues, might not be devised, which
would avoid all constitutional difficulties, and, at
the same time, secure all the advantages to the

government and country that were expected to result from the present Bank."[1]

The administration of the second bank of the United States, chartered by an act of April 10, 1816, was not at first successful, partly because of the difficult economic conditions which prevailed after the war, but principally on account of the bad management of the officers of the institution. Popular opposition, too, was great, many states seeking to check by taxation the operations of the bank; and only the action of the supreme court, which in the cases of McCulloch *vs.* Maryland and Osborn *et al. vs.* The Bank of the United States maintained the constitutionality of the bank, saved the institution from being "taxed out of existence in all of the southern and western States."[2] Under the presidency of Langdon Cheves, 1819–1823, the bank recovered; but the policy of Cheves, though successful as far as conservative management of the business was concerned, increased rather than allayed popular antagonism in the south and west.[3]

Nicholas Biddle, who succeeded Cheves as president of the bank in January, 1823, continued the conservative policy of his predecessor. He devoted himself to collecting the balances due from the state banks, providing better means of controlling the

---

[1] Richardson, *Messages and Papers*, II., 462.
[2] Catterall, *Second Bank*, 65.
[3] See Babcock, *American Nationality* (*Am. Nation*, XIII.), chap. xiii.

branches, increasing discounts by issuance of bank-notes, and accumulating a surplus. The financial crisis of 1825 was successfully weathered, notwithstanding the redemption of seven million dollars of the national debt in October of that year. Dealings in foreign exchange became of importance in 1826.[1]

There was great difficulty in issuing notes in sufficient quantities to supply the demand, since by law only the president and cashier of the bank could sign the notes. A system of branch drafts was accordingly devised, the first issue being made in June, 1827. The drafts were for five, ten, or twenty dollars each, "signed by the branch presidents and cashiers, drawn on the principal cashier at Philadelphia, and payable to some officer of the branch, or his order. This officer then endorsed the drafts 'payable to bearer,' with the effect of transforming them into a circulating medium." [2] The circulation of the drafts was facilitated by their close resemblance in appearance to bank-notes, and they were received by the secretary of the treasury in payment of taxes and other dues the same as notes. The legality of the branch drafts, though subsequently questioned, was affirmed by a circuit court of the United States in 1831.[3]

The attempt of the general assembly of Maryland, in 1818, to impose a tax on the branch of the Bank

---

[1] Catterall, *Second Bank*, 106–108, 111.   [2] *Ibid.*, 119.
[3] United States *vs.* Benjamin Shellmire, 1 Baldwin, 370; cited in Catterall, *Second Bank*, 121, *n.* 1.

of the United States at Baltimore had already called
forth one of Chief-Justice Marshall's greatest decisions, that of McCulloch *vs.* Maryland.[1] The
affirmation of the constitutionality of the bank did
not, however, prevent further attempts by the
states to interfere with the institution, and a number of cases growing out of these attempts came
before the supreme court. As late as the January
term, 1829, the court, in the case of Weston *et al. vs.*
The City Council of Charleston,[2] held void a city
ordinance imposing a tax on the United States six
and seven per cent. stock held by the bank.

The bank was not always blameless, however.
For example, the branch bank at Lexington, Kentucky, discounted a note at six per cent., paying the
holder of the note, however, in Bank of Kentucky
notes at par, although the market value of the notes
was but fifty-four per cent. of their face value. In
the case of Bank of the United States *vs.* Owens *et
al.*,[3] January, 1829, the supreme court held the
contract void as usurious, the bank being limited
by its charter to interest not exceeding six per cent.
On the other hand, legal refinement was carried a
long way in Bank of the Commonwealth of Kentucky
vs. Wister *et al.*,[4] decided at the same term, where
the state, although the sole owner of the stock of

---

[1] 4 Wheaton, 316–437.
[2] 2 Peters, 449–480.　　　　　　　　[3] *Ibid.*, 527–542.
[4] *Ibid.*, 318–326. See also United States Bank *vs.* The Planters'
Bank of Georgia, 9 Wheaton, 904.

the bank, was held not to be a party to the suit, "the president and directors" alone constituting the body corporate.

Notwithstanding wide-spread and persistent local opposition, however, the bank became, under Biddle's management, a prosperous and powerful institution. Its dividends, from 1816 to 1831, averaged five per cent. The average yearly circulation increased from $4,487,000 in 1823 to $13,102,000 in 1829. The currency had never been so good as in the year when Jackson declared that the efforts of the bank in this direction had been a failure. Of the $14,700,000 cash in the bank, November 1, 1829, nearly half was specie. The holdings of stock were largest, naturally, in the tide-water states. Of the 350,000 shares, 20,853 were held, in 1828, in New England, 46,638 in New York, 70,763 in Pennsylvania, 34,262 in Maryland, 35,495 in South Carolina, and 19,815 in the remaining southern states, while but 1804 were held in Ohio, Indiana, Illinois, Kentucky, and Tennessee. The foreign holdings aggregated 40,412 shares.[1]

Yet however unexpected Jackson's attack on the bank may have been to the institution itself or to its friends, it could hardly have been either unexpected or unwelcome to the general public in the west, the southwest, and the south. The very success of the bank had aroused antagonism. In

[1] Sumner, *Jackson* (rev. ed.), 268; Dewey, *Financial Hist. of the U. S.*, 154, 156; Catterall, *Second Bank*, 508.

New England and the Middle States, where the bank as yet issued but little circulation, and where the notes of the state banks were generally well secured, the interference with the business of the local banks was not great. In the south and west, on the other hand, where the demand for local banking facilities was large and safeguards against excessive note issues and unsafe loans less rigorous, the methods of the Bank of the United States brought the institution constantly into collision with local interests, and bred jealousy and ill-will. Associate-Justice William Johnson, in a dissenting opinion in Osborn *et al. vs.* The Bank of the United States, admitted that "a state of things has now grown up, in some of the States, which renders all the protection necessary that the general government can give to this bank." [1]

Statistics of state banking for this period are defective, but a comparison of the condition of three hundred and twenty-nine state banks, November 1, 1829, with that of the Bank of the United States is suggestive. The state banks, with a combined capital of $110,100,000, had, in round numbers, $48,200,000 of notes in circulation, $40,700,000 of deposits, $137,000,000 of loans, and $14,900,000 of specie. The Bank of the United States, with a capital of $35,000,000, held $7,100,000 of specie, and had $13,000,000 of notes in circulation, $14,700,000 of deposits, and $40,600,000 of loans." [2]

---

[1] 9 Wheaton, 871.　　[2] Dewey, *Financial Hist. of the U.S.*, 154.

In view of the wide-spread popular feeling against
the bank in the south and west, and the repeated
attempts to tax or otherwise interfere with it notwithstanding the decisions of the supreme court,
Jackson was undoubtedly well within the truth in
asserting that "both the constitutionality and the
expediency" of the act creating the bank were
widely doubted.[1] The authority of the supreme
court, however highly regarded by lawyers and
statesmen, sat lightly upon the people of the newer
states when local or personal interests and ambi-
tions were involved; and it was shortly to be made
clear that the court's authority carried no greater
weight with Jackson himself. Moreover, the bank
was a great financial monopoly, and the greatest
corporate power with which the people were familiar;
and democracy has ever been the relentless enemy of
monopolies, corporations, and the money power.
The destruction of the bank was a natural consequence of the democratic revolution which brought
Jackson to the presidency, rather than a sudden
and unwarranted assault upon an institution whose
propriety, constitutionality, and economic usefulness were generally admitted.

The beginning of political opposition to the bank
is undoubtedly to be placed as far back as the congressional session of 1827–1828, in the debate in the
House of Representatives on a motion to sell the
bank stock held by the United States. In Feb-

[1] Sumner, *Jackson* (rev. ed.), 283, disputes this view.

ruary, 1828, and again in December, Benton raised
the question of the sinking-fund, and of compensation for the use of the balances of public money in
the hand of the bank. Of more importance was
the circulation of charges, apparently to be ascribed
to Kendall, Hill, and Blair, that certain branch
banks, particularly those at Portsmouth, Charleston, Lexington, and New Orleans, had used their
influence to defeat Jackson.[1] November 16, 1828,
Jackson wrote to General Thomas Cadwalader, a
friend of Biddle, in response to an inquiry about
the branch at Nashville, that while he knew nothing
about the business of the bank, it would be well to
appoint directors who were better known.[2]

The immediate occasion, if any, of Jackson's opposition to the bank cannot be determined with
exactness. Biddle knew, in 1827, that Jackson had
opposed the repeal of the Tennessee law taxing
branches established in that state.[3] A reference in
the veto of the recharter bill, in September, 1833,
seems to confirm the statement of Polk, that Jackson had intended to animadvert on the bank in
his first inaugural, but was deterred by the advice
of friends.[4] The course of the branch bank at
Lexington, Kentucky, during the election, had led
Jackson to believe that the bank was using its loans
to defeat him. In October, 1829, Felix Grundy,

[1] *Debates of Congress*, IV., 815; Catterall, *Second Bank*, 164,
170, 171.   [2] *Jackson MSS*.
[3] Catterall, *Second Bank*, 183.   [4] *Debates of Congress*, X., 2263.

representative from Tennessee, submitted to Jackson a plan for a national bank, under which the capital of forty millions was to be divided among the states according to population, the state directors to be chosen by the representatives of the state in Congress.[1]

Jackson himself probably revealed his own attitude in the matter when he wrote to Biddle, in November, 1829, that he did not think that Congress had the right to charter a bank outside the District of Columbia, that he did not dislike Biddle's bank more than other banks, but that ever since he had read the history of the South Sea Bubble he had been afraid of banks.[2] In other words, it was opposition to banks as such, and not to this particular bank, that moved him. His ignorance of financial matters in general, together with his belief in "hard" money, may also have influenced him. That his opposition to banks was not inflexible, however, is shown by his request of his friend James A. Hamilton, in December, to draw up plans for two banks, one as a branch of the treasury department, the other for general banking purposes.[3]

The influence of the Portsmouth branch controversy on Jackson's opinions has also, perhaps, been overrated. At the instigation of Senator Woodbury, of New Hampshire, Ingham wrote to Biddle

---

[1] *Jackson MSS.*
[2] Quoted by Catterall, *Second Bank*, 184.
[3] Hamilton, *Reminiscences*, 151, 152.

complaining of the course of Jeremiah Mason, president of the Portsmouth branch.[1] Mason, a close friend of Webster, to whom he owed his appointment, had aroused opposition among New Hampshire merchants by his methods in reorganizing the business of the branch, and it was now intimated that the bank had used its influence against Jackson in the late election. Biddle had no difficulty in disproving the charges, and, in a vigorous correspondence with Ingham, repudiated what he assumed to be the latter's claim to a right on the part of the government to interfere with the choice of officers of the bank or with the conduct of its business. Biddle did not quote Ingham correctly, but the action of the secretary of war in ordering the removal of the pension funds from Portsmouth to Concord, together with complaints against the branches at New Orleans and elsewhere, convinced him that the administration desired a voice in the management of the bank. Jackson wrote to Biddle in November that the controversy was due to the "foolishness" of Isaac Hill—who, unknown to Ingham, had taken part in the affair—and that he should take occasion in his message to declare publicly his appreciation of "the services rendered by the Bank at the last payment of the national debt." [2]

Though the charges of political favoritism were not sustained, it was, of course, a fact that the bank

---

[1] *House Reports*, 22 Cong., 1 Sess., No. 160.
[2] Catterall, *Second Bank*, 179.

officials were in general opponents of Jackson, and that the bank possessed the power to influence elections, even though it had not yet exercised it. Biddle took the precaution, however, to secure the appointment of directors favorable to the administration at a number of the branches. He also sought to improve his personal relations with Jackson, and even went so far as to submit a plan for a recharter; but to this proposal the president again interposed his former constitutional objections.[1]

The pronouncement against the bank in the message of December, 1829, did not express the opinions of a majority of the cabinet; but Jackson refused to omit the paragraphs, though he allowed his friend James A. Hamilton, of New York, to rewrite them.[2] The declaration came as a great surprise to Biddle, who had expected something of quite opposite tenor; and there was a decline in the bank stock. The part of the message relating to the bank was referred in the House to the committee of ways and means, five of the seven members of which were supporters of the administration. April 13, 1830, the committee submitted a report, through McDuffie, of South Carolina — who here for once abandoned his characteristic close-construction doctrine — in favor of both the constitutionality and the expediency of the bank, and against a government bank such as Jackson proposed, the evils of

---

[1] Catterall, *Second Bank*, 190–192.
[2] Hamilton, *Reminiscences*, 149, 150.

patronage in a government institution being especially urged. Thousands of copies of the report were circulated by the bank.[1] Resolutions against paper money, the bank, and a renewal of the charter were tabled, and a call upon the secretary of the treasury for information refused. The Senate committee on finance, three of whose five members, including the chairman, were Jackson men, reported, March 20, that the currency was uniform and sound, and that the objections to Jackson's plan were "insuperable and fatal."[2] The "great debate" on nullification and the discussion over appointments and removals absorbed the attention of Congress, while out-of-doors little attention seems to have been paid to the message.

In the spring of 1830 personal and political relations between Jackson and Calhoun were ruptured. Jackson had for some time been doubtful of Calhoun's loyalty in 1825 and 1828, and began to think that the attitude of Monroe and his cabinet, in the Florida affair of 1818, had not been as favorable to him as Calhoun's correspondence at the time seemed to indicate. A letter from Crawford to Forsyth, dated April 30, 1830,[3] was now put into his hands, which asserted that Calhoun had been in favor of "punishing the general" in 1818, notwithstanding the fact that the Rhea letter to Monroe

---

[1] *House Reports*, 21 Cong., 1 Sess., No. 358; Catterall, *Second Bank*, 199.   [2] *Senate Reports*, 21 Cong., 1 Sess., No. 104.
[3] Calhoun, *Works*, VI., 360–362.

was before the cabinet at the time. The whole affair was apparently the result of the machinations of Lewis, Forsyth, and Hamilton, and designed to shift the whole burden of opposition in 1818 to Calhoun, thereby discrediting Calhoun in the eyes of Jackson and defeating his aspirations for the presidency.

Jackson, his suspicions now become a certainty, demanded an explanation from Calhoun. Calhoun could hardly have been unprepared, for he had corresponded with Monroe about the Florida matter since December, 1827, and on March 7, 1828, wrote to Monroe that he had reason to think that false statements had been made to Jackson about the cabinet discussion of 1818.[1] His reply to Jackson's inquiry was a long and not quite satisfactory defence of his conduct, together with a criticism of Crawford for revealing a cabinet secret. Jackson, in response, disclaimed any intention of calling in question Calhoun's character or motives, but closed the controversy, so far as he was concerned, by stating that, in view of the revelations of Crawford's letter, "no further communication with you on this subject is necessary." The breach was final, Calhoun declining to renew friendly relations unless Jackson would retract, although declaring that "every opening was made" for him to do so. He kept up an active correspondence, however, with Monroe and others, showed the letters to his friends,

---

[1] Calhoun, *Corresp.* (Jameson's ed.), passim., esp. 260.

and in February, 1838, published them in his own
defence.[1]

In his second annual message, December, 1830,
Jackson returned to the attack on the bank, this
time with a more specific statement of his own views.
A Bank of the United States might, he suggests, be
organized "as a branch of the treasury department, based on the public and individual deposits,
without power to make loans or purchase property,
which shall remit the funds of the Government, and
the expense of which may be paid, if thought ad-
visable, by allowing its officers to sell bills of exchange to private individuals at a moderate pre-
mium." Such a bank would have "no means to
operate on the hopes, fears, or interests of large
masses of the community," while the state banks,
though having the sole right of issuing the "local
paper currency," would be compelled to redeem
their notes in specie by the refusal otherwise of the
Bank of the United States to receive such notes on
deposit or for exchange.[2]

Congress paid even less attention to this message than to that of a year before. A motion to refer
the part of the message relating to the bank to a
select committee of the House, instead of to the
committee of ways and means, was lost by a decisive vote, as was Benton's motion in the Senate
for leave to bring in a motion against the renewal

[1] Calhoun, *Corresp.* (Jameson's ed.), 280; *Works*, VI., 358–445.
[2] Richardson, *Messages and Papers*, II., 529.

of the charter.   Newspapers favorable to the bank
were bitter in their attacks on the president and
Van Buren, while the bank published "floods of
articles" in its own behalf.[1]   The controversy began to show its political aspect, however.   The
legislature of New York passed a resolution against
a recharter, to which the legislature of Pennsylvania responded with a resolution in favor of the
bank.   With a presidential election not far distant,
the entanglement of the bank issue with other political questions was of the highest moment, especially in view of the support which Jackson had received
from both Pennsylvania and New York in 1828.

While Congress was sitting in 1831, the cabinet
was breaking up.   Rumors regarding the character
of Mrs. Eaton, wife of the secretary of war, led to
a refusal on the part of the ladies of the cabinet to
call upon her, although the existence of the scandal
was for some time unknown to the public.   Jackson, notably chivalrous in his attitude towards
women, and remembering the attacks on his own
wife, championed the cause of Mrs. Eaton, collected
a mass of evidence to prove her innocence, and did
everything in his power to obtain for her social
recognition; but without avail.   For Van Buren and
Calhoun the consequences were indirectly important.   Van Buren, being a widower, was free to extend to Mrs. Eaton the usual social courtesies, with
the result of rising rapidly in Jackson's esteem;

[1] Catterall, *Second Bank*, 205.

while Calhoun, whose wife had been prominent in
the drawing-room revolt, lost favor.

The Eaton affair, together with the desire to get
rid of Calhoun's friends after the breach between
Calhoun and Jackson, led to the break-up of the
cabinet. Jackson seems to have held Ingham,
Branch, and Berrien responsible for the refusal to
receive Mrs. Eaton; but on submitting a statement
of the case to them, and receiving their assurance
that their influence had not been exercised as he
supposed, but that "their wish was to harmonize
the cabinet," he "determined not to dismiss them." [1]
The final rupture was only postponed, however;
personal relations were difficult, cabinet meetings
became infrequent, and finally ceased altogether.
In the mean time, the "kitchen cabinet" had decided that Jackson must be a candidate again in
1832, if his health, which was then bad, permitted,
and that Van Buren should be brought forward as
a candidate for vice-president, with the possibility
of succession.[2]   April 11, 1831, Van Buren resigned,
alleging the impropriety of remaining in the cabinet
while popularly looked upon as a candidate for vice-
president. Eaton had already resigned four days
earlier, and Ingham and Branch followed on the
19th. Berrien did not resign until June 15. Van
Buren was shortly appointed minister to England,
and Eaton became governor of Florida. The pub-

---

[1] Undated memorandum in *Jackson MSS.*
[2] Parton, *Jackson*, III., 309; Sumner, *Jackson* (rev. ed.), 200.

lic criticism of Jackson by Branch and Berrien after their virtual dismissal called forth bitter denunciation from Jackson in his private letters to Van Buren.[1]

The new cabinet comprised Edward Livingston, of Louisiana, as secretary of state; Louis McLane, of Delaware, secretary of the treasury; Lewis Cass, of Michigan, secretary of war, after the place had been declined by Senator White, of Tennessee;[2] Levi Woodbury, of New Hampshire, secretary of the navy; Roger B. Taney, of Maryland, attorney-general; and Barry, the former postmaster-general and only hold-over from the previous cabinet. Livingston had been in the Senate since 1829. McLane was minister to England when appointed, and did not return to the United States until August. Cass had been governor of Michigan territory since 1813. Taney was attorney-general of Maryland and a former Federalist, but a supporter of Jackson in 1828.[3]

The brief reference to the bank in the annual message of December, 1831, in which Jackson, though still "entertaining the opinion heretofore expressed," left the question "for the present to the investigation of an enlightened people and their representatives," was in part the outcome of an understanding between Livingston, McLane, Biddle, and the president himself. Jackson was will-

[1] *Van Buren MSS.*   [2] McLaughlin, *Cass* (rev. ed.), 138.
[3] Parton, *Jackson*, III., 364.

ing to drop the matter, so far as securing the adoption of his own plan was concerned, and to accept a new charter under which the government should cease to be a stockholder in the bank, and the establishment of branches be made dependent on the consent of the state legislatures. McLane, in his annual report, argued the cause of the bank at length.[1]

Biddle, however, who had expected a colorless message, was alarmed when he read that Jackson's opinion of the bank remained unchanged, and saw the necessity of immediate decision of the question of a renewal of the charter. The difficulty was in determining the political effect of a discussion of the question on the eve of a presidential election, especially if Jackson should show opposition. He unwisely decided to apply for the charter at once, supported by the opinions of Clay, of Webster, a trusted legal adviser, and of McDuffie, chairman of the ways and means committee of the House and a supporter of Calhoun. The address of the National Republican Convention at Baltimore, in December, indorsed the bank; and January 9, 1832, the application of the bank for a renewal of its charter was presented to Congress.

A bill to recharter was reported in the Senate March 13, by Dallas, of Pennsylvania, from a select committee, but was not taken up until May 22, and

---

[1] Richardson, *Messages and Papers*, II., 558; Catterall, *Second Bank*, 208–210; *House Exec. Docs.*, 22 Cong., 1 Sess., No. 3.

was then before the Senate until June 11, when it
passed by a vote of 28 to 20. In the House, a bill
to renew the charter, with modifications, was reported by McDuffie, February 10, from the committee of ways and means. A select committee, of
which Clayton, of Georgia, was chairman, appointed
to investigate the affairs of the bank, reported ad-
versely April 30; [1] but the report was a disorderly
and impotent performance, and helped rather than
hindered the cause of the bank. Minority reports
submitted by McDuffie and John Quincy Adams,
May 11 and 14, ridiculed Clayton's report and defended the bank. On June 30 the House took up
the discussion of the Senate bill, and July 3 passed
it with amendments, in which the Senate concurred, by a vote of 107 to 86, under suspension of
the rules. [2]

The grudging submission of the bank to investigation completed Jackson's conviction that the
bank was unsound; and his opinion but reflected
that of the people. It had been expected that he
would veto the bill, and on July 10 the veto message was sent in. The economic reasoning of this
famous document has been characterized as " in
the main beneath contempt." [3] Neither here nor
elsewhere does Jackson show even elementary

[1] *House Reports*, 22 Cong., 1 Sess., No. 460.
[2] *Senate Journal*, 22 Cong., 1 Sess., 451-453.
[3] Catterall, *Second Bank*, 239; Mason, *Veto Power*, 75. The
message, in *Senate Journal*, 22 Cong., 1 Sess., 433-446.

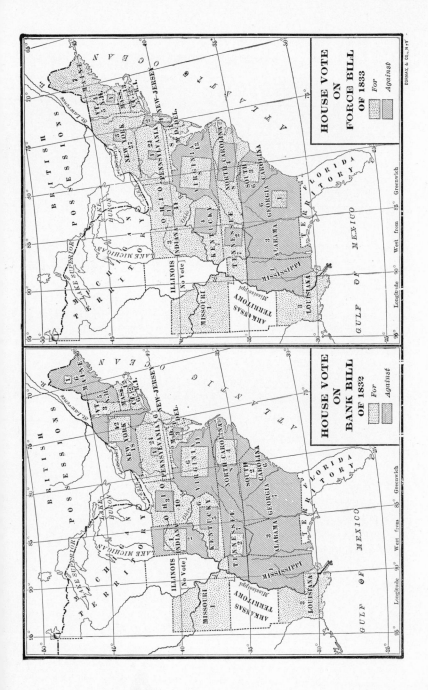

knowledge of the principles of finance or of the practical operations of banking; and it would be useless to refute his financial arguments and objections. The strength of the message is its attack upon the bank as a monopoly, with vast power of control over state banks and the business of the country. To the people of the United States, just beginning to voice the instinctive popular opposition to monopolies and capitalistic combinations, the Bank of the United States appeared as the chief and most familiar illustration of the evils which they feared; and denunciation of the bank as a "money power" and a monopoly was a form of argument which they appreciated.

Even more significant was the attitude of the message towards the supreme court. In a few vigorous and well-phrased paragraphs, Jackson casts aside the notion that a decision of the supreme court is binding upon either the executive or the legislature; for these are co-ordinate departments of the government, and "must each for itself be guided by its own opinion of the Constitution." "The opinion of the judges has no more authority over Congress, than the opinion of Congress has over the judges; and, on that point, the President is independent of both." Moreover, it is contended, the decision of the court in McCulloch *vs.* Maryland extends only to an affirmation of the constitutionality of "a bank"; while the decision as to whether a particular kind of bank is "necessary and proper," and therefore constitutional, or the reverse, is a matter exclusively for the Congress and the executive.

What Jackson insists upon, in other words, is not only the right of the president to reject a bill on constitutional grounds in case he thinks the proposed act unwarranted under a decision of the supreme court, but an independent right of private judgment and official action on constitutional matters, whether the question at issue has been decided by the court or not. The first of these contentions was undoubtedly sound, but if the doctrine of the second were to be maintained, what would become of Webster's contention that the final interpreter of the supreme law of the land was the federal courts? Were the decisions of the courts, though binding upon individuals throughout the land, and even upon the states, of no application to the legislative and executive branches of the general government? Did Jackson mean to declare himself superior to the law?

The veto encountered vigorous, though formal, opposition in Congress. Webster put the case correctly when he said that the veto showed the president to be "against the bank, and against any bank constituted in a manner known either to this or any other country"; and that the responsibility for putting an end to the present bank would rest with him.[1] Clay declared that the veto power was "totally

[1] Webster, *Works* (ed. of 1856), III., 417.

irreconcilable" with "the genius of representative government" "if it is to be frequently employed in respect to the expediency of measures, as well as their constitutionality"; and he later wrote to Biddle that the veto "has all the fury of a chained panther, biting the bars of his cage." [1] Benton, on the other hand, found even his wealth of vocabulary and phrase too small to praise adequately the veto and its author, or to denounce the advocates of the bank.[2] The object of the speeches was, of course, to make political capital, for every one understood that the bank was doomed. The vote in the Senate, July 13, was 22 to 19, less than the two-thirds necessary to pass the bill over the veto.

The bank question was no longer one of finance, but of politics. It remained to be seen whether the bank would continue to regard the interests of the community, or whether, in bringing its career as a national institution to a close, it would use its power to embarrass the administration and the party at whose hands it had suffered.

[1] Clay, *Life and Speeches* (ed. of 1843), II., 90; Clay, *Private Corresp.*, I., 341.
[2] Benton, *Thirty Years' View*, I., 255-265.

CHAPTER VIII

INTERNAL IMPROVEMENTS

(1796–1837)

THE participation of the federal government in what came to be known as internal improvements dates from 1796, when a grant of land was made to Ebenezer Zane in aid of the construction of a road from Wheeling, Virginia, to Maysville, Kentucky. The construction of the Cumberland Road was authorized by Congress in 1806, and appropriations for the road and its extensions were regularly made for a number of years, the total expenditures to 1836, when the road was abandoned to the states, aggregating nearly seven million dollars.[1] Specific appropriations for the improvement of river navigation began in 1809.

A further development of the system took the form of subscriptions by the United States of stock in improvement companies. The Chesapeake and Delaware Canal Company (1825), the Louisville and

[1] The principal acts for the Cumberland Road are in *U. S. Statutes at Large*, II., 173–175, 179, 357–359; III., 489; VI., 27. See also Benton, *Thirty Years' View*, I., 26; Turner, *Rise of New West* (*Am. Nation*, XIV.).

Portland Canal Company (1826), the Dismal Swamp Canal Company (1826), and the Chesapeake and Ohio Canal Company (1828) all received federal aid in this way shortly before Jackson's first administration.   In 1827 a grant of land was made to Illinois in aid of the construction of a canal connecting the Illinois River and Lake Michigan; and in 1828 a similar grant was made to Ohio in aid of the Miami Canal from Dayton to Lake Erie.   Alabama received in 1828 a grant of four hundred thousand acres of land for the improvement of the navigation of the Tennessee River.[1]   The states, as well as the national government, were active in improving their means of communication, though with many of them financial resources were small.   Turnpikes, maintained in part by tolls, were extensively constructed.   Canals were particularly in favor. The Erie Canal, begun in 1817 and finished in 1825, assured the commercial pre-eminence of New York.

In 1817 the movement for internal improvements received a check, when Calhoun's " bonus bill," setting aside the bank dividends and bonus as a permanent fund for the construction of roads and canals, was vetoed by Madison on constitutional grounds.[2]   Calhoun, at this time a nationalist, saw no reason why the expenditure of public money

[1] *U. S. Statutes at Large*, IV., 124, 139, 162. 169, 234, 290, 293, 305–307.

[2] Cf. Babcock, *American Nationality* (*Am. Nation*, XIII.), chap. v.

should be restricted to the enumerated powers.[1]
The scruples of Madison were shared by Monroe,
who in 1822 vetoed a bill appropriating money to
erect toll-gates on the Cumberland Road. Under
John Quincy Adams, however, there was a marked
increase of activity, for Adams shared to the full
the views of Clay, whose "American system" included internal improvements as one of its cardinal
features. His successive annual messages reviewed
with special satisfaction the progress of surveys and
construction of roads and canals, while abundant
revenue made appropriations easy.

A report submitted by the secretary of the treasury, December 20, 1830,[2] showed that there had been
appropriated by the United States to December 31,
1829, for internal improvements—the classification
including the building of piers, preservation of
ports and harbors, making roads, and removing
obstructions from rivers—$1,603,694.21. To this
was to be added $2,443,420.20 for the Cumberland
Road, and $1,263,315.65 for subscriptions to canal
stock and the improvement of the Ohio and Mississippi rivers. More than one-quarter of the expenditures for internal improvements—$490,288.97
—had been in New England and New York, nearly
all, however, for harbors and navigable rivers. Almost an equal amount — $462,965.32 — had been
spent in Ohio. Indiana had received $115,067.49,

[1] Calhoun, *Works*, II., 193.
[2] *House Reports*, 21 Cong., 2 Sess., No 11.

Alabama $92,725.73, Mississippi $53,291.38, Missouri $24,575.09. The expenditures in the territories of Michigan, Arkansas, and Florida, where, of course, no constitutional question could arise, aggregated $234,955.92.

It was reserved for Jackson to give the system its death-blow. As senator from Tennessee he had voted for various works of internal improvement. In the interval from 1824 to 1829, however, perhaps because of his attitude towards Adams and Clay, he had veered towards a strict-constructionist position; and while not yet willing to oppose works of national importance, he seems to have become convinced that a large part of the appropriations were for purely local undertakings. In his inaugural address, indeed, he uttered only the meaningless platitude that "internal improvement and the diffusion of knowledge, so far as they can be promoted by the constitutional acts of the Federal Government, are of high importance," [1] October 18, 1829, however, he wrote to Van Buren, apparently in reference to an act of the previous session appropriating money for light-houses, beacons, and buoys, and for improving harbors and directing surveys: "The most objectionable objects of surveys, in the bill, are those for ascertaining the expediency and expense of improving the navigation of rivers running from navigable streams into a county or neighborhood or even State,—These cannot be considered

[1] Richardson, Messages and Papers, II., 437.

national; nothing can be so considered, but those great leading and navigable streams from the ocean, and passing through two or more States, and an obstruction that prevents commerce from passing through other States, which when removed will give an uninterrupted passage to those other States, can be viewed as coming within the constitutional power of Congress." [1] Van Buren, in 1824, had proposed in Congress an amendment to the Constitution giving Congress the right to construct roads and canals. [2]

Jackson's first annual message, in December, 1829, showed that his ideas on the subject were becoming clearer.   While admitting that "every member of the Union, in peace and in war, will be benefited by the improvement of inland navigation and the construction of highways in the several States," he pointed out that the method heretofore adopted had been questioned on grounds of constitutionality and expediency.   He accordingly recommended the apportionment of the surplus revenue among the states according to their representation in Congress, an amendment to the Constitution to be proposed in case such distribution should otherwise be regarded as unwarranted.   Nothing must be done that would encroach upon "the legitimate sphere of State sovereignty."   The success of the Union thus far he held to be chiefly due "to the watchful and auxiliary operation of the State authorities. . . . It is

[1] *Van Buren MSS.*
[2] *Senate Journal,* 18 Cong., 1 Sess., 124.

our duty to preserve" for the Constitution "the character intended by its framers." [1]

May 27, 1830, Jackson communicated to the House of Representatives his veto of a bill authorizing a subscription of stock by the United States in the Maysville, Washington, Paris, and Lexington Turnpike Road Company.[2] The company had been incorporated by the legislature of Kentucky to build a section of a road planned to run from the Cumberland Road at Zanesville, Ohio, to Florence, Alabama, on the Tennessee River, which had been surveyed by United States engineers in 1827. Maysville, a town on the south side of the Ohio River, about sixty miles above Cincinnati, was an important point for trade between Kentucky and the East. The existing road, admittedly in very bad condition, was much travelled, an average of 351 persons, 33 carriages, and 51 wagons being reported to have passed over it daily in a particular month of which a record was kept. The one hundred and fifty thousand dollars proposed to be subscribed by the United States was not to be paid until an equal amount, subscribed in equal parts by the state of Kentucky and by private individuals, had been paid in. The bill encountered opposition, particularly in the House, where a bill for a road from Buffalo to New Orleans was laid on the table, April 15, after long consideration, by the close vote of 99 to 91. Polk was es-

[1] Richardson, *Messages and Papers*, II., 451.
[2] *Ibid.*, II., 483–493; Mason, *Veto Power*, 97.

pecially aggressive in opposition, insisting that if the Maysville road was a national road, then any road anywhere might with equal propriety be so regarded; and John Tyler, of Virginia, spoke against the bill in the Senate.[1]

Jackson based his veto partly on constitutional grounds, but mainly on the contention that the Maysville road was a work of local, and not national, character. "It has no connection with any established system of improvements; is exclusively within the limits of a State, starting at a point on the Ohio river and running out sixty miles to an interior town, and even as far as the State is interested conferring partial instead of general advantages." Further, lavish appropriations for internal improvements, even if admittedly of national character, can only be sustained by the prospect of a continual surplus; and he thought it would be better to reduce federal taxation and pay the debt before engaging further in such undertakings. If federal aid to roads and canals is deemed necessary to the prosperity of the country, the people should be asked to authorize it by adopting a constitutional amendment.

The veto led to acrimonious debate in the House.[2] Daniel, of Kentucky, though regretting the disappointment to his state, thought the president should be supported, at least until the people could express

---

[1] *Debates of Congress*, VI., 433–435, 806, 820.
[2] *Ibid.*, VI., 1140.

their opinion. Stanbery, of Ohio, on the other hand, bitterly denounced the message, declaring that it could never have been the work of Jackson, but had "every appearance of a low electioneering document." The voice was that of Jackson, but the hands were those of the "little magician," Van Buren. Polk, Barbour, and Bell as vigorously defended the president. The vote of the House showed a small majority in favor of the bill, but the required two-thirds could not be obtained. Five thousand copies of the message were ordered printed, obviously for political use.

The Maysville veto showed Jackson to be still favorable, in general, to internal improvements, but doubting the constitutional power of the federal government to aid them, questioning the effect of such appropriations on taxation and revenue, and in any case opposing federal grants for merely local enterprises. May 31 he vetoed a bill authorizing a subscription to the stock of the Washington Turnpike Road Company, referring the Senate to the Maysville message for his reasons.[1] On the other hand, he approved on the same day a bill appropriating thirty thousand dollars for examinations and surveys, one hundred thousand dollars for the extension of the Cumberland Road, and various sums for other roads, informing Congress, however, that he did so with the understanding that a road from Detroit to Chicago, for which an appropriation was made,

[1] Richardson, *Messages and Papers*, II., 493, 494.

was not to be extended beyond the limits of Michigan territory.[1]

At the end of the session of 1829–1830, Jackson "pocketed" bills authorizing a subscription to the stock of the Louisville and Portland Canal Company, and appropriating money for rivers, harbors, and light-houses. His statement of reasons, embodied in his annual message of the following December,[2] took a decidedly bolder tone. Such bills as that relating to the Louisville and Portland Canal Company were improper, he declared, not only because the corporation was a private one, but also because federal and state or local powers ought to be kept distinct. If such subscriptions are made, the power of the United States in local affairs will become "almost inconceivable," and "dangerous to the liberties of the people." The river and harbor bill was attacked on the ground of its local items, and its provision for the survey of rivers and removal of obstructions which projected canals are intended to avoid. The need of retrenchment was particularly insisted upon. Over five million dollars had already been spent for internal improvements, while the cost of enterprises projected or surveyed aggregated over ninety-six million dollars; yet even with this large outlay the benefits of such undertakings cannot be equitably distributed. A report submitted to the House, February 10,

[1] Richardson, *Messages and Papers*, II., 483.
[2] *Ibid.*, II., 508–517.

1831, controverted these figures, insisted that by "internal improvements" were properly to be understood only roads and canals in the interior of the country and the clearing of rivers above tidewater, and recommended the continuance of appropriations.[1]

The message of December, 1831, again argued at great length the proposed distribution of the surplus revenue among the states for the benefit of internal improvements. It is noticeable that in this connection Jackson reiterates his opinion that no adjustment of the tariff is to be anticipated which will do away with a considerable surplus.[2] Of interest, also, in view of the character of Jackson's veto, is his protestation of "reluctance and anxiety" at the exercise of the "undoubted right" to veto bills on grounds of constitutionality. Most characteristic of all is the frank admission that some of the arguments adduced in the Maysville veto were not essential to the decision of the case in hand, but were brought forward in order to arouse the interest and obtain the judgment of the people. With "full allowance" for "all irregular expressions of public opinion" as "of necessity attended with some doubt as to their accuracy," Jackson is nevertheless convinced that the vetoes have received popular approval. If the wishes of "the people" have been mistaken, the Constitution provides a

[1] *Debates of Congress*, VII., App., xxxv.–xlii.
[2] Richardson, *Messages and Papers*, II., 514.

way by which a more acceptable executive may be obtained. No president ever proclaimed his own consciousness of rectitude more frankly, or challenged popular condemnation more boldly, than did Jackson in these remarkable utterances.

The vetoes were variously received. Grundy wrote to Jackson, July 31, 1830, that the Maysville veto had increased the administration strength in Maine, New Hampshire, and New York, and had "done no harm" in Pennsylvania; Maryland was divided, but that elsewhere in the south there was scarcely any opposition. In Grundy's opinion, the support of Jackson would now rest more on principle and less on personal grounds.[1] Crawford wrote approvingly to Van Buren, but thought a constitutional convention the "best and only means" to give effect to Jackson's views, and urged Van Buren to bring the matter before the legislature of New York as a means of influencing other states. Calhoun, of course, had to admit the propriety of a constitutional amendment. Clay, on the other hand, assured Webster that the Maysville veto would strengthen the opposition, particularly since the road lay through the part of Kentucky most favorable to Jackson; and he suggested a constitutional amendment restricting the veto power.[2]

---

[1] *Jackson MSS.*
[2] Crawford to Van Buren, **January 3, 1831,** *Van Buren MSS.;* Calhoun, *Corresp.* (Jameson's ed.), 297; Webster, *Private Corresp.,* I., 504.

In his annual message of December 4, 1832, Jackson again argued against expenditures for internal improvements without constitutional sanction, and urged Congress not to act favorably in doubtful cases. Two days later he vetoed a river and harbor bill which contravened his principle about local improvements, though stating that he would have signed it had it contained national objects only.[1] Finally, in his sixth annual message, December 1, 1834, he gives his reasons for "pocketing," at the end of the last session, a bill for the improvement of the Wabash River, because it was a local bill and contrary to his previous action. "I am not hostile to internal improvements," he declared, "and wish to see them extended to every part of the country. But I am fully persuaded, if they are not commenced in a proper manner, confined to proper objects, and conducted under an authority generally conceded to be rightful, that a successful prosecution of them cannot be reasonably expected."[2]

The question of federal aid to railroads did not become important in Jackson's time, partly, no doubt, because the railroad was not for some years able to compete with the canal. A bill to authorize a subscription to the stock of the Baltimore and Ohio Railroad, chartered in 1827, was laid on the table in the Senate in the session of 1829–1830. An act of March 2, 1833, authorized the state of

[1] Richardson, *Messages and Papers*, II., 601, 638.
[2] *Ibid.*, III., 118–122.

Illinois to use the proceeds of the sale of canal lands, granted in 1827, to construct a railroad, but the permission was not utilized. A right of way for a railroad in Florida was granted in 1835, and a similar privilege to the New Orleans and Nashville Railroad Company in 1836, but it was not until 1850 that the system of railroad land grants was fairly inaugurated.[1]

Jackson undoubtedly gave effective check to the further progress of internal improvements at the expense of the federal government. With the exception of the Cumberland Road, no appropriation seems to have been made by Congress after 1829, with the approval of the president, for roads in any state, save an item of twenty thousand dollars, in 1833, to be expended in Alabama.[2] Appropriations for roads in the territories, however, and for the improvement of rivers and harbors, continued, on the whole in increasing amount. Gross expenditures for roads and canals, aggregating $2,737,-000 from 1826 to 1830, reached $4,210,000 from 1831 to 1835.[3] It cannot be said that Jackson's opposition achieved consistency. His contention that only works of a national character should receive

[1] *Debates of Congress*, VI., 455; *U. S. Statutes at Large*, IV., 778; V., 65; VI., 662.

[2] *Report of Secretary of War*, January 7, 1847 (*Senate Docs.*, 22 Cong., 2 Sess., No. 44).

[3] Dewey, *Financial Hist. of the U. S.*, 216; *Report on Internal Improvement Bills Reported, 1815-1835* (*House Reports*, 24 Cong., 1 Sess., No. 850).

federal aid was, in practice, little more than a rough general rule, to be honored in the breach as well as in the observance. There was force in Clay's slur that constitutional scruples did not avail to prevent appropriations for favorite objects.[1] What Jackson did, in short, was to put a stop to the development, at federal expense, of interstate communication by means of roads and canals. The larger field of internal river communication, in his day as now a prolific source of extravagance and waste, he left practically untouched.

[1] *Debates of Congress*, VIII., 1183.

CHAPTER IX

NULLIFICATION IN SOUTH CAROLINA
(1829–1833)

HAYNE'S defence of nullification, in the "great debate," was hailed by many in the south as a complete refutation of Webster's argument and a convincing exposition of the doctrine of strict construction. In South Carolina, where personal leadership was most aggressive and jealousy of federal encroachment most keen, opposition to the tariff became identified, as it had not been at first, with nullification. The aristocracy of leading families was largely a unit on the subject; and the control of politics in the state had been thus far largely in their hands. Elsewhere in the south the state of public opinion was not so clear. The general assembly of Kentucky, in February, 1830, resolved in favor of protection and internal improvements, and the legislature of Louisiana passed resolutions, in April, in favor of the tariff of 1828.[1] Such action was explained by the interest of these states in sugar and hemp. In general, however, there was an im-

[1] *Niles' Register*, XXXVII., 428; XXXVIII., 203.

pression that the south was of one mind, and that the mind of South Carolina.

A strong ground of hopefulness for the anti-tariff men lay in the supposed attitude of Jackson, who had not as yet expressed any unequivocal opinion on the subject of the tariff, but who was understood to be a strict constructionist; and his annual message of December, 1829, indicated opposition to protection.   March 31, 1830, he was renominated for president by the Democratic members of the Pennsylvania legislature,[1] and similar action was shortly taken in other states.   When, accordingly, at the banquet in Washington, April 13, 1830, in celebration of Jefferson's birthday, he proposed the toast, "Our Federal Union; it must be preserved!" the shock to his supporters was great.   The toast was at once interpreted as an intimation that the Union was in danger, and that the public must rally to its defence.

If such was Jackson's fear, he was not alone in it.   Webster wrote, in 1833, that he had become "thoroughly convinced" as early as December, 1828, "that the plan of a Southern Confederacy had been received with favor by a great many of the political men of the South."[2]   There is no evidence that Calhoun, against whom Jackson's toast was immediately directed, was a party to any such scheme.   His letters abound with expressions

---

[1] *Niles' Register*, XXXVIII., 169.
[2] Webster, *Private Corresp.*, I., 534.

of sincere attachment to the Union. But he was sad; and disappointed as he was at Jackson's candidacy for re-election, and daily more entangled in the controversy over the Florida affair, he could only write, gloomily: "The times are perilous beyond any that I have ever witnessed. All of the great interests of the country are coming into conflict, and I must say, and with deep regret I speak it, that those to whom the vessel of state is entrusted seem either ignorant, or indifferent about the danger." [1]

The Maysville veto, with its insistence on the necessity of conserving the original powers of the states, was momentarily reassuring. To Hayne it "opened to the Southern States the first dawning of returning hope." [2] Acts of May 20 and 29, 1830, reduced the duties on coffee, tea, cocoa, molasses, and salt, and allowed a drawback on spirits distilled from foreign materials. During the summer the organization of the nullifiers was earnestly pushed, as was that of their opponents, the State Rights and Union party, the issue being the calling of a state convention to consider the propriety of nullification. The union sentiment in South Carolina, though it had been unable to prevent the adoption of the "Exposition" in 1828, was strong. Hayne described it as consisting of "all the Adams and Clay men, a few seceders from the Jackson

---

[1] Calhoun, *Corresp.* (Jameson's ed.), 273.
[2] Ames, *State Docs. on Federal Relations*, IV., 32.

ranks, and the dissatisfied of all parties." [1]   At a
state-rights celebration at Charleston, July 5, the
opposing views were ably expounded by Hayne and
William Drayton. Jackson, who laid the whole movement at the door of "the ambitious Demagogue,"
Calhoun, gave the Unionists his moral support. [2]

The annual message of December 6, 1830, was
not calculated to allay the hostility of South Carolina. Jackson admitted, indeed, that the existing
tariff taxed "some of the comforts of life unneces-
sarily high," attempted "to protect interests too
local and minute to justify a general exaction," and
tried "to force some kinds of manufactures for which
the country is not ripe"; but he also asserted his belief in the right of Congress to levy protective duties,
and declared that the abandonment of protection
"is neither to be expected or desired." [3]   In South
Carolina the Unionists were able to prevent the
passage by the legislature of a bill for calling a convention; but resolutions embodying parts of the
Kentucky and Virginia resolutions of 1798, and declaring the right of a state to "interpose," were
adopted. [4]   In Congress, the house committee on
judiciary reported favorably, January 24, 1831, a
resolution repealing the section of the judiciary
act which provided for appeals from state courts to

---

[1] Hayne to Van Buren, October 23, 1830, *Van Buren MSS.*
[2] Sumner, *Jackson* (rev. ed.), 259; *Niles' Register*, XXXVIII.,
375–392.   [3] Richardson, *Messages and Papers*, II., 524.
[4] *Niles' Register*, XXXIX., 304, 305, 330.

the federal courts; but the proposition was rejected by the House.

Jackson, though refraining as yet from public expression of his opinions, did not hesitate to let his views be known privately. He refused to appoint as United States district attorney for South Carolina a candidate who had denied the constitutionality of the tariff, declaring to Hayne that while he did not proscribe any one on account of political opinions, he thought opinions such as those in question rendered the candidate unsuitable. Nullification, he maintained, was an untenable doctrine.[1] Hayne's reply was a defence of state rights. The party contest in South Carolina continued, and a dinner to McDuffie, May 19, at Charleston, was made the occasion of extreme state-rights toasts. Elaborate celebrations on July 4 were held by both parties. Jackson's letter to the committee of the Union party, June 14, in response to an invitation to attend the dinner, intimated his belief that force might properly be used in case nullification were attempted—a remark which provoked a heated reply from the legislature in December.[2]

Calhoun, though despairing of relief through tariff revision, and hopeless of aid from Jackson, still sought to reconcile nullification and union, notwithstanding the steady progress of disunion sentiment in his own state. Before Congress met in Decem-

[1] Jackson to Hayne, February 8, 1831, *Jackson MSS.*
[2] Ames, *State Docs. on Federal Relations*, IV., 35, 37.

ber he had prepared three elaborate statements of
the nullification theory: the "Address on the Relation of the States and the Federal Government,"
the "Address to the People of South Carolina," and
the "Report on Federal Relations." [1] In August
a public meeting of his friends in New York nominated him for the presidency.   In the fall two
great conventions spread the tariff issue before the
country. The "Free Trade" convention at Philadelphia, September 30 – October 7, adopted a memorial to Congress prepared by Albert Gallatin,
while a convention of "Friends of Domestic Industry" issued an address to the people, besides a memorial to Congress and various reports.

In his annual message in December, 1831, Jackson again urged the revision of the tariff as "one of
the principal objects" before Congress in view of the
reduction of the debt.   The various bills submitted
in Congress showed a "maze of conflicting opinions." [2] McDuffie, for the House committee of ways
and means, proposed a system of ad valorem duties,
with a reduction to a uniform duty of twelve and
one-half per cent. after June 30, 1834.   Two of the
committee, Ingersoll, of Connecticut, and Gilmore, of
Pennsylvania, presented a minority report, while
Verplanck, of New York, could agree with neither.
McLane, secretary of the treasury, submitted a
compromise plan, and Adams proposed to repeal

[1] Calhoun, *Corresp.* (Jameson's ed.), 281, 307, 317; *Works*, VI.,
59–144.   [2] Dewey, *Financial Hist. of the U. S.*, 184.

the act of 1828 and reduce duties on a number of important articles. The tariff finally embodied in the act of July 14, 1832,[1] was in many respects an improvement over the act of 1828, but its reduction or abolition of some millions in revenue taxes was not accompanied by any important modification of the protective system. Clay's views, which were presented at great length,[2] showed no material change on his part. An inspection of the vote— 132 to 65—in the House, shows that in New England and the south the vote was evenly divided, while the middle, western, and southwestern states were overwhelmingly in favor of the measure. Virginia and North Carolina voted strongly in the affirmative, South Carolina and Georgia as strongly in the negative.[3] The fact that Jackson, who had vetoed the bank-charter bill July 10, did not oppose the tariff bill must be taken as indicating his approval of its provisions.

"I no longer consider the question one of free trade, but of consolidation," wrote Calhoun in May.[4] South Carolina echoed his words. In a letter to Governor Hamilton, August 28, Calhoun gave "the final and classical exposition of the theory of state sovereignty."[5] On the passage of the tariff bill,

---

[1] *U. S. Statutes at Large*, IV., 583–594.

[2] Clay, *Life and Speeches* (ed. of 1843), II., 9–67.

[3] See table in Dewey, *Financial Hist. of the U. S.*, 185.

[4] Calhoun, *Corresp.* (Jameson's ed.), 321.

[5] Von Holst, *Calhoun* (rev. ed.), 97. For the letter, Calhoun, *Works*, VI., 144–193.

in July, the South Carolina members in Congress issued an address to the people of the state, expressing their conviction that protection "must now be regarded as the settled policy of the country," that "all hope of relief from Congress is irrevocably gone," and that it was for the people to decide "whether the rights and liberties which you received as a precious inheritance from an illustrious ancestry shall be tamely surrendered without a struggle, or transmitted undiminished to your posterity."[1] The state campaign which ensued resulted in the victory of the nullification party. The legislature assembled October 22, 1832, listened to a message by Governor Hamilton recommending a convention, and by large majorities in each house passed the necessary act.

Jackson had not been an idle spectator of these ominous proceedings. The Union party in South Carolina, though beaten at the polls, was still strong, and the friends of Jackson kept him informed of what was taking place. September 11 he wrote from the "Hermitage" to Woodbury, the secretary of the navy, that there were rumors of an attempt to "seduce" the naval officer at Charleston, and that the United States should be prepared.[2] October 6 special instructions were sent to the collector of customs at Charleston. On the 16th Poinsett wrote that the nullifiers would use force "under law," and that the Union men needed arms—a request several

[1] *Niles' Register*, XLII., 412-414. [2] *Jackson MSS.*

times repeated. October 29 Major Heileman, in
command of Fort Moultrie, in Charleston harbor,
was warned by Major-General Macomb that an attempt might be made to seize the fort. November
7 the garrison at Fort Moultrie was strengthened.
A special agent was also sent to Charleston to learn
the plans of the nullifiers and investigate the reported opening of government mail. November 18 General Scott was sent to the scene of disturbance. It
is hardly possible that the leaders of the nullifiers
could have been unaware of these proceedings, or
of the evident intention of the president to resist
by force any interference with the authority of the
United States.

The convention met at Columbia, November 19,
1832. Of the 162 delegates, 136 were in favor of
nullification.[1] On the 24th the convention, by a
vote of 136 to 26, adopted the famous ordinance
"to nullify certain acts of the Congress of the
United States, purporting to be laws, laying duties
and imposts on the importation of foreign commodities."[2] The ordinance declared the tariff acts
of 1828 and 1832 to be "null, void, and no law, nor
binding upon this State, its officers, or citizens."
The enforced payment of duties under the acts was
held to be unlawful, and the legislature was called
upon to pass such measures as might be necessary to
give effect to the ordinance, and arrest the operation

[1] Houston, *Nullification in South Carolina*, 109.
[2] MacDonald, *Select Documents*, 268-271.

of the obnoxious acts from and after February 1,
1833. No case in law or equity, involving either
the validity of the ordinance or the action of the
legislature under it, might be appealed to the supreme court of the United States; and any attempt
to take such appeal was made punishable as for
contempt of court. All office-holders, except members of the legislature, were required to take an
oath to obey and uphold the ordinance and the
laws passed to give it effect.

Finally, to cap the arch of protest, it was declared, in the name of the people of the state, that
"we will not submit to the application of force, on
the part of the Federal Government, to reduce this
State to obedience; but that we will consider the
passage, by Congress, of any act authorizing the
employment of a military or naval force against the
State of South Carolina, her constituted authorities
or citizens, or any act abolishing or closing the ports
of this State, or any of them, or otherwise obstruct-
ing the free ingress of vessels to and from the said
ports, or any other act, on the part of the Federal
Government, to coerce the State, shut up her ports,
destroy or harass her commerce, or to enforce the
acts hereby declared to be null and void, otherwise
than through the civil tribunals of the country, as
inconsistent with the longer continuance of South
Carolina in the Union, and that the People of this
State will thenceforth hold themselves absolved
from all further obligation to maintain or preserve

their political connection with the people of the other States, and will forthwith proceed to organize a separate Government, and to do all other acts and things which sovereign and independent States may of right do."

The legislature reassembled November 27, three days after the adjournment of the convention, and promptly passed the acts necessary to give effect to the ordinance.[1] A replevin act provided for the recovery of goods seized or detained for non-payment of duties. In case of refusal to deliver the goods, the personal estate of the offender to double the amount of the goods might be seized. Persons arrested or imprisoned on any judgment or decree of any federal court for duties were to be entitled to the privilege of the writ of habeas corpus, with the right to maintain an action for damages. Another act authorized the use of the military force of the state, including volunteers if necessary, under direction of the governor, in case armed force were employed or threatened against the state; the purchase of arms and ammunition was also authorized. A form of oath, especially obnoxious to the Union men, was prescribed for all state officers, both civil and military.

Jackson's message of December 4, 1832, again urged readjustment of the tariff, so that the protection afforded might not exceed "what may be necessary to counteract the regulations of foreign

[1] *Senate Docs.*, 22 Cong., 2 Sess., No. 30.

nations and to secure a supply of those articles of manufacture essential to the national independence and safety in time of war." [1]   The reference to the situation in South Carolina was brief, but pointed. The opposition to the revenue laws "in one quarter of the United States" had risen, it was said, "to a height which threatens to thwart their execution, if not to endanger the integrity of the Union"; but it was believed that the federal laws were probably sufficient to deal with the matter.

December 10, six days later, came Jackson's proclamation to the people of South Carolina. [2]   In a bold, vigorous, and admirably reasoned argument, the proclamation swept aside the bad logic and impracticable theory of the ordinance of nullification, and proclaimed the doctrine of the supremacy of the Union.   "I consider the power to annul a law of the United States, assumed by one State, incompatible with the existence of the Union, contradicted expressly by the letter of the Constitution, unauthorized by its spirit, inconsistent with every principle on which it was founded, and destructive of the great object for which it was formed"—this was the text, printed in bold type that it might not be overlooked.   It is no argument against the tariff, urged the president, that it was passed with improper motive, for the motive of the legislature cannot be ascertained save from the act, nor may any

[1] Richardson, *Messages and Papers*, II., 598.
[2] *Ibid.*, II., 640-656.

state impugn it. It is no objection that the tariff operates unequally, for so do all taxes which the wisdom of man has ever contrived; or that the proceeds of the tax will be improperly applied, for the law makes no particular disposition of the revenue. As for the compact theory, that can be as little maintained as the theory of secession derived from it. In words of solemn earnestness, the chief magistrate of the nation appealed to the people of South Carolina to beware of the danger into which they were running, and to stop before resort must be had to force.

The proclamation, apparently the joint production of the president and his secretary of state,[1] is unquestionably the ablest and most impressive state paper of the Jackson era. If the people of South Carolina who favored nullification had imagined that Jackson would sit quietly by while the state went out of the Union, their eyes must have been holden that they could not see. With Jackson, love for the Union and jealous regard for the dignity of his high office were predominant passions, and an attack upon them was an affront to him. The language of the proclamation was not, indeed, wholly characteristic of Jackson, nor were the constitutional doctrines enunciated in accord at all points with Jackson's views as elsewhere expressed; but there can be no doubt that he approved the general tone and purport. There is no doubt, too, that he

[1] Parton, *Jackson*, III., 466; Tyler, *Taney*, 188.

was prepared promptly to act under the proclamation. The day before the proclamation was issued he wrote to Poinsett that in forty days "from the date of my orders," if force should become necessary, "I will have forty thousand men in the State of South Carolina" to put down resistance and enforce the law.[1]

To the nullifiers the proclamation was like a blow in the face, but they did not at once recoil. Hayne, who had resigned from the Senate to become governor of the state, was inaugurated December 13. Two weeks later Calhoun resigned the vice-presidency, and took Hayne's seat in the Senate. December 17 a series of ten resolutions in reply to the proclamation was adopted by the legislature, and the purpose was declared of meeting force with force.[2] Governor Hayne put forth a counter-proclamation. A call for a general convention of the states to consider questions of disputed power between the states and the federal government was also issued. The replies of the states, however, through their legislatures, were an emphatic condemnation of nullification and secession, and in most cases also an equally emphatic indorsement of the president's proclamation.[3] South Carolina had taken the lead in attempting to carry its doctrine into effect, only to find that, once the step was

[1] *Jackson MSS.*
[2] Ames, *State Docs. on Federal Relations*, IV., 42–44.
[3] The replies are in *State Papers on Nullification* (Boston, 1834).

taken, none of the "co-States" would follow it, but that it stood alone. Would it still persist when the first day of February, the date on which the ordinance was to go into effect, arrived?

The question was not to be answered directly, for the forces of compromise were already at work. December 13 a letter, probably written by Cass at Jackson's request,[1] appeared in the Richmond *Inquirer*, urging that Virginia propose a reduction of the tariff. On the 27th the House committee of ways and means reported, through Verplanck, of New York, a bill to reduce the duties, within two years, to about half the existing rates. A special message of January 16, 1833, reviewed at length the course of events in South Carolina, pointed out that the duties could not be collected, and suggested additional legislation to enforce the revenue laws. Three days later Poinsett wrote that, so strained was the feeling between the parties, a conflict in the streets of Charleston seemed imminent.[2] On the 21st a bill to enforce the collection of the revenue was reported in the Senate. On the 26th the general assembly of Virginia voted to appoint a commissioner to proceed to South Carolina and offer friendly mediation.[3] In the mean time, moved by the attitude of the other southern states, and alarmed at the prospect of a "force bill," a public meeting at Charleston, January 21, though without

[1] McLaughlin, *Cass* (rev. ed.), 149.   [2] *Jackson MSS*.
[3] Ames, *State Docs. on Federal Relations*, IV., 53-56.

legal authority in the premises, voted a suspension
of the ordinance until the action of Congress were
known. February 13 the president of the convention, James Hamilton, issued a call for a meeting of
the convention on March 11 — seven days after the
adjournment of Congress.

February 12, while the "force bill" was before
the Senate, and Verplanck's bill still under consideration in the House, Clay submitted a compromise
tariff. Clay, who foresaw danger to the protective
system from the election of an anti-protection majority in the next Congress, and who dreaded the
exercise of military power by Jackson, is said to have
planned during the recess a compromise which, while
materially lowering the duties, would keep the tariff
in the hands of its friends and help to avert the
threatened collision in South Carolina. Calhoun,
now thoroughly alarmed at the course events were
taking, gave his support to his old enemy. Webster,
on the other hand, held that the bill, with its provision for horizontal reduction, was not protective
in character, that one Congress could not bind its
successors, and that in any case the difference with
South Carolina ought not to be compromised. He
at once introduced resolutions against the bill,
though supporting Jackson on the constitutional
issue. Adams, who had denounced Jackson's reference to South Carolina in his annual message as
"dissolving the Union into its original elements,"
and "in substance a complete surrender to the

nullifiers of South Carolina," [1] moved to strike out
all but the enacting clause of the tariff bill, and
in a minority report from the committee on manufactures severely censured the course of the administration. The manufacturing interests were
strongly opposed to the bill, yielding only on the
condition that the southern senators, including Calhoun, should vote for the bill.

The Senate passed the "force bill," February 20,
by a vote of 32 to 1, Tyler, of Virginia, casting the
only negative vote. Nearly one-half of the senators refrained from voting. In the House, the text
of Clay's compromise tariff was substituted for
the Verplanck bill, and in this form passed the
House on the 26th, the vote being 119 to 85. The
Senate passed the bill, March 1, by a vote of 29 to
16; and on the same day the "force bill," by a vote
of 149 to 47, passed the House.

The tariff act of 1833 provided that, in all cases
where the duty exceeded twenty per cent., the excess should be reduced, one-tenth after December
30, 1833, one-tenth after September 30, 1835, and
one-tenth every second year thereafter until September 30, 1841; after which date one-half of the
remaining excess over twenty per cent., and after
September 30, 1842, the remaining one-half, should
be removed. Some immediate additions were made
to the free list, and the number was to be consider-
ably increased after 1842; but the duty on cer-

---

[1] Adams, *Memoirs*, VIII., 503.

tain coarse woollens, which had been reduced to
five per cent. by the tariff of 1832, was raised to
fifty per cent. before the reduction began. The
credit system of paying duties was to be abolished
after 1842. The provision for home valuation after
1842, added as an amendment to Clay's bill in the
interest of increased protection, was strenuously
resisted by Calhoun, but the threat of Clayton, of
Delaware, to let the bill fail unless this particular
provision, as well as the bill as a whole, received
Calhoun's vote compelled him to submit.[1] As an
illustration of "horizontal" reduction, the act was
open to criticism, while its limitation of the control
of the revenue by future Congresses was of doubtful constitutionality. As a matter of fact, however, the tariff of 1833 never went fully into operation, because of general financial disturbance after
1836.

The "force bill"[2] empowered the president to
change the location of a custom-house to any place,
on land or aboard ship, in case the collection of
duties was resisted, and to use military or naval
force to collect the duties. The jurisdiction of the
circuit courts of the United States was extended to
all cases arising under the revenue laws. In case
copies of the record of proceedings in any state
court were refused, the circuit court might allow
the plaintiff to proceed *de novo*. Should the opera-

[1] Benton, *Thirty Years' View*, I., 343.
[2] *U. S. Statutes at Large*, IV., 632–635.

tion of any law of the United States, or the process of any federal court, be obstructed by military force or other unlawful means, and the proclamation of the president directing the dispersal of such force be disregarded, the president was authorized to enforce the laws or uphold the courts by means of the militia or the army and navy. So much of the act as provided for the use of force was, however, limited in its duration to the end of the next session of Congress.

The passage of the "force bill" was strenuously resisted in debate. Calhoun denounced it in a great speech, February 15 and 16, as vesting in the president unlimited power of the sword, authorizing him to treat the states "as a mere lawless mass of individuals," prostrating all the barriers of the Constitution, and decreeing a massacre. Should the bill pass, he predicted that South Carolina would resist even unto death.[1] Webster talked on the general issue of nullification and secession,[2] in regard to which Calhoun had again stated his position and defended his course. The representatives of South Carolina in the House were bitterly defiant, while McDuffie proposed to change the title of the bill to read, as the epitaph of state rights and the Constitution, "An Act to Subvert the Sovereignty of the States of this Union, to Establish a Consolidated Union Without Limitation of Powers, and to

[1] Calhoun, *Works*, II., 197–262.
[2] Webster, *Works* (ed. of 1851), III., 448–505.

Make the Civil Subordinate to the Military Power." [1]
But argument and defiance alike were unavailing,
for the vote in both houses on the passage of the
bill was overwhelming.

The convention of South Carolina met March 11,
Hayne replacing Hamilton as president. A committee of twenty - one, appointed to consider the
proper steps to be taken, reported on the 13th
an ordinance rescinding the ordinance of nullification and the legislative acts passed to give effect
to it. On the 15th, by a vote of 153 to 4, the rescinding ordinance was adopted.[2] To nullify the
"force bill" was difficult, and, in McDuffie's opinion, ridiculous, but an ordinance [3] to that effect, together with a report calling upon the legislature to
pass laws to prevent its enforcement, were adopted on the 18th by a vote of 132 to 19. The same
day the convention adjourned, and nullification in
South Carolina was at an end.

Both sides claimed the victory, and with some
reason. The supremacy of the Union had been
maintained, and attempted resistance by a state
defeated. If the course of events could settle a
question of law, then a protective tariff was constitutional. On the other hand, the tariff complained
of had been greatly modified, and force had not
been used by the federal government. On the

---

[1] *Debates of Congress*, IX., 1903.
[2] *Statutes of South Carolina*, I., 390.
[3] Houston, *Nullification in South Carolina*, 149.

whole, the greater victory lay with South Carolina. Alone, unaided by its "co-States," it had challenged the constitutionality of a federal policy, formally refused longer to submit to it, and prepared itself to resist by force of arms.   In response, the president had declared that the law must be obeyed, and had taken steps to secure obedience, if necessary, by force; but before the test came Congress had pushed through in two weeks a compromise measure which would shortly reduce duties to a revenue basis. Politically, nullification cost something. Calhoun ceased to belong to any party, and South Carolina did not again join with the Democracy until 1840. As to the "force bill," much as men might wish to forget the circumstances which called it out, it was in every way a proper addition to the body of federal law. Calhoun was correct in writing, December 12, 1833, that he saw little prospect of repealing the act; and the principle of the act is a part of the federal law to-day.

CHAPTER X

INDIAN AFFAIRS

(1825–1837)

WHILE Jackson was reconstituting the civil service, undermining the Bank of the United States, and circumventing nullification by mingled threats and concessions, a controversy with Georgia and Alabama came also to a head. In the act by which Georgia, in 1802, ceded its western lands to the United States, it was agreed that the United States should extinguish the Indian title to lands within the state "as early as the same can be peaceably obtained upon reasonable terms." By a series of treaties, the United States succeeded in extinguishing the title to a considerable portion of the lands; but in 1825 the Creeks still held 4,245,760 acres, and the Cherokees 5,292,160 acres, in Georgia. Much of this was among the best land in the state. In addition, the two tribes held 5,995,200 acres in Alabama, the Cherokees 1,055,680 acres in Tennessee, and the Choctaws and Chickasaws 15,-705,000 acres in Mississippi and 1,277,376 acres in Alabama. At that time the Creeks in Georgia and Alabama numbered about 20,000; the Cherokees in

Georgia, Alabama, and Tennessee, 9000; the Choc-
taws in Mississippi and Alabama, 21,000; and the
Chickasaws in Mississippi, 3600.[1]   In 1827, after a
controversy between Georgia and the federal gov-
ernment which had gone on since the beginning of
Adams's administration, the remaining lands of the
Creeks in Georgia were purchased by the United
States.[2]

The position of the Cherokees, the most highly
civilized of all the southern Indians, was substantially identical with that of the Creeks, and their
leaders early recognized that the overthrow of their
neighbors would be the signal for immediate encroachment upon their own territory.   Against such
encroachment, to be sure, they held indisputable
constitutional guarantees.   By a series of treaties
extending from 1785, the United States had "recognized the Cherokees as a nation, capable of making peace and war, of owning the lands within its
boundaries, and of governing and punishing its own
citizens by its own laws."[3]   These treaties were a
part of the supreme law of the land, and the state
of Georgia, as one of the parties to them, was clearly bound by them.

Jackson was not long in declaring his policy.   A
Georgia statute of December 20, 1828, annexed the
Cherokee lands to five adjacent counties, and de-

---

[1] *Am. State Papers, Indian*, II., 546.
[2] Turner, *Rise of the New West* (*Am. Nation*, XIV.).
[3] Cherokee Nation *vs.* State of Georgia, 5 Peters, 17.

clared that after June 1, 1830, all laws of the Cherokee nation should be null and void, and all Indians
resident in the Cherokee country should be subject
to the laws of the state.[1] A protest against the
encroachments of Georgia had been presented to
Adams by the Cherokees in February, 1829, but had
been left without action. April 18, Eaton, the secretary of war, informed the Cherokee representatives that their only course was either "to yield to
the operation of those laws which Georgia claims,
and has a right, to extend throughout her own
limits," or else to remove beyond the Mississippi.
The right of the Indians to maintain an independent government within the limits of a state, but
outside its jurisdiction, could not, it was declared,
be conceded by the United States.[2] Similar views
were expressed in Jackson's annual message of
the following December, where the case of the
Indians in Georgia and Alabama was discussed at
length.

For the welfare of the Indians the message of
1829 expressed kindly consideration; indeed, there
is nothing in any of Jackson's official utterances
to support the charge that he viewed the Indians
with contempt or indifference, or that he was regard-
less of their treatment. Justice and humanity, he
averred, required that they be saved from the destruction which must fall upon them if they re-

---

[1] Lalor, *Cyclopædia*, II., 392; Worcester *vs.* Georgia, 6 Peters,
525.   [2] *Niles' Register*, XXXVI., 258.

mained surrounded by the whites, or continued to
be driven "from river to river and mountain to
mountain" by persuasion or force. The best provision for them would be to set apart an ample territory west of the Mississippi for their permanent
occupancy, where each tribe could have its own
limits and its own government, "subject to no
other control from the United States than such as
may be necessary to preserve peace on the frontier
and between the several tribes." Their emigration
thither should be voluntary; forcible removal would
be as cruel as it would be unjust. If, however, they
chose to remain within the limits of a state, they
must submit to the laws of the state and relinquish
their claim to all lands which they had not improved.[1]

In the paragraphs of this first annual message
are to be found all the essential points of Jackson's
Indian policy. The Indians were to be given the
choice of remaining on so much of their lands as
they could use, or of emigrating westward to lands
set aside for their special occupancy. If they remained, however, they must submit to the laws of
the state in which they lived; for the supremacy of
the state throughout all its borders could not be
questioned. Of the rights which they enjoyed by
treaty they were not to be violently deprived, but
every effort was to be made to induce them to surrender such rights for an equitable consideration,

[1] Richardson, *Messages and Papers*, II., 458.

in order that conflicts with the whites might be avoided and the progress of settlement be unimpeded. The policy was at least humanely conceived, so far as Jackson was concerned, and represented an earnest effort to deal justly with the difficult problem of the relations between superior and inferior races.

The immediate results, however, were far from happy. The discovery of gold in the Cherokee country, in July, 1829, gave a powerful stimulus to the desire for the possession of the Indian lands, and by the summer of 1830 some three thousand persons were searching for gold in northeastern Georgia, where the United States, Georgia, and the Cherokee nation now all claimed jurisdiction.[1] A touching memorial of the Cherokees to Congress, protesting against the conduct of Georgia as a violation of their ancient rights in the soil and of their treaty guarantees as well, was met by an opinion of Attorney-General Berrien, March 10, 1830, that the Indian title was one of occupancy merely.[2] A bill providing for the exchange of the Indian lands for lands west of the Mississippi, and appropriating five hundred thousand dollars for the removal of the Indians thither, provoked extended argument in Congress, and passed the Houses by small majorities, but became law May 28.[3] Mississippi had al-

[1] Phillips, *Georgia and State Rights*, 72.
[2] *Niles' Register*, XXXVIII., 421.
[3] *U. S. Statutes at Large*, IV., 411.

ready, January 19, passed an act extending the jurisdiction of the state over the Indians within her limits, and incorporating them within the free population of the state. The federal troops who had been sent to keep order in the Cherokee region were withdrawn in November, at the request of the governor of Georgia.

The Cherokees still refused to emigrate, and accordingly became, June 1, 1830, subject to the laws of Georgia, provided, of course, that they acknowledged the right of the state to exercise jurisdiction over them. A proclamation of the governor, June 3, asserted that the state of Georgia held a fee-simple title to the Indian lands, and forbade trespassing or unlawful taking of gold and silver.[1] In December the lands were ordered to be surveyed, the improvements of the Cherokees being seized by the state. Severe penalties, aimed at the Indians themselves, were decreed against such persons as should interfere with the emigration of the Indians or the sale of their lands. An attempt was shortly made to obtain relief from the supreme court of the United States; but the court held, in the case of Cherokee Nation vs. State of Georgia,[2] decided at the January term, 1831, that the Cherokees, who were described in the complaint as "a foreign state," were not such within the meaning of the Constitution, and therefore were not entitled to sue in that character in a federal court. They were,

[1] *Niles' Register*, XXXVIII., 328.   [2] 5 Peters, 1–80.

rather, a "domestic dependent" nation, occupying
a territory to which the United States asserted "a
title independent of their will, which must take effect in point of possession when their right of possession ceases." Marshall did, indeed, declare that,
in the opinion of the majority of the judges, the
argument which had aimed to prove that the
Cherokees were "a distinct political society, . . .
capable of managing its own affairs and governing
itself," had been "completely successful," and that
the courts were "bound" by the acts of the federal
government which "plainly recognize the Cherokee
nation as a state." This was *obiter dictum*, in view
of the decision on the question of jurisdiction, and
hence was not binding upon the state of Georgia or
its officers; but there was nothing in the decision
which upheld the claim of Georgia to extend its
jurisdiction over the Cherokees or their lands.

The contempt with which Georgia regarded the
federal courts had just had striking illustration.
An Indian named Tassel was tried before a state
court on a charge of murder, committed in resisting
the execution of a law of Georgia within the Cherokee country, and sentenced to death. A writ of
error to the supreme court of the United States was
sued out in December, 1830, and the state of Georgia, through its governor, cited to appear. The
legislature denounced the action of the court as a
"flagrant violation" of the rights of the state, and
declared that no obedience ought to be rendered to

the mandate, but that "every invasion, from whatever quarter, upon the administration of the criminal laws of this State" ought to be forcibly resisted; and authorized the governor to have the sentence of the state court carried into effect.[1] Tassel was accordingly hanged. When the case of Cherokee Nation *vs.* State of Georgia was heard by the supreme court, the conduct of Georgia in the matter of Tassel was presented in a supplementary bill of complaint; but as no counsel appeared for the state in either cause, and no further action was taken by the court, the nullification of a federal judicial mandate by the state was complete.

Among the numerous acts of Georgia directed against the Cherokees was one of December, 1830, which forbade white persons, except agents of the federal government, to reside within the former Cherokee reservation without a license from the governor and an oath to support the constitution and laws of the state. One Worcester, a Presbyterian missionary, was arrested under the act, and on his refusal to leave within ten days, was sentenced to four years' imprisonment at hard labor. The case was appealed to the supreme court of the United States, which rendered its decision in March, 1832. In an elaborate opinion,[2] Marshall affirmed the status of the Cherokees as "a nation," within whose territory" the laws of Georgia can have no

---

[1] *Am. Annual Register*, 1830–1831, pp. 356–358.
[2] Worcester *vs.* Georgia, 6 Peters, 521–579.

force, and which the citizens of Georgia have no right to enter but with the assent of the Cherokees themselves or in conformity with treaties and with the acts of Congress." The Georgia statute was, accordingly, held unconstitutional, and Worcester was ordered to be discharged. Georgia again defied the mandate of the court: the state court refused to issue a writ of habeas corpus, and Worcester and his companions remained in prison until January, 1833, when they were pardoned by the governor.

Jackson declined to support the court. "John Marshall has made his decision; now let him enforce it!" he is reported to have said.[1] The equivocal position of Jackson, engaged as he was at the moment in breathing out threatenings and slaughter against the nullifiers in South Carolina, did not escape the keen eye of Calhoun. In the debate on the "force bill" he remarked that a great change seemed to have come over the opinion of the executive in the past twelve months. In South Carolina, where the tariff was a sore grievance, the decision of the supreme court as the "final arbiter" was to be supported, if necessary, by the full military and naval power of the federal government. In Georgia, where the position of the Indians was involved, "the will of the executive is to be supreme." There was truth in the charge, for in no part of his public policy did Jackson show less regard for law and consistency, or less respect for a co-ordinate department

[1] Greeley, *American Conflict*, I., 106.

of the federal government, than in the case of the Cherokee Indians.

That the open defiance of the supreme court by the state of Georgia did much to encourage nullification is clear. As to Jackson's course in the matter, rational considerations fail to afford a satisfactory explanation. Jackson strongly disliked Marshall, and the latter was known to be opposed to Jackson's re - election in 1832. An article in the *Globe*, in March, 1832, apparently written by Cass,[1] offered an elaborate argument against the position of the supreme court. The insults of Georgia, moreover, were hurled at the court rather than at the president. Doubtless, too, Jackson's own views about the Indian influenced his conduct. On the whole, however, the affair seems to illustrate the erratic character of Jackson's political mind. He chose to ignore the threats and denunciations of Georgia. He chose to take notice of the threats and denunciations of South Carolina. In the one case he offered no explanation, while in the other he framed a bold and convincing justification of his course. That the two positions were mutually contradictory seems not to have given him concern.

Jackson appears to have been committed from the first to the policy of removal, although he felt it necessary repeatedly to defend his course and to argue the case, often at considerable length. His annual messages of 1829, 1830, 1833, and 1835 de-

[1] McLaughlin, *Cass* (rev. ed.), 161.

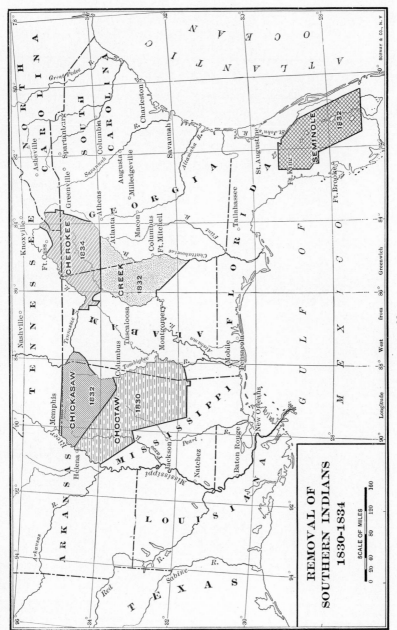

REMOVAL OF
SOUTHERN INDIANS
1830-1834

SCALE OF MILES

0 20 40   80   120   160

39

vote special attention to the subject. Cass discussed the matter fully in his annual report for 1831.
The line of argument is in each case the same—consideration for the Indians as such and regret at their
disappearance, but denial of their right to impede
the development of the country and of their claim
to legal equality with the whites. Congress supported the policy by an act of June 30, 1834, creating
an Indian territory west of the Mississippi.[1]

The Cherokees, encouraged by the decision of the
supreme court in Worcester *vs.* Georgia, and by
Jackson's proclamation to South Carolina, long refused to go. The painful struggle was at last terminated by a treaty of December 29, 1835,[2] by
which the Indians relinquished to the United States
all their lands east of the Mississippi, receiving in
return five million dollars, an additional grant of
land in the Indian territory, and the expenses of
removal to their new home. Even so, some of the
Cherokees refused to leave and had to be removed
by force. Members of the tribe in North Carolina,
Tennessee, and Alabama, who did not wish to remove, were granted pre-emption rights to land in
those states. With the Choctaws and Chickasaws
there was not much trouble. By March 1, 1833,
both of these tribes had accepted the liberal terms
offered by the United States for the cession of their
lands east of the Mississippi, and begun their removal westward. In the case of the Choctaws,

[1] *U. S. Statutes at Large*, IV., 740.   [2] *Ibid.*, VII., 478, 479.

Jackson took the unusual course of submitting some modifications of the agreement proposed by the Indians, and asking the advice of the Senate as to which line negotiations should take. All the lands of the Creeks east of the Mississippi were ceded to the United States in 1832.

Further to carry out the same policy, the early extinguishment of the Indian title in all of the states was urged, not only as sound public policy, but also as a fulfilment of the contract between the federal government and the states when the latter entered the Union. There was steady progress in this direction throughout Jackson's terms. In his annual message in December, 1835, Jackson was able to state that, "with the exception of two small bands living in Ohio and Indiana, not exceeding fifteen hundred persons, and of the Cherokees, all the tribes on the east side of the Mississippi, and extending from Lake Michigan to Florida, have entered into engagements which will lead to their transplantation."[1] Between 1829 and 1837, ninety-four Indian treaties, most of them treaties of cession, were concluded.

The policy of removal was not carried out without opposition. Members of the Society of Friends and other religious bodies, who were interested in the education and conversion of the Indians, opposed Jackson's course, as did anti-administration members of Congress. Clay, though holding opinions

[1] Richardson, *Messages and Papers*, III., 171.

about the Indians substantially identical with those of Jackson, was in opposition for political reasons.[1] On the whole, however, Jackson's Indian policy undoubtedly met with the approval of the great majority of the people of the United States. There could be little question that the claim of the Cherokees to independent sovereignty within the limits of Georgia, while good in law and solemnly guaranteed by the action of the United States during fifty years, was nevertheless contrary to public policy, and constitutionally an anomaly which could not last. Sooner or later, by fair means or foul, the jurisdiction of the state would be coextensive with its boundaries. On the other hand, the compulsory removal of the Indians from their homes to the region beyond the Mississippi, attended as it often was with distressing incidents, seemed needlessly harsh, and made a painful impression. It was fortunate, on the whole, for the Indians that they received from Jackson, an old frontier soldier, as generous treatment as they did.

The most serious armed collision with the Indians in Jackson's time was the Black Hawk War, in 1832.[2] During the War of 1812, the Sac and Fox Indians had allied with the English, but a treaty of peace made in 1816 was for many years faithfully observed. The removal of the tribe to the west, however, in enforcement of a treaty of cession of

---

[1] Schurz, *Clay* (rev. ed.), II., 59.
[2] Winsor, *Narr. and Crit. History*, VII., 406, 439.

1804, roused the bitter opposition of their chief, Black Hawk, who sought to reoccupy the ceded lands in Illinois and Wisconsin. The result was a devastating frontier war during the summer of 1832, in which the Indians were defeated and large numbers of them, including women and children, mercilessly killed on their retreat beyond the Mississippi. Black Hawk, finding further resistance hopeless, surrendered to the United States. After being exhibited about the country as a captive, he was imprisoned for a time at Fortress Monroe, but was finally released through the efforts of a rival chief, Keokuk, who had opposed the violation of the treaty of 1804. The Seminole War, breaking out again in 1835, cast its wretched shadow over the remaining years of Jackson's term, and was not ended until 1842.[1]

[1] Schouler, *United States*, IV., 488.

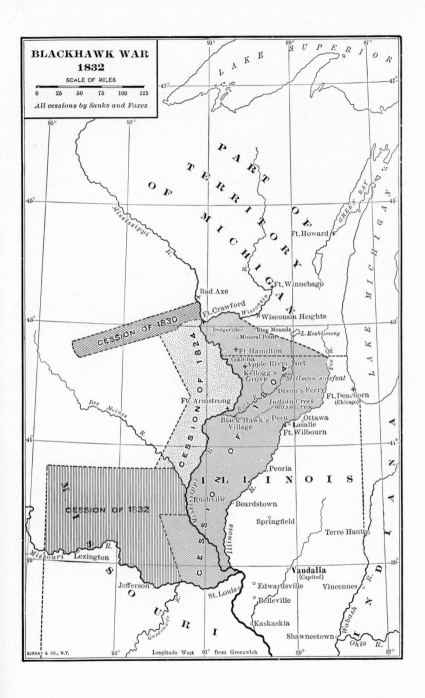

BLACKHAWK WAR
1832

SCALE OF MILES

0   25   50   75   100   125

All cessions by Sauks and Foxes

LAKE SUPERIOR

PART

OF

TERRITORY

OF

MICHIGAN

GREEN BAY

Ft. Howard

Ft. Winnebago

LAKE MICHIGAN

Bad Axe

CESSION OF 1830

Ft. Crawford

Wisconsin Heights

Dodgeville

Blue Mounds

L. Koshkonong

Mineral Point

CESSION OF 1824

Ft. Hamilton

Galena

Apple River Fort

Kellogg's Grove

Stillman's defeat

Ft. Armstrong

Dixon's Ferry

Indian Creek massacre

Ft. Dearborn (Chicago)

Black Hawk's Village

Peru

Ottawa

Lasalle

Ft. Wilbourn

Fox R.

ILLINOIS

Peoria

Mississippi R.

Des Moines R.

Rushville

Beardstown

Springfield

Terre Haute

CESSION OF 1832

Missouri

Lexington

MISSOURI

CESSION

Illinois R.

Vandalia (Capital)

Vincennes

Jefferson

St. Louis

Edwardsville

Belleville

Kaskaskia

Gasconade R.

Shawneetown

Wabash R.

INDIANA

Ohio R.

BORMAY & CO., N.Y.

93°   Longitude West   91° from Greenwich   89°   87°

CHAPTER XI

ELECTION OF 1832

(1830–1833)

IN his first annual message, Jackson urged upon
Congress the propriety of an amendment to the
Constitution limiting the eligibility of the president
to a single term of four or six years. There is no
reason to suppose that Jackson was not sincere in
making this recommendation, or that he was conscious of any inconsistency in repeating it in his
annual messages of 1830 and 1831, when he was
known to be a candidate to succeed himself; or in
that of 1832, when he had just been triumphantly
re-elected.[1] The amendment of the Constitution
was a matter for the people to act upon, and if they
did not choose, even after repeated invitation, to
make a change in this respect, Jackson had no
scruples about availing himself of all the privileges
which the instrument accorded to him.

Jackson was hardly warm in the presidential chair,
however, before his friends, particularly those of the
"kitchen cabinet," began to plan for his re-election
in 1832. There were reasons for this early prepara-

[1] Richardson, *Messages and Papers*, II., 448, 519, 557, 605.

tion. The vote for Jackson in 1828 had indicated an immense popular support, and the scenes at the inauguration had emphasized the extent and enthusiasm of the popular idolatry. Calhoun, who stepped aside for Jackson and accepted second place with the understanding that he was to be supported by the Jackson following four years later, never had the entire confidence of the party managers; and his breach with the president over the Seminole affair shortly put him out of the question as a presidential possibility. Adams could not hope to run again. The opponent most to be feared was Clay. From 1829 to 1831, Clay was in private life; but his position as representative of the protected interests, the respect paid to him wherever he went, and the popular enthusiasm which the mention of his name evoked in many quarters, marked him as a formidable candidate if he should enter the field. That he would accept a nomination if it were tendered him no one doubted.

The issues of the campaign, with a single important exception, were mainly supplied by Jackson himself. The overturning of the civil service, while obviously unprincipled and demoralizing, broke the hold of the official class which had supported Adams and was supposed to be favorable to Clay, and gave the people a chance at the federal treasury. Official inaction in the face of the defiance of Georgia, as to the Cherokee Indians, appealed to the many who attached little weight to the authority of the supreme court, and opened the way to all too-willing appropriation of the Indian lands. Most of all, perhaps, the attack upon the Bank of the United States brought Jackson before the country as the foe of monopoly, special privilege, and the "money power," and as the friend of the people of the states. Jackson's opposition to internal improvements, to be sure, was dangerous to his popularity, but even here his arguments were so phrased as to make his opposition appear to be, as it was, for the ultimate benefit of the people. In foreign affairs, too, there had been successes, and — most potent of all with the masses — a vigorous tone, especially towards smaller powers.

The election of 1832 was more than a personal victory, however. The course of the administration, while it made Jackson a logical candidate to succeed himself, was also the great agency in bringing about a reformation of political parties. With all his hesitancy, inconsistency, and vagary, Jackson was essentially a strict constructionist, and in committing himself to this position he made possible a new drawing of party lines. It was not, indeed, the simple, Arcadian, strict construction of Jefferson that Jackson preached. The federal administration was too vast a machine to be run save with a large force and at great expense. Neither the navy nor the army suffered at Jackson's hands. But in its insistence on the constitutional rights of the states, its imposition of restraints on the exercise of federal powers, and its appeal to the people as the tribunal of last resort, Jacksonian strict construction marked out ground upon which the new Democracy could stand. Jackson was hardly a great party leader in the narrow sense in which we now commonly use the term, but he made possible a reconstitution of parties on broad national lines, and a reformulation of political opinions such as had not been seen since the close of the War of 1812.

The candidacy of Jackson was skilfully inaugurated by Lewis and the "kitchen cabinet," and as skilfully nursed. March 15, 1830, Webb, in the New York *Courier and Enquirer*, announced that Jackson would be a candidate for re-election. On the 31st the Democratic - Republican members of the Pennsylvania legislature met and resolved that "the unanimity and harmony of the great democratic party of the union" would be "greatly promoted" by Jackson's candidacy. This action of the Pennsylvania legislature was indorsed, April 13, by a caucus of the Republican members of the legislature of New York.[1]

These pronouncements gave opportunity to feel the public pulse. A month later Calhoun professed himself "perfectly uncertain" whether Jackson would "offer again or not," on the ground that "it will be difficult to reconcile the course to his previous declarations, unless there should be the strongest considerations of the publick good to justify

[1] *Niles' Register*, XXXVIII., 110, 169, 170.

him." [1] "Considerations of the publick good" did
not wait long for expression. June 15 the Democratic-Republican members of the New Hampshire
legislature approved the action of Pennsylvania and
New York. December 17 the Alabama House of
Representatives approved of Jackson's course as
president and recommended him for re - election.
In January, 1831, fifty-two members of the Ohio
legislature asked him to be a candidate. The legislature of North Carolina was divided, the House of
Commons favoring him, while the Senate disagreed
to the resolution indorsing him. February 3 sixty-
eight members of the Pennsylvania legislature signed
a letter to Jackson, prepared by Lewis, soliciting
him to become a candidate. Six days later Jackson
accepted the nomination tendered by both Pennsylvania and Ohio. New York nominated him again
February 21.[2] The Tammany Society of New York,
at its anniversary on May 12, expressed itself in favor of Jackson, as did his friends in Tennessee at a
public dinner in Nashville in November.[3]

The opposition, meantime, particularly those who
favored Clay, were not idle. In September, 1830, a
Republican convention at Hartford, Connecticut,
nominated Clay—a nomination repeated, December
13, by a public meeting in New York. A meeting in

---

[1] Calhoun, *Corresp.* (Jameson's ed.), 273.
[2] These various nominations in *Niles' Register*, XXXVIII.,
393; XXXIX., 341, 424; XL., 126, 127.
[3] *Ibid.*, XL., 221, 229–232.

Fayette County, Kentucky, June 21, condemned the course of the administration in regard to internal improvements and the Indians, and, while declining to nominate Clay by name, adopted a resolution clearly indicating its preference for him. Members of the legislature of Maryland, February 17, 1831, invited all from other states who "deprecate the re-election of Andrew Jackson" to send delegates to a convention at Baltimore, in December, to nominate candidates "the best established in public confidence." On the same day Clay was nominated by a convention in Boston. On the 22d a Republican state convention at Portland voted confidence in Clay, as did also a convention at Hartford the following day. A candidate favorable to internal improvements, domestic manufactures, and the "preservation of national faith with the Indian tribes" was called for by the council and general assembly of New Jersey. Five thousand persons assembled in convention at Philadelphia, April 4, disapproved of Jackson's course and voted confidence in Clay. National Republicans in Connecticut and New York added their indorsement at meetings in June.[1]

The rupture of relations between Jackson and Calhoun, in the spring of 1830, put an end to any hope of support for Calhoun from the Jackson party.

[1] The various nominations of Clay in *Niles' Register*, XXXVIII., 360; XXXIX., 94, 303; XL., 28, 91, 126, 127, 254, 274.

Throughout the campaign, the attitude of Calhoun was that of a man conscious of his own rectitude and scorning to curry favor by modifying his views, yet keenly interested in the contest, noting with eager satisfaction every manifestation of public confidence in himself, and fatuously blind to the trend of events. May 16, 1831, he wrote to his friend James H. Hammond, of South Carolina: "In the present state of things, I have but little ambition to administer the Government. I cannot support Clay, who in my opinion has done great mischief to the country, and I have no confidence in Jackson, who is too ignorant, too suspicious, and too weak to conduct our affairs successfully. He must fail. Loosing [sic] as he has done, how can he go through six years more?" On August 5 he wrote: "If the country wants an individual to carry on the sectional conflicts, I am not their man. I would not advance myself by sacrificing its true interests; but if they look to the higher considerations of peace, harmony, and liberty, it would be the proudest incident of my life, to be instrumental in promoting these great objects." [1] Four days later a public meeting in New York nominated him for president. [2]

The obvious Jacksonian candidate for vice-president was Van Buren. Of the first group of advisers whom Jackson called about him, Van Buren was

[1] Calhoun, *Corresp.* (Jameson's ed.), 291, 297.
[2] *Niles' Register*, XL., 417.

in every respect the ablest. He was the shrewdest political manager in the country. The political power of New York was at his command. He had opposed Adams and the bank, though maintaining friendly relations with Clay. He was a capable official and an agreeable gentleman. He had probably contributed more than any other man to secure Jackson's election, and was credited with an influence second only to that of Jackson in the formulation of the new Democratic creed. Jackson liked and trusted him from the first, and maintained an active and intimate correspondence with him through all the changing relations which the two occupied to each other.

Jackson's health was extremely bad during the first months of his administration, and his friends feared that he might not live to serve out his term. To provide for this contingency, and to secure from Jackson an expression of preference regarding the succession, Lewis induced Jackson to write to Judge Overton, of Tennessee, in December, 1829, a letter commending Van Buren in warm terms, and declaring that, in Jackson's opinion, he was "well qualified to fill the highest office in the gift of the people." [1] The letter, not intended for immediate use, but available for publication when needed, expressed the opinion of Jackson as well as that of his confidential advisers. Unfortunately for Van Buren, the opinion was not widely shared. To many peo-

[1] Parton, *Jackson*, III., 293–295.

ple the secretary of state was a "little magician," a
consummate political intriguer, a schemer not to
be trusted; and not all the arts of the "kitchen cabinet" could make him popular.

To what extent Van Buren had a hand in the
break-up of the cabinet in 1831 cannot be determined with precision.[1] The cabinet, however, was
inharmonious, and, with the Eaton affair and the
Calhoun quarrel to harass it, could hardly have
lasted long. Politically, Van Buren's resignation
was a shrewd move. Circumstances beyond his
control, he wrote, had brought forward his name
in connection with the succession, and he felt that
it would be improper for him to embarrass the administration by remaining longer in the cabinet.
Jackson, in accepting the resignation, admitted the
sufficiency of the reasons, coupling this, however,
with an expression of the hope that Van Buren's
retirement would be but "temporary," and "that
if in any other station the government should have
occasion for" his services, his consent would "not
be wanting." [2]

When McLane returned from England, in the
summer of 1831, to become secretary of the treasury in the reconstructed cabinet, Van Buren was
appointed to the vacant mission. A period of absence from the country would perhaps help to reconcile the public to his candidacy. He reached

[1] Cf. Benton, *Thirty Years' View*, I., 214.
[2] Parton, *Jackson*, III., 348–352.

London in September, where he met Washington Irving, who had just resigned his post as minister to Spain.[1] In February he received the mortifying news that his nomination had been rejected by the Senate, on the ostensible ground of an alleged insult to the United States in Van Buren's instructions to McLane regarding the negotiations for the opening of the West India trade, but really because of his supposed hostility to Calhoun, his sympathy with the spoils system, and his share in the dissolution of the cabinet. The vote was so arranged as to produce a tie—23 to 23—thus giving Calhoun an opportunity to avenge himself, by a casting vote, on his rival. "It will kill him, sir, kill him dead. He will never kick, sir, never kick," said Calhoun to a doubting friend.[2] He was mistaken. The rejection was a huge political blunder. Benton put the case in a nutshell when he said: "You have broken a minister and elected a Vice-President."[3]

The new element in the campaign was the appearance of the Anti-Masons as a party of national importance. Starting in New York, in 1826, with the excitement caused by the mysterious disappearance of William Morgan, who had written a book said to reveal the secrets of freemasonry, the organized opposition to secret societies of all

---

[1] Shepard, *Van Buren* (rev. ed.), 224–227.
[2] Benton, *Thirty Years' View*, I., 215, 219.
[3] Shepard, *Van Buren* (rev. ed.), 234.

sorts spread rapidly in Vermont, Massachusetts, Connecticut, Pennsylvania, and Ohio, and exercised considerable influence in state elections.[1] As a political dogma, Anti-Masonry afforded but a scanty basis on which to build a national political party; and not all of those who approved the sentiment could be relied upon to support the party. The chief effect of the party in the election of 1832 was to draw votes from the other candidates, particularly from Clay.[2]

In the summer of 1830 the Anti-Masons formally appeared in New York as an anti-Jackson party. In September a national convention of Anti-Masons, representing ten states and the territory of Michigan, met at Philadelphia, and voted to hold a further convention at Baltimore, September 26, 1831, for the purpose of nominating candidates for president and vice-president. The number of delegates from each state was to be equal to the number of senators and representatives from the state in Congress. One hundred and thirteen delegates met at the appointed time, nominated William Wirt, of Maryland, for president, and Amos Ellmaker, of Pennsylvania, for vice-president, and issued an address to the people.[3] Wirt, who was not a willing candidate, had been a mason, and in a speech before the convention virt-

---

[1] Stanwood, *Hist. of the Presidency*, 155.
[2] Webster, *Letters* (Van Tyne's ed.), 164–168; McCarthy, *Anti-Masonic Party* (Am. Hist. Assoc., *Reports*, 1902, I.), 442–454.
[3] *Niles' Register*, XLI., 83–85, 107–110, 166–174.

ually defended the order.   To the Anti - Masons, therefore, belongs the honor of originating the national nominating convention with a fixed representation and a platform.

December 12 a convention of National Republicans, as the anti - administration following now called itself, met at Baltimore. The hundred and sixty-seven delegates represented all the states except South Carolina, Georgia, Alabama, Mississippi, Illinois, and Missouri. Clay, who had just been returned to the Senate by a narrow majority,[1] was unanimously nominated for president. The candidate for vice-president was John Sergeant, of Pennsylvania. It is interesting to note that the vote was taken *viva voce*, each member rising in his place and announcing his choice, and that a committee of one delegate from each state was appointed to notify the presidential nominee.[2] In an address to the public, the convention arraigned the administration for its course regarding removals from office, internal improvements, the tariff, the Georgia Indians, and the bank.

In May, 1832, a national convention of young men at Washington approved the nomination of Clay and Sergeant, and framed a series of ten resolutions which constitute the first formal party platform. The resolutions declared in favor of protection and internal improvements, and of the main-

---

[1] Schurz, *Clay* (rev. ed.), II., 350.
[2] Stanwood, *Hist. of the Presidency*, 157.

tenance unimpaired of the rights of the supreme
court and the Senate; denounced "the indiscriminate removal of public officers" as "a gross
abuse of power"; and condemned the conduct
of the administration in the negotiations relative
to the northeast boundary and the West India
trade.[1]

At the suggestion of Major Lewis, the Republican members of the New Hampshire legislature, in
June, 1831, adopted resolutions indorsing the administration and recommending a convention at
Baltimore the following May. Three hundred and
twenty-six delegates, representing every state except Missouri, met May 21, and "cordially concurred" in the "repeated nominations" of Jackson.
The test of party loyalty, however, was the willingness to support Van Buren, who had no popular
support whatever, and who was especially obnoxious
to Pennsylvania. For the taking of the vote, the
convention adopted the famous "two-thirds rule,"
under which each state was to be entitled, in the
nomination of a candidate for the vice-presidency,
to a number of votes equal to the number to which
it would be entitled in the electoral college under the
new apportionment; two-thirds of the whole number of votes in the convention to be necessary to
a choice. So skilfully had the plans been laid, and
so powerful was the influence of Jackson, that Van
Buren received on the first ballot 208 votes out of

[1] Stanwood, *Hist. of the Presidency*, 158.

283. No platform was adopted by the convention.[1]

In the campaign that followed, violent abuse of the candidates was mingled with spectacular appeals to the voters. Each party had its newspaper organs, to which great importance was attached. Clay insisted on keeping to the front the tariff and the bank, hoping thereby to divide the Jackson forces in Pennsylvania, which favored the bank, in Ohio and Kentucky, which favored protection, and in the south, which opposed both. Of the two issues, that of the bank turned out to be the most potent; for while the merits of a banking policy could never afford sufficient ground for party divergence among the masses, the attempt to force a recharter gave Jackson a powerful weapon against his enemies. The veto of the bank-charter bill, in July, 1832, together with the inability of Congress to pass the bill over the veto, afforded convincing popular proof that the institution was the menace to the country that Jackson had claimed, and that Jackson was the champion to be relied upon to destroy it.

The struggle, accordingly, was between Jackson and the bank, and the anti-administration leaders showed little political wisdom in affecting to believe that in such a contest the people would not side with Jackson. Between Wirt and Clay there was

---

[1] Stanwood, *Hist. of the Presidency*, 161; Sumner, *Jackson* (rev. ed.), 156–160, 273. Kendall apparently wrote an address (*Autobiography*, 296–303).

good understanding, and the former would probably
have withdrawn in favor of Clay had there been opportunity to do so.[1] Clay's hold on Kentucky, even,
was sadly shaken. At the state election in August
the Clay candidate for lieutenant - governor was
elected, but the governorship was captured by the
Jackson forces, a result which Clay attributed to a
corrupt use of patronage and money, "an irruption
of Tennessee voters" in some of the border counties,
and, chief of all, to the fact that the Clay candidate
was a Presbyterian, against which sect "most deep-
rooted and inveterate prejudices exist, the weight
of which had not been sufficiently estimated when
he was selected."

The national election was a great Democratic triumph. Jackson received 219 electoral votes, Clay
49, John Floyd, of Virginia, 11, and Wirt 7. Of the
twenty-four states, all except Vermont, Massachusetts, Rhode Island, Connecticut, Delaware, Maryland, South Carolina, and Kentucky voted for Jackson. The Pennsylvania electors voted, according to
instructions, for William Wilkins for vice-president,
the 30 votes so cast reducing Van Buren's vote to
189. Of the other candidates for the vice-presidency, Sergeant received 49 votes, Henry Lee, of Massachusetts, 11, and Ellmaker 7. The votes for Floyd
and Lee, neither of whom was a candidate, came
from South Carolina, where the nullifiers had carried the legislature which chose the electors; in other

[1] Webster, *Letters* (Van Tyne's ed.), 175.

words, South Carolina deliberately threw away its vote. Maryland, which alone adhered to the district system, gave five of its eight votes for Clay and Sergeant. Vermont alone chose Anti-Masonic electors. There was no Jackson ticket in opposition to Wilkins in Pennsylvania. In New York the National Republicans indorsed the electoral ticket of the Anti-Masons, but without winning a single electoral vote for Jackson.[1]

The popular vote was 687,502 for Jackson against 530,189 for Clay and Wirt. Clay carried only Massachusetts, Rhode Island, Connecticut, Delaware, Kentucky, and part of Maryland. In Rhode Island and Delaware the majority for Clay was extremely small; in Maryland it was only four in a total vote of 38,616. In some of the Jackson states, too, the majorities were small; but Pennsylvania gave the Jackson ticket 90,983 votes against 56,716 for Clay, Virginia 33,609 against 11,451, North Carolina 24,862 to 4563, Tennessee 28,740 against 1436, Indiana 31,552 against 15,472, and Illinois 14,147 against 5429. In Georgia and Alabama there was no opposition.[2]

On September 5, 1831, Jackson had written to Van Buren: "I hope circumstances will occur to enable me to retire to the Hermitage in due season, and to set an example, worthy to be followed, and give an evidence to my country, that I never had any other ambition but that of serving my country

[1] Stanwood, *Hist. of the Presidency*, 164.   [2] *Ibid.*, 163.

when she requested, and when I knew it could be
better served by others, to open the door for their
employment—*you will understand me.*" [1]   The election of 1832 had opened the door, and not only Van
Buren, but the whole country as well, understood.

[1] *Van Buren MSS.*

CHAPTER XII

FOREIGN AFFAIRS UNDER JACKSON
(1829–1837)

IN his inaugural address, Jackson declared that with foreign nations it would be his aim "to preserve peace and to cultivate friendship on fair and honorable terms, and in the adjustment of any differences that may exist or arise to exhibit the forbearance becoming a powerful nation rather than the sensibility belonging to a gallant people." The same sentiment was more pithily put in his first annual message, where he stated it to be his "settled purpose to ask nothing that is not clearly right and to submit to nothing that is wrong." [1] The dictum accorded well with the reputation of the man who had defeated the British at New Orleans, invaded Spanish territory in Florida, hung British subjects on tinsel evidence, set the military power above the federal courts, and quarrelled with the commanding general of the army. Apparently it would not be the fault of Jackson if the United States failed to maintain, under his rule, a vigorous foreign policy, and "cause all our just rights to be respected."

[1] Richardson, *Messages and Papers*, II., 437, 443.

That he would mingle, with extraordinary skill, in his conduct of diplomatic business, tact, forbearance, and firmness, few could foresee.

Several important questions were pending in 1829. Ever since the close of the war for independence, the United States had coveted the lucrative direct trade with the British West Indies, from which, however, American vessels were excluded, save as smugglers, by the English navigation acts. Repeated attempts, from the time of Washington down, to secure the prize had ended in failure. In 1822 an act of Parliament repealed existing statutes regulating the trade of the English colonies in America, and opened certain West Indian ports to direct trade with the United States, although heavy duties were still imposed and some important articles of American export excluded altogether.[1] The United States promptly opened its ports to goods of the British West Indies imported in British bottoms, and allowed exports to the islands to be carried in British vessels. In 1825, however, an act of Parliament limited importation in foreign ships to those countries only which granted to Great Britain the "most favored nation" privilege, established a new schedule of duties, and imposed upon American vessels in Canadian ports the same tonnage duties as were imposed upon British vessels in American ports.[2] The terms of the act were not complied with by the

---

[1] Pickering, *Statutes*, LXII., 196–207.
[2] *Ibid.*, LXV., 905–935.

United States, and on July 27, 1826, an order in council closed the West Indian ports to American vessels after December 1. Thereupon Adams, by a proclamation of March 17, 1827, revived the prohibitory provisions of acts of 1818 and 1820.[1] As a result of this battle of legislation and decree, neither British nor American vessels could trade directly between the United States and the West Indies.

McLane, Jackson's first minister to Great Britain, was instructed to apply for a reopening of the trade on the terms laid down in the act of Parliament of 1825. The reason assigned for the renewed application was that there was a new administration, that public opinion had changed, and that the United States was prepared to receive as a "privilege" what had hitherto been demanded as a "right."[2] It was a new thing in American diplomacy, this invocation of the political opinion of the country as a reason for seeking concessions abroad, and it later cost Van Buren his confirmation as McLane's successor.

The move was adroitly followed up. The annual message of December, 1829, saluted Great Britain, "alike distinguished in peace and war," as a country with which "we may look forward to years of peaceful, honorable, and elevated competition." At Jackson's request, Congress in May authorized

---

[1] *Am. State Papers, Foreign*, VI., 247–249; Richardson, *Messages and Papers*, II., 375.

[2] *Senate Docs.*, 21 Cong., 2 Sess., No. 20, pp. 1–64.

the president, on evidence that the British colonial
ports in America were open to the vessels of the
United States without discrimination, to open by
proclamation the ports of the United States on re-
ciprocal terms.[1] Not to be left without recourse,
however, in case the negotiations failed, Jackson
directed Van Buren, April 10, 1830, to "let a communication be prepared for Congress recommending
a non - intercourse law between the United States
and Canada, and a sufficient number of cutters
commanded by our naval officers and our midship-
men made revenue officers, and a double set on every vessel." In six months Canada and the West
Indies would "sorely feel" the effects of this strin-
gent policy.[2]

Jackson's frank course was completely successful.
The West Indian colonies suffered from the loss of
American products, while the tariff of 1828 narrowed
the demand for English manufactured goods. The
act of May 29, 1830, together with McLane's repre-
sentations, was favorably received, and on October
5 Jackson was able to announce by proclamation
that the trade was open.[3] Vessels of the United
States might import into the British West Indian
colonies from the United States any articles which
could be imported by a British vessel from the
United States, and export therefrom, to any country except the British possessions, any article which

[1] *U. S. Statutes at Large*, IV., 419.   [2] *Van Buren MSS.*
[3] Richardson, *Messages and Papers*, II., 497–499.

any British vessel could export. The annual message of December, 1830, referred in flattering terms to the action of Great Britain, and praised McLane for the "talent and exertion" which he had displayed. The value of imports from the West Indies increased from $101,843 in 1830, to $873,855 in 1831, and the value of exports to the West Indies from $140 to $1,439,593.[1]

The settlement of pending claims against France was more difficult. These claims had their origin in the injury wrought to American commerce by the arbitrary orders and decrees of France during the Napoleonic Wars, and ever since 1815 had been the subject of negotiation. The claims of the United States, however, had been met by counter-claims of France on account of alleged violation of the "most favored nation" privilege accorded by the eighth article of the treaty of 1803, for the cession of Louisiana. In his message of December, 1829, Jackson referred to the claims as still unsettled, and therefore likely to "continue to furnish a subject of unpleasant discussion and possible collision between the two Governments." He had already, however, instructed the American minister to France, William C. Rives, to press for the satisfaction of the claims. The July revolution of 1830, which brought Louis Philippe to the throne, gave Jackson an opportunity, in his message of the fol-

[1] *Summary of Commerce and Finance*, Treasury Dept., August, 1901, p. 620.

lowing December, to flatter the French people by praising the new sovereign, "borne . . . to the throne" by "the paramount authority of the public will."

July 4, 1831, a treaty was concluded by which France agreed to pay to the United States, in full satisfaction of the claims of American citizens, twenty-five million francs, payment to be made in six annual instalments, beginning one year from the exchange of ratifications of the treaty. The United States, in satisfaction of claims against it by France or French subjects, agreed to pay one million five hundred thousand francs, also in six annual instalments. In consideration of a reduction of the duties on French wines imported into the United States, France abandoned the reclamations which it had formed in relation to the treaty of 1803.[1] The signature of the treaty was announced to Congress in the message of December, 1831. Ratifications were exchanged at Washington, February 2, 1832. An act of July 13 reduced the duties on wines, as provided in the treaty,[2] and on the same day the treaty was proclaimed.

But the treaty was unpopular in France, and no provision was made by the Chambre for payment. The first instalment became due February 2, 1833; but a draft on the French minister of finance, drawn by the secretary of the treasury and presented through the Bank of the United States, was refused

[1] *Treaties and Conventions* (ed. of 1889), 330, 345-347.
[2] *U. S. Statutes at Large*, IV., 574-576.

on the ground of no appropriation. A communication from the king, urging that provision be made for the payments, was left without action by the Chambre. There was at the moment no American minister in France, but in August, Livingston, who had resigned the office of secretary of state at the end of May, was sent out. In April, 1834, the necessary appropriations were again refused. The king, however, remained friendly, and the French minister was instructed to promise that "all the constitutional powers of the king and his cabinet should be exerted" to secure favorable action from the next Chambre. This promise was not fulfilled.[1]

A year of inaction and delay exhausted Jackson's patience. In his annual message of December, 1834, he declared that the executive had reached the limit of its authority, and recommended reprisals on French property in case the appropriations were not made at the approaching session of the Chambre. The Senate, under the lead of Clay, voted it "inexpedient at present to adopt any legislative measures" on the subject. The House, on the contrary, followed Adams in declaring that the execution of the treaty ought to be insisted on; but a bill appropriating three million dollars for extraordinary military expenses was lost.[2]

---

[1] Richardson, *Messages and Papers*, III., 27, 103, 104; on the action of the bank, see below, chap. xiii.

[2] Richardson, *Messages and Papers*, III., 106; *Senate Journal*. 23 Cong., 2 Sess., 94; *House Journal, ibid.*, 500.

Jackson's message caused great excitement and irritation in France, where the moderate tone of previous messages had been quite misunderstood. A bill making the appropriation was promptly rejected by the Chambre, and the French minister was shortly recalled. April 25, 1835, the appropriation was voted on condition that satisfactory explanation be offered of the expressions concerning France in the message. Livingston remained long enough to write an able note to the Duc de Broglie, defending Jackson, and then withdrew.[1] Jackson met the affront of France with characteristic vigor. "The honor of my country," he wrote in his annual message of December 7, "shall never be stained by an apology from me for the statement of truth and the performance of duty; nor can I give any explanation of my official acts except such as is due to integrity and justice and consistent with the principles on which our institutions have been framed." A special message of January 15, 1836, again recommended reprisals, and urged the increase of the navy and the completion of the coast defences.[2]

Jackson had not failed, however, to leave a loophole through which France might escape. Any "intention to menace or insult the Government of France" was declared "unfounded," and the curi-

---

[1] Livingston to Forsyth, November 22, 1834; Richardson, *Messages and Papers*, III., 130, 184.

[2] Richardson, *Messages and Papers*, III., 160 188-193.

ous doctrine asserted that the discussions between the president and Congress were matters of domestic importance only, and that they became of public international character only when they "terminate in acts." "The principle which calls in question the President for the language of his message would equally justify a foreign power in demanding explanation of the language used in the report of a committee or by a member in debate."[1] If Jackson could urge such claptrap, France could afford to accept it. January 27, 1836, Great Britain offered to mediate. The offer was accepted, and on February 25 the British minister had the satisfaction of informing the secretary of state that the "frank and honorable manner" in which Jackson had expressed himself had removed the "difficulties" which had interfered with the execution of the treaty of 1831.[2] On May 10, Jackson was able to apprise Congress that four instalments of the indemnity had been paid.

In the session of 1834–1835 claims to the amount of five million dollars, arising from alleged depredations of France on American commerce prior to 1800, were presented to Congress. The basis of the claim to indemnity was the exclusion from the provisions of the treaty of 1800, between the United States and France, of claims on account of captures or condemnations, and the surrender of these claims

---

[1] Richardson, *Messages and Papers*, III., 157.
[2] *Ibid.*, III., 217–221.

by the United States in return for benefits received
from France under the treaty.   In other words, the
United States, "having appropriated to itself a benefit resulting from the losses of its citizens, should
make compensation to the sufferers." [1]   The case
for the claimants was ably argued by Webster, and
vigorously opposed by Tyler, Benton, Wright, and
others.   A bill for the relief of the claimants passed
the Senate January 28, 1835, but was not acted on
by the House.   The "French spoliation claims,"
as they were called, were brought before Congress
from time to time until 1885, when provision for
their examination by the court of claims was finally
made.[2]

Claims against other European countries, similar
in origin and character to those against France,
were also prosecuted, and in some cases settled,
during Jackson's administrations.   Diplomatic relations with Portugal, which had been suspended
after the seizure of the throne by Don Miguel, in
June, 1828, were resumed in the summer of 1829.
Depredations on American commerce by Portu-
guese armed vessels continued, and diplomatic intercourse was again broken off, to be renewed in 1835.
A treaty for the arbitration of claims growing out
of the destruction of the American privateer brig
General Armstrong by British vessels in the harbor

---

[1] *Treaties and Conventions* (ed. of 1889), 335–338, and J. C. B.
Davis, note at 1309; Webster, *Works* (ed. of 1851), IV., 152–178.
[2] *U. S. Statutes at Large*, XXIII., 283.

of Fayal, in September, 1814, was not concluded until 1851, and the decision was against the United States. A convention with Denmark for the payment of claims to the amount of six hundred and fifty thousand dollars was concluded in 1830. A convention with the Two Sicilies, in 1832, provided for the payment of claims for depredations on American commerce by Murat in 1809-1812. The claims against Spain were settled in 1834.[1]

Commercial relations were further improved by the negotiation of a number of commercial treaties —with Austria-Hungary in 1829, with the Ottoman Porte in 1830, with Mexico in 1831, with Chili and Russia in 1832, with Siam and Muscat in 1833, and with Morocco, Venezuela, and the Peru-Bolivian Confederation in 1836. Commercial treaties with Prussia and Brazil, concluded in 1828, were ratified in March, 1829. In May, 1829, discriminating tonnage duties on Austrian vessels were suspended under reciprocity arrangements. Similar suspension was proclaimed regarding the Grand Duchy of Oldenburg in September, 1830, the Grand Duchy of Mecklenberg-Schwerin in 1835, and Tuscany in 1836. Spain in 1832 made the tonnage duties on American vessels the same as those imposed on the vessels of Spain. Tonnage dues on American vessels were abolished by an act of May 31, 1830.[2]

---

[1] Richardson, *Messages and Papers*, II., 445; *Treaties and Conventions* (ed. of 1889), 235-237, 1023, 1100.

[2] *U. S. Statutes at Large*, III., 425.

The northeast boundary controversy continued to be a subject for diplomatic consideration under Jackson, without, however, arriving at any settlement. In 1827 a convention between Great Britain and the United States provided for the submission of the dispute to arbitration.[1] The king of the Netherlands was chosen as arbitrator, but his decision, made in 1831, was rejected by the United States and not insisted on by Great Britain. No further progress in the matter was made during Jackson's administrations, although frequent reference was made to the subject in the annual messages. The boundary was finally settled in 1842.[2] The northwest boundary dispute, which was also pending, rested under an agreement, first made in 1818, and renewed in 1827, for joint occupation of the territory in controversy, subject to a termination of the agreement on twelve months' notice by either party.[3]

The movement for the annexation of Texas, though originating before Jackson became president, was materially advanced during his administrations. The treaty of 1819 with Spain, under which the United States acquired the Floridas, had fixed the boundary between the two countries, west of the Mississippi, in the Sabine River, from its mouth to the parallel 32° north latitude.[4] In 1821 certain of

---

[1] *Treaties and Conventions* (ed. of 1889), 429–432.
[2] Garrison, *Westward Extension* (*Am. Nation*, XVII.).
[3] *Treaties and Conventions* (ed. of 1889), 1331.
[4] *Ibid.*, 1017.

the northern colonies of Spain established their independence as the United States of Mexico. Three years later the importation of slaves from foreign countries was prohibited, and children of slave parents were declared free. A considerable emigration from the southern states set in, notwithstanding the interdiction of slavery, and an agitation began for the acquisition of Texas with a boundary extending to the Rio Grande del Norte. Under Adams, various suggestions looking to a readjustment of the boundary and the purchase of the territory were made to Mexico, but that country naturally refused to entertain them. In 1827 the provinces of Coahuila and Texas were united as a state, with a constitution which embodied the antislavery provisions of the Mexican constitution of 1824.[1]

It seems to have been expected in the south that Jackson would aid the annexation movement, and he apparently connived, in 1830, at a scheme, originated by Samuel Houston, formerly governor of Tennessee and a lieutenant in Jackson's command in 1814, for bringing about a revolution in Texas.[2] A treaty with Mexico, reaffirming the Sabine boundary of 1819, concluded January 12, 1828, was delayed until April 5, 1831, when the time for the exchange of ratifications was extended to one year

---

[1] Von Holst, *United States*, II., 553; Bugbee, "Slavery in Texas" (*Pol. Sci. Quart.*, XIII., 389–412, 648–668).

[2] Sumner, *Jackson* (rev. ed.), 415; Mayo, *Political Sketches*.

from the latter date. In the summer of 1829
Poinsett was instructed to attempt to purchase
Texas,[1] but an offer of five million dollars was refused. Mexico shortly forbade Americans to settle
in Texas, but without effect; land companies organized in New York issued stock on the basis of
grants acquired from Mexican empresarios, and
found ready purchasers for securities of most uncertain value.[2] On the Arkansas border, especially,
there was danger of collision, but Jackson assumed
to inform Congress, in December, 1830, that "the
unfortunate and unfounded suspicions" which Mexico had entertained of the "disposition" of the
United States had been "entirely removed," and
that "friendship and mutual confidence" had been
established. A commercial treaty between the two
countries was concluded April 5, 1831, and ratified
a year later, together with the delayed treaty of
limits.[3]

From 1833 Mexico was torn by civil war. An
offer to purchase Texas, the boundary to follow the
Rio Grande to 37°, and thence west on that parallel
to the Pacific, was authorized by Jackson in July,
1835;[4] but Mexico refused to entertain any proposition. In March, 1836, Texas declared itself an
independent republic, with a constitution permit-

[1] *Exec. Docs.*, 25 Cong., 1 Sess., No. 42, pp. 10–16.
[2] Von Holst, *United States*, II., 560.
[3] *Treaties and Conventions* (ed. of 1889), 664–675.
[4] Von Holst, *United States*, II., 566.

ting the introduction of slaves, and forbidding the residence in the republic of free negroes without the consent of Congress.[1] The massacre of Texas soldiers at Fort Alamo and Goliad the same month greatly stirred public feeling in the United States. April 21 a Texas force under Houston defeated a Mexican force under Santa Anna at San Jacinto, and the authority of Mexico in the new republic came practically to an end.

Public sympathy in the United States was undoubtedly on the side of Texas, and numerous petitions in favor of annexation were presented to Congress. Adams, however, in a great speech, May 25, 1836, declared his opposition to annexation at the cost of war with Mexico.[2] The speech made a deep impression, particularly in the north; and Jackson later credited his "arch enemy" with having defeated annexation at the time.[3] Webster, though favorable to annexation, counselled delay until it was known whether Texas had a *de facto* government. Calhoun, on the contrary, advocated immediate recognition of independence and admission into the Union. The first part of his proposal was carried out by a resolution, reported in the Senate June 18, 1836, and unanimously adopted, favoring an acknowledgment of the independence of Texas "whenever satisfactory information should

---

[1] *Senate Docs.*, 24 Cong., 1 Sess., No. 415, pp. 1–23.
[2] *Debates of Congress*, XII., 4036–4049.
[3] Sumner, *Jackson* (rev. ed.), 418.

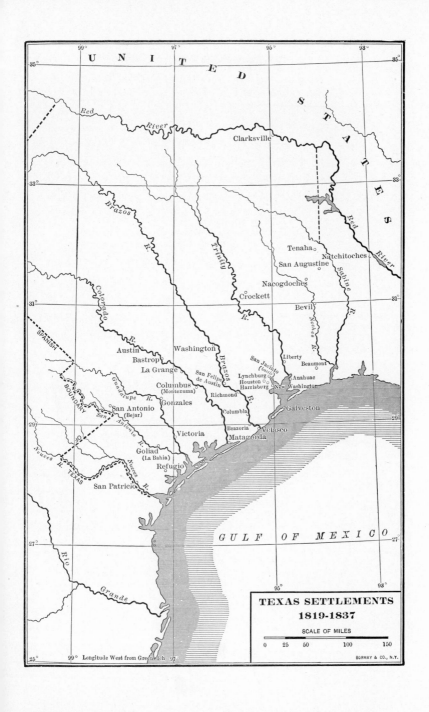

TEXAS SETTLEMENTS
1819-1837

SCALE OF MILES

0   25   50   100   150

BORMAY & CO., N.Y.

be received that it has in successful operation a civil government, capable of performing the duties and fulfilling the obligations of an independent power." A similar resolution was adopted in the House by a vote of 113 to 22, all but one of the opposition being from the free states.[1]

Throughout the war between Texas and Mexico, the United States gave hardly more than formal heed to its obligations as a neutral. Volunteers were openly recruited and ships of war fitted out.[2] Under pretence of danger from the Indians, United States troops under General Gaines had been ordered to enter Texas, but the vigorous remonstrance of the Mexican minister, followed by the rupture of diplomatic relations, caused their recall. Jackson's defence of his course in his message of December, 1836, was utterly specious. The "Mexican functionary" had withdrawn, it was stated, because in his opinion "the honor of his country will be wounded by American soldiers entering, with the most amicable avowed purposes, upon ground from which the followers of his Government have been expelled, and over which there is at present no certainty of a serious effort on its part being made to re-establish its dominion."[3]

December 19, 1836, an act of the Texan congress declared the western boundary of the republic to

---

[1] *Senate Journal*, 24 Cong., 1 Sess., 516; *House Journal, ibid.*, 1220. [2] Von Holst, *United States*, II., 573.
[3] Richardson, *Messages and Papers*, III., 238.

be the Rio Grande from its mouth to its source,
thence north to latitude 42°, and thence west on the
line between the possessions of the United States
and Spain fixed by the treaty of 1819. Two days
later Jackson sent a special message to Congress in
which he stated that "no steps have been taken by
the executive towards the acknowledgment of the
independence of Texas." The question of recognition he left to Congress, with the suggestion that it
would be well to proceed in this instance "with even
more than our wonted caution."[1] The Senate,
however, March 1, by a vote of 23 to 19, voted in
favor of recognition.[2] The House laid a similar
resolution on the table by a vote of 98 to 86, but at
the same time voted, 171 to 76, as an amendment
to the civil and diplomatic appropriation bill, an appropriation for the salary and outfit of a diplomatic agent to Texas, in case the president should find
that Texas was an independent power and deemed
the appointment of an agent expedient.[3]

February 6, 1837, Jackson called the attention of
Congress to the claims upon Mexico for public and
private injuries inflicted during the war, which were
still unsatisfied. "The length of time since some
of the injuries have been committed, the repeated
and unavailing applications for redress, the wanton

---

[1] Richardson, *Messages and Papers*, III., 266, 268.
[2] *Senate Journal*, 24 Cong., 2 Sess., 310.
[3] *House Journal*, 24 Cong., 2 Sess., 546; *U. S. Statutes at Large*,
V., 170.

character of some of the outrages upon the property and persons of our citizens, upon the officers
and flag of the United States, independent of recent insults to this Government and people by the
late extraordinary Mexican minister, would justify in
the eyes of all nations immediate war." He accordingly recommended reprisals, enforced by the
use of the navy in case Mexico should refuse to settle "upon another demand . . . made from on board
one of our vessels of war on the coast of Mexico." [1]
Congress, just happily freed from the possibility of
war with France, was in no mood for a war with
Mexico, and passed resolutions favoring another
demand before resort to coercion, as provided for
by article thirty-four of the treaty of 1831. No
further action was taken.

Jackson's limitations as a diplomatist were offset, in the popular estimation, by the general success of his policy. No international questions of
the first order arose during his administrations, and
the personnel of the diplomatic service was not distinguished; but a number of important differences,
some of them of long standing, were adjusted and
respect for the United States appreciably enhanced.
Towards powerful states Jackson used frowns or
smiles as best suited his mood, while weak states
like Mexico were treated with scant regard; but there
was unceasing watchfulness over American interests
and a jealous care for national honor and standing.

[1] Richardson, *Messages and Papers*, III., 278.

CHAPTER XIII

REMOVAL OF THE DEPOSITS

(1832–1837)

IN a speech on the bank veto, July 13, 1832, Benton declared to the supporters of Jackson that "they might continue to be for a bank and for Jackson, but they could not be for *this* bank and for Jackson." [1] The speech emptied the Senate, but Benton's words stated the situation with exactness. The attitude of Jackson towards the bank had done more than anything else to consolidate his followers into a party and give them a slogan; and henceforth those who were not for him were to be regarded as against him. Whether or not the bank would be allowed to run the remainder of its course in peace depended mainly on its own conduct; but there was no real hope of a renewal of the charter, nor of the establishment of any other similar institution with monopolistic privileges. Whatever it did, however, the bank was under Jackson's eye, and no amount of preoccupation with South Carolina and the nullifiers, or with the details of a presidential campaign, could lessen his

[1] Benton, *Thirty Years' View*, I., 262

vigilance, as no amount of good conduct on the part of the institution could allay his instinctive, deep-rooted, and merciless hostility.

The bank itself invited a renewal of the attack. In March, 1832, as the public debt was nearing extinction, the directors authorized an arrangement by which the bank was to obtain the certificates of foreign holders of five million dollars of three-per-cent. stock, and turn them over to the United States; and to hold the money thus advanced to the government as a loan on its own account, with interest, for one year. The government would thus be free of obligation on account of the debt, while the bank would assume a new loan for five million dollars.[1] In August, however, General Cadwalader, who had been sent by the bank to England to negotiate with the firm of Baring Brothers, arranged with that house to secure from the foreign holders of the stock an extension of their loan for a year. and to buy up as much of the stock as could be had at an agreed figure. The plan contemplated by the bank was unobjectionable, but Cadwalader's contract not only violated the provision of the bank-charter act which forbade the bank to purchase any public debt, but also prevented the discharge of the debt of the United States.[2]

The contract was repudiated by the bank in

---

[1] Catterall, *Second Bank*, 270.

[2] For the correspondence, *House Exec. Docs.*, 22 Cong., 2 Sess., No. 9.

October, but its announcement greatly intensified the popular hostility to the bank, and led to charges of deliberate violation of the charter. In his annual message in December, Jackson called the attention of Congress to the transaction, raised the question whether the public deposits were "entirely safe" in such an institution, and recommended an inquiry into the affairs of the bank and its branches. The disposal of all stocks held by the United States in corporations, state or federal, was also urged. "As a source of profit," the message declared, "these stocks are of little or no value; as a means of influence among the States, they are adverse to the purity of our institutions. The whole principle on which they are based is deemed by many unconstitutional, and to persist in the policy which they indicate is considered wholly inexpedient." [1]

McLane, the secretary of the treasury, had already appointed a special agent, Henry Toland, to investigate the condition of the bank. Toland's report, submitted on the same date as Jackson's message, showed that the bank had assets of $79,-593,870 with which to meet $37,296,950 of liabilities—obviously a solvent and safe condition. [2] February 13, 1833, in the House, a bill authorizing the sale of the bank stock held by the United States, reported by Polk from the committee of ways and

---

[1] Richardson, *Messages and Papers*, II., 599.
[2] *House Exec. Docs.*, 22 Cong. 2 Sess., No. 8.

means, was rejected by a vote of 102 to 91; and on March 2 the House voted, 109 to 46, "that the Government deposits may, in the opinion of this House, be safely continued in the Bank of the United States."[1]

In the election of 1832 the bank took no part beyond the circulation of literature favorable to its interests; and, after the result was known, no radical change of policy was planned.[2] The suggestion of removing the deposits created some excitement, and preparations were made to meet a run on the branches, but it was not yet believed that removal would actually be directed. Jackson had become thoroughly convinced, however, that the bank was unsound, that it had sought to influence the election against him, and that bribery would probably be resorted to to secure a recharter. The result of the election confirmed him in his purpose to break all connection between the government and the bank; and even the warning of friends that no combination of state banks could take the place of the Bank of the United States, and that the removal of the deposits would be the signal for a panic, could not deter him.[3] His course from this time was laid with his eyes open, and he must in consequence be held responsible for its outcome. Only the profoundest ignorance of public finance could have led Jackson to believe that the removal of the deposits, under the circumstances, would result

[1] *House Reports*, 22 Cong., 2 Sess., No. 121.
[2] Catterall, *Second Bank*, 285.   [3] *Ibid.*, 291.

otherwise than in a dangerous shock to the financial interests of the country.

The charter of the Bank of the United States provided that the public moneys should be deposited in the bank and its branches, unless the secretary of the treasury should direct that they be deposited elsewhere, in which case he should lay before Congress at its next session a statement of his reasons for ordering the removal. Action under this provision had been suggested in 1819; Ingham had reminded Biddle, in 1828, of the power which the secretary of the treasury possessed in this particular; and in New Hampshire, Massachusetts, and New York a part of the funds had actually been removed to state banks, or attempts at removal had been made, in connection with the political warfare against the bank. The project was revived soon after the meeting of Congress in December, 1832. The secretary of the treasury, McLane, being opposed to removal, it was planned to replace him by William J. Duane, of Philadelphia, a lawyer of good standing who had never held office. Duane was to take office January 30, and was at once informed by Reuben M. Whitney, on behalf of the president, that the deposits were to be removed; but the appointment was delayed.[1] In March, 1833, questions regarding the organization of a new bank and the regulation of the deposits were submitted to the

[1] Sumner, *Jackson* (rev. ed.), 346; Catterall, *Second Bank*, 292.

cabinet, and the opinions of the members requested in writing.[1]

At the end of May, McLane succeeded Livingston as secretary of state, and Duane took the treasury portfolio. A tour by Jackson of the Atlantic states, from Virginia to New Hampshire, in May and June, was made the occasion for enthusiastic display of affection and esteem for the "old hero," and may well have strengthened his conviction that the people were with him. Rumors of the intended removal of the deposits were rife.[2] The matter was taken up with Duane as soon as Jackson returned from New England. On July 10, in a letter to Jackson, Duane stated his reasons for opposing the removal, and asserted that he was "prepared to make any personal sacrifice, except an acquiescence in a measure, that he positively believes to be at variance with his obligations to the country, the president, and himself." He was thereupon asked to suggest an alternative plan, but was unable to do so. July 22, Jackson wrote objecting to a part of Duane's instructions to an agent appointed to inquire into the state of the deposits, "unless you are determined not to acquiesce in the decision" which the president had reached. Duane at once replied that he could not change his opinions, but that when the decision had been made he would either concur or resign.[3]

[1] *Jackson MSS.*   [2] *Niles' Register*, XLIV., 353.
[3] *Jackson MSS.*

Before the summer was over, the bank had given further ground of offence.[1] February 7, 1833, the secretary of the treasury undertook to collect the first instalment of the French indemnity, due under the treaty of 1831, by drawing on the French minister of finance and selling the draft to the bank. No appropriation having been made by the French Chambre, payment of the draft was refused. The bill went to protest, but was taken up by Hottinguer & Company, the continental agents of the bank, and returned. The bank demanded of the treasury repayment of the principal, with interest and other charges, and fifteen per cent. damages under a law of Maryland in force in the District of Columbia. McLane paid the principal and admitted the validity of the claim for charges, but was advised by Taney, the attorney-general, that the claim to damages was unfounded. Nothing was done until July, 1834, when the amount claimed by the bank was deducted from the bank dividend due the United States at that time. No further action in the case was taken during Jackson's term; but in 1838 suit was brought against the bank to recover, and, after several trials, the supreme court, in 1847, gave judgment against the bank.

In August, 1833, Kendall made a tour of the eastern cities to consult with the state banks about their willingness to undertake the care of the public funds in case the deposits should be removed from

[1] Catterall, *Second Bank*, 299–301, and references there given.

the Bank of the United States. On the 5th, Taney wrote to Jackson, urging removal. Van Buren wrote, September 7, to express the hope that Jackson would not forget to take the opinion of the attorney-general about the contracts to be made with the state banks. Taney not only assured the president on this point, but wrote to him on the 17th: "I am fully prepared to go with you firmly through this business, and to meet all its consequences." Jackson indorsed the letter: "to be filed with my private papers—As evidence of his virtue, energy and worth."[1]

On September 18, Jackson read to the cabinet a paper,[2] prepared by Taney,[3] containing an elaborate exposition of his reasons for thinking that the deposits should be removed from the Bank of the United States. After reviewing the controversy with the bank, particularly over the attempt to obtain a renewal of the charter, the paper urged that the power of the secretary of the treasury over the deposits is "unqualified," and that while it is for Congress "to decide upon the best substitute" for the present bank, the responsibility is devolved upon the executive branch of the government "of deciding how long before the expiration of the charter the public interests will require the deposits to be placed elsewhere." The career of the bank,

[1] *Jackson MSS.*
[2] Richardson, *Messages and Papers*, III., 5-19.
[3] Tyler, *Taney*, 204.

as evidenced by the charges against it, together with
the fact that the charter had but little more than
two and a half years to run, showed that removal
ought not to be longer delayed. The state banks,
it was declared, were willing to assume the responsibility on the same terms as those now made with
the Bank of the United States. Should the bank
attempt the ruin of the state banks, the result would
be disaster to its own stockholders. Such action,
however, was deemed improbable. "The funds of
the government will not be annihilated by being
transferred. They will immediately be issued for
the benefit of trade, and if the Bank of the United
States curtails its loans, the state banks, strengthened by the public deposits, will extend theirs.
What comes in through one bank will go out through
others, and the equilibrium will be preserved." If,
however, the bank possessed the power which has
been feared, that was but another reason for shak-
ing off the despotism at once. "The struggle can
never come with less distress to the people, or
under more favorable auspices than at the present
moment."

In thus pressing his views upon the cabinet, Jackson, while asserting his undoubted right to express
to those "whom the laws and his own choice have
made his associates in the administration of the
government, his opinion of their duties under circumstances as they arise," expressly disclaimed any
intention to coerce them. The support which they

give him should be such only as "their reason approves and their conscience sanctions." The secretary of the treasury will, he trusts, see in his remarks "only the frank and respectful declarations of the opinions which the President has formed on a measure of great national interest, deeply affecting the character and usefulness of his administration, and not a spirit of dictation." The measure is his own, and in the support of it "he shall require no one" of the cabinet "to make a sacrifice of opinion or principle." Having thus stated his views, Jackson concluded by designating October 1, or sooner if practicable, as the date when the transfer might properly be made.

The paper read to the cabinet is the most explicit statement we have of Jackson's theory regarding the status and function of a cabinet officer in our constitutional system. In his view, the head of an executive department is the agent through whom the president acts in matters relating to that department. As such, he may properly hold and express an independent opinion on any question regarding which his advice is sought. The president, however, is the responsible head of the administration, and the acts of his cabinet are his acts. In the event, accordingly, of an irreconcilable difference of opinion between the president and his cabinet, the will of the president must prevail; and if the cabinet officer cannot submit, he should resign, or may be removed. The fact that the secretary

of the treasury was required by law to report to
Congress instead of to the president did not, in
Jackson's opinion, exempt him from obligation to
support the president in matters of public policy.
Whatever the circumstances of this particular case,
the doctrine itself was sound constitutional law,
and is neither dictatorial nor imperialistic.[1] How
far the theory was originally Jackson's own cannot
be determined. Taney was undoubtedly Jackson's
principal adviser at this time; but the president's
adoption of Taney's statement of it made it his
own.

The cabinet was deeply stirred. McLane and
Cass were opposed to the removal of the deposits,
and Cass would have resigned, but was dissuaded by
Lewis and Jackson. Duane refused to give the order for removal, and on September 23 was formally
removed and replaced by Taney, who would have
preferred to become a justice of the supreme court.[2]
Duane later published parts of the correspondence
between himself and Jackson, thereby earning the
abuse of the administration press. Four years later
he wrote that he found himself "ostracised, dis-
owned, outlawed on all sides, a warning to all persons to adhere to party, right or wrong."[3] The
post of attorney-general, left vacant by the transfer

[1] Sumner, *Jackson* (rev. ed.), 353, disagrees.
[2] McLaughlin, *Cass* (rev. ed.), 154; Kendall, *Autobiography*,
186.
[3] *Narrative and Correspondence*, etc. (1838); *Niles' Register*,
XLV., 236; Sumner, *Jackson* (rev. ed.), 358.

of Taney, was taken by Benjamin F. Butler, of New York, who held it until the end of Jackson's term.

September 26 the paper read to the cabinet was printed in an extra of the Albany *Argus*. On the same day Taney issued the first order for removal, designating the Girard Bank of Philadelphia as a place of deposit [1] The collector was directed to procure, with the assistance of the United States district attorney, the execution of a contract with the Girard Bank, and to deposit in the bank, after September 30, all public money which should come into his hands, together with bonds taken for the payment of customs duties. Bonds to the United States, payable on or after October 1, in the possession of the Bank of the United States, were to be withdrawn and deposited in the Girard Bank. The latter institution agreed to give satisfactory collateral security whenever the government deposits exceeded one-half of the capital stock paid in; to make weekly reports to the secretary of the treasury; to pay all warrants or drafts drawn upon it by the treasurer of the United States, and transfer any portion of the deposits without charge; to furnish foreign bills of exchange; and, in general, to perform any or all of the services hitherto rendered by the Bank of the United States within its vicinity. The secretary of the treasury might terminate the contract whenever, in his judgment, the public interest

[1] MacDonald, *Select Documents*, 295-300.

required it. Similar contracts were shortly made with other banks.

The deposits in the Bank of the United States were not "removed" in the sense of being withdrawn and placed elsewhere, but were drawn upon "in the ordinary course of paying government debts." To guard, however, against the possible action of the bank in compelling the payment in coin of balances held by state banks, drafts on the bank were deposited with state banks in New York, Philadelphia, and Baltimore; and these were shortly cashed.[1] The demand for payment of these drafts embarrassed the bank, and the more because Taney had trickily neglected to include them in the weekly list of drafts issued which had hitherto been furnished to the bank.

In July, 1833, the condition of the bank was as follows: discounts on personal security, $37,032,000; discounts on bank stock, $827,000; other discounts, $3,833,000; domestic exchange, $21,676,000; balances with European bankers, $1,911,000; balances with state banks, $485,000; circulation, $19,366,000; public deposits, $6,512,000; other deposits, $9,868,-000; specie, $10,098,000.[2]

In his communication to the Girard Bank, September 26, Taney expressed the hope that the bank would "adopt the most liberal course which circumstances will admit towards other moneyed in-

[1] Catterall, *Second Bank*, 302–305.
[2] *Ibid.*, 501–503.

stitutions," and suggested that, "as the duties which are payable to the Government arise from the business and enterprise of the merchants engaged in foreign trade," such borrowers should be given a preference "in the additional accommodation which the public deposits will enable your institution to give, whenever it can be done without injustice to the claims of other classes of the community." Twenty-three banks had been chosen as places of deposit by the end of the year. Charges of political favoritism were, of course, promptly made; but the "pet" banks, as they were popularly styled, seem to have been selected with care, and the interests of the government carefully safeguarded.[1]

In his annual message of December 3, 1833, Jackson assumed responsibility for the removal of the deposits, and defended his action on the ground that the bank "had been actively engaged in attempting to influence the elections of the public officers by means of its money," and had, "by a formal resolution, placed its funds at the disposition of its president, to be employed in sustaining the political power of the bank."[2] Taney, in a special report, made an elaborate statement of his reasons, mainly, however, political.[3] In the Senate, friends of state rights and nullification, under Calhoun, united with

[1] Sumner, *Jackson* (rev. ed.), 356; Dewey, *Financial Hist. of the U. S.*, 209.

[2] Richardson, *Messages and Papers*, III., 30.

[3] *Senate Docs.*, 23 Cong., 1 Sess., No. 2.

the National Republicans, under Clay, to give a majority against Jackson and for the bank. In the House there was overwhelming support for the administration. Not all, however, of those who were opposed to a recharter favored the removal of the deposits.

December 11 the Senate, by a vote of 23 to 18, called for a copy of the paper read to the cabinet. Jackson refused to transmit it, declaring that "the executive is a co-ordinate and independent branch of the Government equally with the Senate, and I have yet to learn under what constitutional authority that branch of the Legislature has a right to require of me an account of any communication, either verbally or in writing, made to the heads of Departments acting as a Cabinet council."[1] On the 26th, Clay introduced two resolutions declaring that, in the dismissal of Duane and the subsequent removal of the deposits, "the President has assumed the exercise of a power over the treasury of the United States, not granted to him by the constitution and laws, and dangerous to the liberties of the people"; and, further, that Taney's statement of reasons was "unsatisfactory and insufficient."[2] A three days' speech in support of the resolutions opened a debate which occupied most of the time of the Senate for three months, while both houses were flooded with petitions and memorials for or

[1] Richardson, *Messages and Papers*, III., 36.
[2] *Debates of Congress*, X., 58.

against the recharter of the bank and the removal
of the deposits.

A memorial from the bank, protesting against the
removal of the deposits as a violation of its charter, and traversing the arguments of the paper read
to the cabinet, was presented December 18.[1] Nine
days later the nominations of five government directors of the bank were sent in. Of these, Bayard,
of Delaware, was confirmed January 21; the other
nominations were not finally acted upon until February 27, 1834, when they were rejected by votes
of about 20 to 25. An attempt by Benton, January
8, to have Biddle, the president of the bank, brought
before the Senate for examination was defeated,
however, by a decisive vote of 12 to 34. February
5, Webster brought in a report from the committee
on finance, declaring Taney's reasons insufficient,
and recommending the adoption of Clay's second
resolution.[2] In the House, a report of the committee
of ways and means against the restoration of the
deposits and in favor of the continuance of the deposits in state banks, was debated from March 4 to
April 4, when its recommendations were agreed to;
and a proposition, submitted by Webster, to extend
for six years the charter of the bank was rejected
by the Senate, March 25.

The heated discussion in the Senate culminated,
March 28, in the adoption of the following resolu-

[1] *Debates of Congress*, X., 2207.
[2] *Ibid.*, X., Pt. iv., App., 146–156.

tions, based upon Clay's first resolution and the resolution reported February 5 by the committee on finance: 1. "*Resolved*, That the reasons assigned by the Secretary of the Treasury for the removal of the money of the United States deposited in the Bank of the United States and its branches, communicated to Congress on the fourth day of December, 1833, are unsatisfactory and insufficient." 2. "*Resolved*, That the President, in the late Executive proceedings in relation to the public revenue, has assumed upon himself authority and power not conferred by the constitution and laws, but in derogation of both." The vote on the adoption of the first resolution was 28 to 18; on the second resolution, 26 to 20.[1]

April 15, 1834, Jackson entered a formal protest against the resolution of censure.[2] With a vigor at once adroit and merciless, the message dissected the resolution, criticised its form, resented the implication that the action of the president had been taken with "unlawful and corrupt" intent, and inquired why the constitutional process of impeachment was not resorted to for the punishment of what was clearly an impeachable offence. As grounds of solemn protest, the proceedings of the Senate were characterized as "unauthorized by the constitution; contrary to its spirit and to several of its express provisions; subversive of that distribution of the

---

[1] *Senate Journal*, 23 Cong., 1 Sess., 197.
[2] Richardson, *Messages and Papers*, III., 69–93.

powers of government which it has ordained and established; destructive of the checks and safeguards by which those powers were intended on the one hand to be controlled, and on the other to be protected; and calculated by their immediate and collateral effects, by their character and tendency, to concentrate in the hands of a body not directly amenable to the people, a degree of influence and power dangerous to their liberties, and fatal to the constitution of their choice." The Senate was respectfully requested to enter the message and protest at length on its journal.

The reception of the protest on April 17 provoked a heated debate, which continued until May 7. On that date the Senate, in a series of four resolutions, declared that the protest "asserts powers as belonging to the President which are inconsistent with the just authority of the two Houses of Congress" and with the Constitution; that the right of protest could not be recognized; and that the protest, being a breach of the privileges of the Senate, be not entered on the journal.[1] The renominations of bank directors, submitted March 11, were again rejected, and June 24 the nomination of Taney as secretary of the treasury was also negatived.

With the episode of censure and protest the acute struggle between Jackson and Congress reached its climax. The personal and political aspects of the case were significant, but the constitutional aspects

[1] *Senate Journal*, 23 Cong., 1 Sess., 252.

were no less important. In directing the removal
of the deposits, Jackson undoubtedly acted within
his naked right as executive head of the government, though for the action, from any other point
of view, there can be little save condemnation. The
right of either house of Congress to express, by formal resolution, its opinion of an executive act is
neither granted nor withheld by the Constitution;
but the right to censure would seem to be precluded
by the grant to Congress of the power of impeachment, since no act meriting censure could, apparently, fail to afford sufficient ground of impeachment. To deny to the president the right of protest
against legislative censure, whether bestowed with
propriety or not, would be to restrain a natural
and honorable human impulse; but it is not within
the province of the president or of any one else to
demand that a protest be either received or entered
on the journal of the Senate or House, and the
Senate very properly refused the request.

Jackson's own opinion of his performance was
probably best expressed in a passage in his annual
message of December, 1835: "Although clothed with
the legal authority and supported by precedent, I
was aware that there was in the act of the removal
of the deposits a liability to excite that sensitive-
ness to Executive power which it is the characteristic and the duty of freemen to indulge; and I relied on this feeling also, directed by patriotism and
intelligence, to vindicate the conduct which in the

end would appear to have been called for by the best interests of my country. . . . The result has shown how safe is this reliance upon the patriotic temper and enlightened discernment of the people."[1]

The remaining history of the Bank of the United States need not be followed in detail. The bank was now thoroughly unpopular, and without support even among the many who discountenanced Jackson's dealings with it. All projects for obtaining a renewal of the national charter failed, and the bank, by a judicious collection of its debts, readjustment of loans, accumulation of specie, and gradual closing of branches, indicated a purpose quietly to wind up its affairs. In February, 1836, however, it obtained a charter from Pennsylvania, under the name of the Bank of the United States of Pennsylvania, and planned to continue its business. In June, the fourteenth section of the bank-charter act, making the bills of the bank receivable in all payments to the United States, was repealed.[2] A controversy over the payment to the United States of the government stock was settled in 1837, when four bonds, payable in September, 1837, 1838, 1839, and 1840, were accepted as security for the indebtedness of $7,886,145.49.[3] The bonds were duly paid, and the connection between the bank and the government ceased.

In December, 1834, and again in 1835, Jackson

[1] Richardson, *Messages and Papers*, III., 167.
[2] *U. S. Statutes at Large*, 48. [3] Catterall, *Second Bank*, 375.

urged upon Congress the necessity of providing by law for the regulation of the public deposits in the state banks. The deposit act of June 23, 1836,[1] required the secretary of the treasury to designate at least one bank in each state and territory, if possible, as a place of public deposit. No bank, however, was to be allowed to hold such deposits to an amount greater than three-quarters of its capital stock paid in; nor might any bank be selected which did not redeem its notes and bills on demand in specie. The deposit banks were to credit as specie all government deposits, and pay in specie all checks, warrants, or drafts drawn on such deposits; to afford facilities for transferring the funds without charge from place to place, and for distributing the same in payment of the public creditors; and, in general, to render to the government the services previously rendered by the Bank of the United States and its branches. With the provisions for the regulation of the deposits went also, as part of the same act, a plan for the distribution of the surplus revenue among the states. Efforts to divide the measure in the House failed.

In the debate in the Senate on Jackson's protest, Benton, the most aggressive champion of the president, announced his intention to introduce, at each succeeding session, a motion to expunge the resolution of censure. Motions to this effect in 1835 and 1836 were tabled, but a third, prefaced by long

[1] *U. S. Statutes at Large*, V., 52–56.

preambles which repudiated and abjured all that the Senate had done, was passed January 16, 1837, after a debate of nearly thirteen hours, by a vote of 24 to 19.[1] The manuscript journal of the session of 1833–1834 was brought into the Senate, and the secretary, in obedience to the resolution, drew black lines around the resolution of censure, and wrote across the face thereof, "in strong letters," the words: "Expunged by order of the Senate, this sixteenth day of January, in the year of our Lord 1837." Many members withdrew rather than witness the proceeding; but a crowded gallery looked on, while Benton strengthened his supporters by providing "an ample supply of cold hams, turkeys, rounds of beef, pickles, wines, and cups of hot coffee" in a near-by committee-room.[2] Jackson gave a dinner to the "expungers" and their wives, and placed Benton at the head of the table. That the action of the Senate was unconstitutional interested no one save the lawyers, for the bank was dead, Jackson was vindicated, and "the people" were enthroned.

[1] *Senate Journal*, 24 Cong., 2 Sess., 81–83.
[2] Benton, *Thirty Years' View*, I., 727.

CHAPTER XIV

CHANGES AND REFORMS

(1829–1837)

WHEN, in his first inaugural address, Jackson declared that the circumstances of his election imposed upon him the task of reform, he held forth the characteristic which was to distinguish his administrations from those of all other presidents. From the beginning of his presidential career to its close, he was incessantly occupied with projects of change, some of the most fundamental of which he was able to carry out with more or less completeness. The establishment of the spoils system in national affairs, the removal of the Indians beyond the Mississippi, the settlement of claims against France and other countries, the opening of the West India trade, the discouragement of internal improvements at federal expense, the destruction of the Bank of the United States, and the payment of the national debt were conspicuous examples of his reforming zeal; and for his success the people, whose idol he was, did him honor.

It would be a mistake, however, to suppose that Jackson concerned himself only with these weightier

matters of the law. On the contrary, his annual
and special messages show intelligent and ceaseless
watchfulness of the public welfare, and attention
to varied details of government business.   Congress,
too, though rarely a unit in supporting the president, spent much time in debating projects of reform; and while it negatived more than one praise-
worthy proposal, and did not scruple to resort to
factious opposition, it could not avoid lending its
approval to many of the most important recommendations of the executive.   The Jacksonian period was pre - eminently one of political and administrative change, of tearing down and building
up, of investigation and reorganization.   What was
done, whether evil or good, was significant of the
pervasive power of a new democratic impulse of
which Jackson was the leader.   The administration
was often far from blameless, and Congress a forum
for recrimination and intrigue; but the fruits of success accrued in the main to Jackson and his supporters.

Some important parts of the Jackson programme
failed altogether to win either popular or legislative
countenance.   Thus, the amendment of the Constitution so as to provide for the election of president
and vice-president by popular vote was urged by
Jackson in each of his eight annual messages, and
with a wealth of argument that fairly exhausted
the subject.   The participation of the Senate or
House of Representatives in presidential elections,

in case of the failure of the electors to choose a candidate, opened the way, in his opinion, to bargain and intrigue, and made possible the defeat of the popular will. The key-note of his political creed was the direct action of the people in political affairs, and whatever interfered with such action was condemned. The principle of secondary election had, to be sure, long since ceased to work as the framers of the Constitution anticipated, and certainly became less defensible as the means of communication increased. In his advocacy of change, however, Jackson stood practically alone; there is no evidence of any deep or wide-spread interest in the question in Jackson's time. Various propositions embodying the executive recommendations, or proposing other forms of popular election, were presented to Congress, but none received favorable consideration.[1]

Propositions for amending the Constitution in one particular or another were numerous in Jackson's time. The limitation of the eligibility of the president to a single term, the exclusion of members of Congress from office, the tenure of office of federal judges, the apportionment of representatives, internal improvements, the distribution of the surplus, the rights of the Indians, the chartering of a national bank, aid to African colonization, the revocation of a veto by a majority vote of all the members of Congress, tenure of civil office, removals from office,

[1] Ames, *Proposed Amendments*, 87–90.

the election of the secretary of the treasury by Congress, and the election of senators by the people were among the subjects of the proposed amendments. The discussion of protection and nullification was productive of a number of resolutions for amendments relating to those subjects, while the legislatures of South Carolina, Georgia, and Alabama called for a convention to amend the Constitution, or to delimit anew the powers of the state and federal governments. None of these proposals passed beyond the initial stage.[1]

In his annual messages of 1830 and 1831, and again in that of 1835, Jackson recommended a change in the form of government of the District of Columbia. The district comprised three local governments—namely, the city of Washington, the town of Georgetown, and a levy court having jurisdiction over the area not included within the other two. The basis of the law of the district was the laws of Maryland and Virginia at the time of the cession. As a consequence, there was vexatious divergence of practice, particularly in criminal matters, the same offence being in some cases punished differently on the two sides of the Potomac;[2] while Congress had thus far failed to supply a uniform code. The recommendations of Jackson comprised a delegate in Congress, an extension of the suffrage to the inhabitants of the district, and perhaps a

---

[1] Ames, *Proposed Amendments*, 343–348.
[2] Richardson, *Messages and Papers*, II., 528.

local legislature. Nothing was done, however, and the tripartite government continued until 1871.

The administration of the executive departments opened a wide range of suggestion, and offered a fertile field for congressional interference. The annual message of December, 1829, reported that since the last session numerous frauds on the treasury had been discovered, but that the attempts to bring the offenders to trial under existing law had failed. A revision of the laws for the protection of the treasury was urged. Attention was also called to the large volume of outstanding debts due the United States by individuals. To remedy this evil, provision was made, in 1830, for the appointment of a solicitor of the treasury.[1] A suggested revision of the consular laws, however, was not made. The administration of the finances did not present special difficulties until near the close of Jackson's second term. There were some annoying defalcations, however, that of Swartwout, collector of the port of New York, being the most notable; but these natural results of unprincipled favoritism in appointments did not disturb Jackson's equanimity. An order to the secretaries of war and of the navy, August 6, 1831, directing them to report for dismissal "every clerk in your office who shall avail himself of the benefit of the insolvent debtors' act for debts contracted during my administration,"[2]

[1] *U. S. Statutes at Large*, IV., 414–416.
[2] Richardson, *Messages and Papers*, II., 544.

showed a vigorous purpose to cure one of the evils of the federal service, though dealing with the surface rather than the root of the matter.

The career of the post - office department was checkered. An investigation of the department was ordered by the Senate in December, 1830. An amendment to the resolution, framed by Grundy and Livingston, was agreed to February 15, forbidding an inquiry "into the reasons which have induced the postmaster-general to make any removals of his deputies." The report of the committee, submitted March 3, instanced thirty-six cases of extra allowances to contractors, in violation of law. The documents showed that the name of Barry, the postmaster-general, had been originally written in as authority for the allowances, but that the signature had been "rubbed out" and the name of "Abraham Bradley, acting postmaster-general," substituted.[1] Bradley had been acting head of the department for a few days between the retirement of McLean and the appointment of Barry; he remonstrated against the printing of the documents, and the printing was suspended.

The matter was soon taken up again. January 27, 1835, the committee reported that the department was in debt to the amount of eight hundred thousand dollars, mainly on account of maladministration and favoritism in letting contracts and making extra allowances; and that the reports were "so

[1] *Debates of Congress*, VII., 4–8, 208, 337.

confused and imperfect" as to be untrustworthy.
The minority of the committee fixed the amount
of the deficit at three hundred thousand dollars,
and, while recommending reorganization, claimed
that Barry had made numerous improvements. A
part of the deficit, however, was fairly chargeable
to the cost of the large number of post-offices and
post-routes established in 1832.[1] A bill to reor-
ganize the department was passed by the Senate
February 10. Amos Kendall, who succeeded Barry
in May, 1835, undertook a thoroughgoing reformation.[2] A committee of the House of Representatives reported that the finances of the department
had been managed "without frugality, system, intelligence, or adequate public utility," and that the
practice of granting extra allowances had "run into
wild excesses." An act of July 2, 1836, finally
effected the needed reorganization.[3] By the close
of Jackson's term the department was free from
debt, the service had been largely increased, and the
deficit had been turned into a surplus.

The organization of a bureau of Indian affairs,
the reorganization of the general land office, and
the codification of the laws relating to copyrights
and patents were substantial achievements in other
departments.[4] The Sac and Fox war in 1832 showed

[1] *Debates of Congress*, XI., App., 341–394; *U. S. Statutes at Large*,
IV., 534.   [2] Kendall, *Autobiography*, 331–369.
[3] *U. S. Statutes at Large*, V., 80–90.
[4] *Ibid.*, IV., 436–439, 735–738; V., 107–112, 117–125.

the insufficiency of the militia system, but Jackson's recommendations for improvement were not acted upon. In 1830, however, the military code was softened by the exemption of deserters in time of peace from punishment by death.[1]

In the legislative department of the government there was, naturally, little change. Three additional standing committees—on invalid pensions (1831), roads and canals (1831), and militia (1835)—were created in the House. In December, 1833, the election of standing committees in the Senate was substituted for appointment by the president *pro tempore*.[2] The apportionment act of May 22, 1832,[3] increased the membership of the House of Representatives from 213 to 240, a figure which was not again reached until 1860. A bill fixing the times of the annual meeting and adjournment of Congress was vetoed, June 9, 1836, on the ground that the power to legislate regarding adjournment was believed to be withheld.[4] It is interesting to note that while the administration controlled the House throughout the period from 1829 to 1837, there was an opposition majority in the Senate from 1831 until the middle of the session of 1836–1837. The opposition in the twenty-third Congress, 1833–1835, was composed of National Republicans and Calhoun

[1] *U. S. Statutes at Large*, IV., 418.
[2] McConachie, *Congressional Committees*, 353; Kerr, *Senate*, 28; *Debates of Congress*, X., 19–42.
[3] *U. S. Statutes at Large*, IV., 516.
[4] Richardson, *Messages and Papers*, III., 231.

State Rights Democrats, while that of the twenty-fourth Congress, 1835–1837, was a combination of Whigs, Nullification Democrats, and Anti-Masons.

The attitude of both the executive and the legislative departments towards the federal courts was hostile throughout the Jacksonian period; and while the ordinary operations of the courts were not as a rule interfered with, the courts were subject to a sort of moral coercion which insensibly affected their independence. The supreme court consisted in 1829 of six members, the most notable of the associate justices being Joseph Story, a jurist in no way inferior to Chief-Justice Marshall in learning and expository power, and Bushrod Washington. Washington died in November, 1829, and two associate justices, John McLean and Henry Baldwin, were appointed. When Durale resigned in January, 1835, Taney was nominated for the vacant post, but the Senate, which had already refused to confirm him as secretary of the treasury, rejected him. He was then appointed chief-justice, December 28, and confirmed March 15, 1836.

Ever since 1815, the trend of decision in the supreme court had been strongly in favor of loose construction and a broad extension of the federal powers, and of a corresponding restriction of the sphere of the states. Such opinions as those in McCulloch *vs.* Maryland (1819), Dartmouth College *vs.* Woodward (1819), Gibbons *vs.* Ogden (1824), Brown *vs.* Maryland (1827), Martin *vs.*

Mott (1827), Ogden *vs.* Saunders (1827), and American Insurance Company *vs.* Canter (1828) had given the federal authority a scope such as even the early Federalists had not claimed; while the cases affecting the Bank of the United States and the Indians, already cited, were in the same line.[1] There can be little question that such decisions predjudiced the people of the south and west against the court, and prepared them to accept Jackson's policy of independence. The attempt in 1830–1831 to repeal the twenty-fifth section of the judiciary act of 1789, with the object of preventing appeals from state courts to the federal courts, though made primarily in the interest of the South Carolina nullifiers, was an illustration of the popular feeling. Nor was the supreme court always consistent, especially in financial cases, as in Briscoe *vs.* Bank of the Commonwealth of Kentucky, where it virtually reversed its previous decisions and gave "wild-cat banking . . . standing ground under the Constitution."[2]

There was further ground for popular complaint in the failure of Congress to extend the system of circuit courts throughout the United States. Jackson took up the matter in his first annual message, pointing out that but fifteen of the twenty-four states had at the time the full benefit of the federal

[1] Cf. Babcock, *American Nationality* (*Am. Nation*, XIII.), chap. xviii.
[2] Sumner, *Jackson* (rev. ed.), 426; Cf. Smith, *Parties and Slavery* (*Am. Nation*, XVIII.), chap. xiv.

judicial system, while to three states the system of circuit courts had been "imperfectly extended," and to six "denied altogether." Some relief was granted by an act of February 19, 1831, under which the United States district courts for northern New York, western Pennsylvania, Indiana, Illinois, Missouri, Mississippi, western Louisiana, eastern Louisiana, northern Alabama, and southern Alabama were given circuit court jurisdiction in all cases save appeals and writs of error.[1] Jackson reiterated his criticism and recommendation, however, in 1831, 1832, 1834, and 1835, until Congress was at last spurred to action. An act of March 3, 1837, supplementary to the judiciary act of 1789, increased the number of members of the supreme court from seven to nine, extended the circuit courts throughout the states, and abolished the circuit jurisdiction of the district courts.[2]

An important episode in the history of the federal courts was the attempt to impeach James H. Peck, judge of the district court of the United States for the district of Missouri. A decision of Judge Peck in the case of Soulard vs. United States, in 1825, arising from claims against the United States under Spanish land grants, was criticised by the counsel for the plaintiff, Luke E. Lawless, in an anonymous article in a newspaper. For this Lawless was brought before the court, subjected to personal abuse from the judge, held guilty of contempt, and ordered to be imprisoned for twenty-four hours and

[1] *U. S. Statutes at Large*, IV., 444.   [2] *Ibid.*, V., 176–178.

suspended from the bar of the court for eighteen months.[1] Lawless twice laid his complaint before the House of Representatives, but without obtaining a hearing. In 1829, however, the House, under the lead of Buchanan, voted to impeach Judge Peck. Among the managers on the part of the House were James Buchanan and George McDuffie, while William Wirt was of counsel for the respondent.

As it appeared that Judge Peck, according to English and American precedents, had legal authority for his action, and as malice was not proved, he was, January 31, 1831, acquitted, though by the significant vote of 21 "guilty" to 22 "not guilty." [2] Inasmuch as Grundy and White, the senators from Tennessee, had voted for acquittal,[3] Adams inferred that Jackson was favorable to Peck, and did not wish to see him impeached by Buchanan's efforts, lest the influence of the latter in Congress should be increased. An act of March 2, 1831, proposed by Buchanan, limited the power of the federal courts to punish for contempt to misbehavior in the presence of the court, or so near it as to obstruct the administration of justice, misbehavior of officers of the court in official transactions, and disobedience or resistance to any lawful mandate or process of the court.[4] The case of Soulard vs. United States had

[1] Foster, *Commentaries on the Const.*, I., 543.
[2] Stansbury, *Report of the Trial of James H. Peck; Debates of Congress*, VII., passim.   [3] Adams, *Memoirs*, VIII., 306.
[4] *U. S. Statutes at Large*, IV., 487.

been, meantime, appealed to the supreme court, which in 1836 reversed Peck's decision.[1]

The personnel of the executive departments underwent frequent changes after the break-up of the cabinet in 1831. In June, 1834, McLane retired from the department of state, and was replaced by John Forsyth of Georgia, who served until the end of Jackson's term, and subsequently for four years under Van Buren. Taney, the secretary of the treasury, was replaced at the same time by Woodbury, the secretary of the navy, while Woodbury's place was given to Mahlon Dickerson, senator from New Jersey. In June, 1836, Cass, the secretary of war, was appointed minister to France. Two other appointments in the diplomatic service brought much criticism upon the administration. John Randolph of Virginia, who succeeded Henry Middleton as minister to Russia in 1830, left his post after nine days at St. Petersburg, though not until he had brought both himself and his office into contempt by his eccentric behavior. A motion to strike out the appropriation for the salary of the minister to Russia for that year was debated in the House for some weeks, and finally lost.[2] The nomination of Andrew Stevenson of Virginia, the notoriously partisan speaker of the House, to the English mission, vacant since the return of Van Buren in 1832, was rejected by the Senate in 1834,

[1] 10 Peters, 100–106.
[2] *Debates of Congress*, VII., 484–678, passim.

on the ground that for a year, and at the time he was elected speaker, he held the promise of the post, and was therefore guilty of official impropriety. Stevenson had resigned the speakership in May, 1834. A combination of opposition members with those who, though supporters of Jackson, were opposed to Van Buren for president, chose John Bell of Tennessee as speaker. The English mission remained in charge of Aaron Vail, secretary of legation, until March, 1836, when Stevenson was again nominated and confirmed.

Jackson's annual messages dwelt much upon the prosperity of the country, the economical administration of the finances, and the surplus available for the extinguishment of the debt. The gross ordinary receipts of the government rose from $24,827,000 in 1829 to $33,948,000 in 1833. In 1834 they fell to $21,791,000, then rose to $35,430,000 in 1835, and to $50,826,000 in 1836, most of the increase being in the receipts from land sales. Far the larger portion of the revenue came from customs duties, the receipts from this source expanding from $22,-681,000 in 1829 to $29,032,000 in 1833, then dropping to $16,214,000 in 1834, and again rising to $23,409,000 in 1836. Gross expenditures increased more slowly, from $15,183,000 in 1829 to $23,017,-000 in 1833. They then fell to $17,573,000 in 1835, only to rise to $30,868,000 the following year. Naval expenditures showed little fluctuation throughout the period. Military expenditures, on the other hand, increased from $5,759,000 in 1835 to $11,-747,000 in 1836, principally in consequence of the Seminole War. The expenditures for pensions were large in 1833 and 1834.[1] For two years, 1836 and 1837, there was the only freedom from interest charges that the United States has ever known.

The distribution of the surplus revenue, engrafted upon the deposit act of June 23, 1836, was obviously only a temporary expedient for meeting a trouble-some situation. The volume of the surplus, now that the debt was paid, was estimated at nine million dollars annually for eight years. There was re-luctance to disturb the compromise tariff, but it was clear that the tariff was the great cause of the surplus, and that a large surplus with no debt was bad public finance, an indefensible drain on the wealth of the people, and a dangerous incitement to speculation and extravagance. Benton argued, with his customary vehemence, in favor of devoting the temporary surplus to public works, especially fortifications and coast defences; but no one listened to him.

The plan finally agreed upon provided that the surplus in the treasury January 1, 1837, in excess of five million dollars, should be distributed among the states as a loan, in proportion to their representa-tion in Congress. No one expected, however, that the money so distributed would ever be recalled.

[1] The figures are from tables in Dewey, *Financial Hist. of the U. S.*, 168, 169, 246.

Benton put the case exactly when he said: "It is, in name, a deposit; in form, a loan; in essence and design, a distribution . . . It is known to be so, and is intended to be so; and all this verbiage about a deposit is nothing but the device and contrivance of those who have been for years endeavoring to distribute the revenues, sometimes by the land bill, sometimes by direct propositions, and sometimes by proposed amendments to the constitution. . . . It has no feature, no attribute, no characteristic, no quality of a deposit." [1] The majorities for the bill were large—38 to 6 in the Senate, 155 to 38 in the House.

Jackson had repeatedly urged the distribution of the surplus revenue among the states as the most equitable method of getting rid of it; but he now signed the act, according to Benton, at the solicitation of friends of Van Buren, and "with a repugnance of feeling, and a recoil of judgment, which it required great efforts of friends to overcome; and with a regret for it afterwards which he often and publicly expressed." [2] His annual message of December contained a long and severe arraignment of the act. Three instalments of the surplus, amounting to twenty-eight million dollars, were paid in January, April, and July, 1837; then came the panic, and the distribution ceased. The deposits have never been recalled.[3]

[1] Benton, *Thirty Years' View*, I., 652.
[2] *Ibid.*, I., 657.   [3] Bourne, *Surplus Revenue*.

CHAPTER XV

THE STATES IN JACKSON'S TIME

(1829–1837)

STUDENTS of American politics have more than once commented on the comparative unimportance of the internal history of the states. While national affairs are eagerly studied, state affairs are either neglected or else relegated to an insignificant place. The great movements and crises in national history are, indeed, reflected with more or less of distinctness in local politics, social life, and economic trend. Federal law has profoundly affected the law and practice of every state, the employment of capital and labor, the direction of industrial development, the encouragement of invention, and the interchange of commodities between the states and with foreign nations. But the superior authority and power of the central government, the ever widening scope of its operations, its steady pressure in the direction of uniformity, the undoubted prestige of its public service, and its practically unlimited financial resource, have tended, and naturally, to dwarf the smaller interests of the states; and have led the mass of people to think more often and more interestedly of the nation.

This tendency was the more noticeable in Jackson's time because of the unique importance, and the immediate and universal appeal to popular interest, of the great issues of his administrations. No consecutive eight years in the history of the United States had been so crowded with stirring events as were those from 1829 to 1837. The wide-spread popular reaction which brought Jackson's election to pass; the wholesale reconstitution of the civil service; the struggle with nullification in South Carolina; the war on the bank; the defeat of internal improvements; the removal of the Indians; the aggression upon Mexico and Texas; and the forcible inauguration of a policy of specie payment—these were events which almost completely filled the political stage, and made the issues of state politics relatively unimportant. Jackson himself, to be sure, was never weary of dwelling on the importance of the states, and the necessity of guarding jealously the powers and privileges secured to them by the Constitution; but while the genuineness of his opinions in the matter cannot be doubted, the whole course of events in his time was such as to leave to the states little opportunity for distinction.

Two states, Arkansas and Michigan, were admitted during Jackson's administrations. In each case the bills provoked long and heated debate. The territory of Michigan had been organized by act of

January 11, 1805. Unsuccessful attempts were
made in 1833 and 1834 to secure admission as a
state. In May and June, 1835, a convention, called by the legislative council of the territory, met
at Detroit and framed a state constitution, which
was ratified by the people November 2, and transmitted by Jackson to Congress December 10.[1]
Joined with the question of admission was the question of the northern boundary of Ohio, the long-
standing controversy in regard to which had several times threatened open outbreak. A bill to fix
the northern boundary of Ohio and admit Michigan
as a state was taken up in the Senate March 29.
Objection was at once made that the bill changed
the boundaries indicated in the state constitution,
yet gave to the legislature the right to assent to
the act of Congress; that the proposed boundary
deprived Michigan of territory, and hence was unjust; that the northern boundaries of Indiana and
Illinois were also involved; and that the extension
of the franchise to free white male inhabitants who
had declared their intention to become citizens of the
United States permitted aliens to vote. The debate
was not protracted, however, and the bill passed the
Senate April 2. In addition to fixing the disputed
boundaries, the bill provided that the boundaries of
Michigan should be accepted by a convention, elected
for that purpose, before the act should take effect.[2]

[1] *Senate Docs.*, 24 Cong., 1 Sess., Nos. 5, 6.
[2] *Debates of Congress*, XII., 1050-1052.

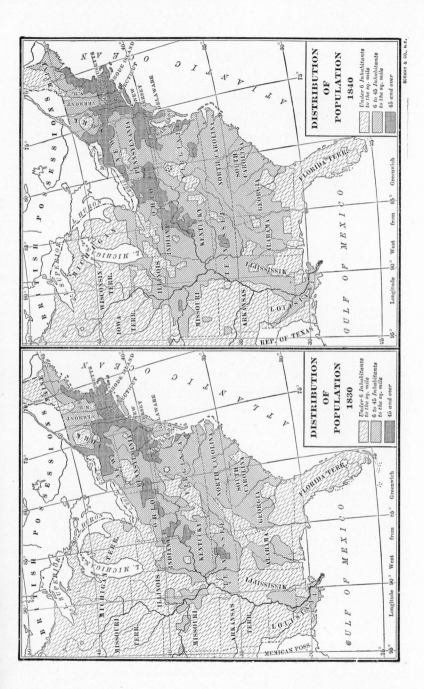

DISTRIBUTION
OF
POPULATION
1840

Under 6 Inhabitants
to the sq. mile
6 to 45 Inhabitants
to the sq. mile
45 and over

DISTRIBUTION
OF
POPULATION
1830

Under 6 Inhabitants
to the sq. mile
6 to 45 Inhabitants
to the sq. mile
45 and over

BORMAY & CO., N.Y.

In the mean time, the people of Arkansas had taken the first steps in the direction of statehood. The territory of Arkansas, formed from the southern part of the territory of Missouri, was organized by act of March 2, 1819.   In January, 1836, a convention met at Little Rock, drew up a state constitution, and applied for admission to the Union.[1] As the convention had been authorized by the territorial legislature without the consent of the governor and without a previous enabling act of Congress, the attorney-general, Butler, held the action to have been unlawful.   A bill for the admission of Arkansas, however, was reported in the Senate March 22, 1836, and passed that body, April 4, by a vote of 31 to 6.[2] The only material objection to the bill was on the ground that the proposed constitution of the state recognized slavery, and forbade the emancipation of slaves without the consent of their owners.

The two bills came up together in the House of Representatives June 8.   The character of the debate is sufficiently indicated by a remark of Wise of Virginia, that he objected to the course of the majority "in pressing this question upon a House, sleepy, tired, and drunk," but that though, on account of the lateness of the hour and the protracted session—it being then between nine and ten o'clock in the evening—it was "true that he was in an unfit condition to continue his remarks, . . . so help him

[1] *House Exec. Docs.*, 24 Cong., 1 Sess., Nos. 133, 144, 145, 164.
[2] *Debates of Congress*, XII., 934, 1057.

God, he would persevere, if he died by it."[1] The
objections to the bills were the slavery provisions
for Arkansas, and the irregular nature of the proceedings in each territory; but the real point of contention was the determination of the southern members to defeat the admission of Michigan unless
slavery were recognized without restriction in Arkansas. Both bills passed the House June 13, the
Michigan bill without a division, the Arkansas bill
by a vote of 143 to 50.[2] The vote on the third
reading of the Michigan bill was 153 to 45. Adams, who had admitted the right of Arkansas to
have slavery, but had denounced the prohibition of
emancipation in the Arkansas constitution, voted
against both bills.

A supplementary act of June 23[3] set aside certain
propositions made by the Arkansas convention regarding the public lands, and in their place offered
the state section sixteen in every township for the
support of schools; all salt-springs in excess of twelve,
the same not to be leased, however, for more than
ten years without the consent of Congress; five per
cent. of the net proceeds of the sale of lands of the
United States within the state, for making roads and
canals; an additional grant of five sections for the
erection of public buildings at Little Rock; and the
confirmation of a grant of two townships of land,
made in 1827, for the use of "a seminary of learning."

---

[1] *Debates of Congress*, XII., 4279.   [2] *Ibid.*, XII., 4294.
[3] Poore, *Charters and Constitutions*, I., 117.

The condition of these grants was that the state should never interfere with the disposal of the public lands therein by the United States, nor tax the lands of the United States, nor tax non-resident proprietors higher than those resident, nor tax military bounty lands, if held by the patentees or their heirs, for three years from the date of the patents.   The conditions of the act were accepted by the general assembly of Arkansas, October 18, as "articles of compact and union" between the state and the United States. The Michigan enabling act was accepted by a convention December 15, and on January 26, 1837, the state became a member of the Union.

The constitution of Arkansas[1] fixed the term of senators at four years, and of representatives at two years.   All free white male citizens of the United States who had resided in the state six months might vote.   Votes in general elections were to be viva voce, unless otherwise directed by law.   Bills might originate in either house of the general assembly. The term of the governor was four years, with ineligibility for more than eight years in any twelve. The election of judges of the supreme and circuit courts was vested in the general assembly.   Lotteries and the sale of lottery tickets were prohibited.   The general assembly was authorized to incorporate a bank, with branches, as a repository of the public funds, and also a bank "calculated to aid and promote the great agricultural interests of the country";

[1] Poore, *Charters and Constitutions*, I., 101-115.

the faith and credit of the state being pledged to raise the necessary funds. In addition to the slavery provisions already referred to, the constitution gave to slaves the benefit of counsel and jury trial, and prescribed in cases of capital offence the same degree of punishment as would be inflicted upon a free white person.

The constitution of Michigan,[1] though prohibiting slavery, limited the suffrage to white persons, conferring the privilege, however, upon all such persons who were residents of the state at the time of the adoption of the constitution, or who should reside in the state for six months previous to an election. The term of representatives was one year, and of senators two years, one-half of the senators retiring annually. No member of the legislature might receive any civil appointment during the term for which he was elected. The governor was given a biennial term. Judges of the supreme court were to be appointed by the governor, with the consent of the senate, and hold office for seven years; and they were subject to removal on the address of two-thirds of each branch of the legislature. A common-school system and libraries were specially provided for, and internal improvements encouraged. As in most of the constitutions of the period, amendment of the fundamental law depended on the initiative of the legislature.

There were some other significant constitutional

[1] Poore, *Charters and Constitutions*, I., 983–993.

changes in the Jacksonian period. In 1830, Virginia replaced its antiquated constitution of 1776 by
a new one.[1] In the composition of the House of
Delegates, in order to give special representation to
slave property, thirty-one members were given to
the twenty-six counties west of the Alleghany Moun-
tains, twenty-five to the fourteen counties between
the Alleghanies and the Blue Ridge, forty-two to
the twenty-nine counties east of the Blue Ridge
and above tide-water, and thirty-six to the counties,
cities, towns, and boroughs lying upon tide-water—
a device which for the first time took account of the
natural geographical divisions of the state.   In the
composition of the Senate, thirteen of the thirty-two
members were to be chosen from the counties west of
the Blue Ridge.   In the reapportionment of members, to be made in 1841 and every ten years thereafter, no change was to be made in the number of
members from the respective districts.   The suffrage was limited to whites who possessed a moderate
property qualification.   The term of the governor
was fixed at three years, and he was made ineligible
for re-election for the three years immediately following his term.   Judges were to hold their offices
during good behavior, but could be removed by impeachment or by concurrent vote of the two houses
of the general assembly.

The Delaware constitution of 1831,[2] though in

[1] Poore, *Charters and Constitutions*, II., 1912–1919.
[2] *Ibid.*, I., 289–302.

form a new instrument, was essentially an amendment of the constitution of 1792. The terms of representatives and senators, originally one and three years, were lengthened to two and four years, respectively; and the property qualification for representatives was given up. The governor had been elected for three years, with disqualification for three years thereafter; the term was now fixed at four years, and his service limited to a single term. The jurisdiction and procedure of the courts were elaborately defined.

The Mississippi constitution of 1832[1] also lengthened the term of senators from three to four years, and of representatives from one to two years. The property qualification for governor was abolished, and the period of eligibility restricted to two biennial terms in any six years. An attempt was made, as in the constitution of Virginia, to restrain the practice of duelling. Appointment to any office for life or during good behavior was prohibited. The provision of the constitution of 1817 which reserved to the state the right to subscribe to at least one-quarter of the capital stock of any bank incorporated by the legislature, was stricken out; and the requirement of a two-thirds vote of both houses on appropriations for internal improvements was added. The introduction of slaves as merchandise, or for sale, was prohibited after May 1, 1833; but actual settlers might purchase and bring in slaves from other states until 1845.

[1] Poore, *Charters and Constitutions*, II., 1067-1078.

The Tennessee constitution of 1834,[1] replacing that of 1796, was a much more elaborate document than its predecessor. Until the population of the state exceeded a million and a half, the number of members of the lower house of the general assembly was not to exceed seventy - five; and thereafter the maximum was to be ninety-nine. The number of senators was not to exceed one-third of the number of representatives. Bills might originate in either house, but every bill must be read once on three different days, and be passed each time in the house where it originated, before transmission to the other. No article manufactured from the produce of the state was to be taxed, save for the purpose of inspection. The term of the governor was two years, with eligibility for not more than six years out of eight. The property qualifications for holding office, imposed by the constitution of 1796, were dropped. Free negroes were exempted from military service in time of peace, and from the payment of a poll-tax; and no person of color was to be debarred from voting who was, at the time of the adoption of the constitution, a competent witness in court against a white person. The latter exemption covered the case of persons whose blood showed only a small negro admixture.

North Carolina, which still retained its original constitution of 1776, adopted in 1835 an extended series of amendments which materially modified the

[1] Poore, *Charters and Constitutions*, II., 1677–1688.

earlier instrument.[1] The general assembly was to
be composed of a senate of fifty members, chosen by
districts, and a house of commons of one hundred
and twenty members, chosen by counties, in each
case according to population as reckoned by the
federal Constitution. Elections were to be by ballot. No free negro, free mulatto, or free person of
mixed blood descended from negro ancestors to the
fourth generation inclusive (though one ancestor
of each generation might have been white), could
vote for members of the assembly. The sessions of
the assembly were to be biennial. The term of the
governor was two years, with the privilege of eligibility for four years in any six. The prohibition on
the tenure of civil office by Catholics was removed,
but the provision which excluded all who did not
believe in God, or in the truth of the Christian religion or the inspiration of the Bible, was retained.

No other state except Arkansas and Michigan
adopted a new constitution during this period.
Rhode Island tried to do so in 1835, but failed. A
number of states, however, adopted constitutional
amendments. Alabama in 1830 fixed the tenure
of judicial offices at six years, instead of for good
behavior. Connecticut in 1832 provided for the
election of a treasurer and secretary in the same
manner as the governor, and in 1836 for the similar
choice of a comptroller. The property qualification
for members of the general assembly of Georgia was

[1] Poore, *Charters and Constitutions*, II., 1415–1418.

abolished in 1833, and the judicial system reorganized in 1835. Maine revised its electoral system in 1834.[1] Massachusetts in 1833 changed the beginning of its political year from the last Wednesday of May to the first Wednesday of January, and set aside the provisions of the bill of rights of the constitution of 1780, which provided for an established church. The representation of the towns in the general court was reconstituted in 1836. The New York constitution of 1821 had reserved the proceeds of a salt tax as a contribution towards the maintenance of canals. In 1833 a reduction of the tax was provided for, while in 1835 provision was made for diverting the salt revenue to the general fund. An oath of allegiance to the state was required of all officials in South Carolina in 1834. The legislative system of Vermont was revised in 1836.[2]

An examination of these various constitutional changes shows a general, though not predominant, trend towards democracy. The lengthening of the term of legislatures and executives indicates no fondness for frequent elections, and the powers of governors are not largely curtailed. On the other hand, the basis of representation is appreciably widened, and the responsibility of executive and judicial officers to the legislatures or to the people enhanced. There is marked jealousy of the judiciary, as shown by the popular choice of judges and the

[1] Poore. *Charters and Constitutions*, I., 46, 267, 399, 803.
[2] *Ibid.*, I., 975; II., 1350, 1636, 1883–1885.

stricter drawing of jurisdictional lines. The property qualification for voting or holding office becomes discredited, and in most states disappears altogether. The disestablishment of the church in Massachusetts marked the completion of the religious emancipation of that state. On the other hand, the new constitutions grow somewhat in length, and there are signs of the tendency, very marked after another generation, to embody in the constitution provisions which fall more properly within the domain of statute law.

The most noticeable change in political methods in the states was the general adoption of the convention system in nominations for office, and the increased effectiveness of political machinery. By 1835 the nomination of state and local officers by legislative caucus or informal presentation of candidates had generally given place to nomination by convention, although the nomination of candidates for president and vice-president by state legislatures continued. A complete system of state and local committees was to be found in many states as early as 1830, and was extended as national party lines were more definitely drawn.[1] Voting by written or printed ballot was general, although Virginia, in its constitution of 1830, required viva voce voting in all elections.

In all matters of political organization, New York was the leading state. No state could show such an array of prominent names. To Enos T. Throup,

[1] Dallinger, *Nominations for Elective Office*, 29, 31, 44.

governor from 1829 to 1832; Azariah C. Flagg and
John A. Dix, secretaries of state from 1826 to 1839;
William L. Marcy, comptroller from 1823 to 1829,
and governor from 1833 to 1839; Silas Wright,
comptroller from 1829 to 1834, and Greene C. Bron-
son, attorney-general from 1829 to 1836, are to be
added William H. Maynard, Nathaniel P. Tallmadge,
Albert H. Tracy, and William H. Seward, state
senators, and John C. Spencer and Millard Fillmore,
assemblymen.[1] The "Albany regency," the most
skilful group of political mechanicians that had yet
appeared in the United States, remained throughout
a state organization, touching national politics chiefly through its control of federal patronage, but lending the powerful weight of its example to the movement for closer party organization. Van Buren's
success as secretary of state and vice-president added greatly to the influence of the regency, and
opened the way for the imitation of its methods by
other states and in federal affairs. Pennsylvania
and Massachusetts, however, were not far behind
New York, while in Virginia and South Carolina the
solidarity of the great planters gave to that class
effective control of the party organizations, and, for
the most part, of electons as well.

New York was a strong protectionist state in 1828.
The electoral vote in that year was divided, twenty
of the thirty-six votes being given for Jackson and
Calhoun, and the remainder for Adams and Rush.

[1] Roberts, *New York*, II., 583.

The popular vote was close—140,763 for Jackson, 135,413 for Adams. From 1833, the main issues between parties were banks and canals. The Whigs were favorable to banks; the "regency" Democrats favored state banks, but opposed the Bank of the United States; while the wing of the Democracy known as "Loco-Focos" demanded free banking and the abolition of special privileges. On the question of canals the Democrats were again divided, the conservative faction, or "Hunkers," advocating an extension of the canal system, and the radicals, or "Barnburners," opposing further expenditures for unprofitable canals.[1] The safety-fund system of banking, established in 1829, provided a fund, equal to three per cent. of the capital stock of a bank, for the redemption of the notes of insolvent banks; and the early success of the system did something to allay the opposition to banks. The objections to appropriations for canals came principally from the counties not reached by the Erie Canal and its branches. A plan for a southern highway, designed to meet this objection, was withdrawn in favor of the New York and Erie Railroad, to which a loan of three million dollars was made in 1836. Similar loans to other railroads followed.

State aid to railroads was also extended in New England, and nearly forty railroad companies were incorporated between 1829 and 1837. Governor Lincoln, in his message of 1829, advocated the con-

[1] Johnston, in Lalor, *Cyclo. of Polit. Science*, II., 1022.

struction of railroads by the state, and the Western, Norwich and Worcester, Andover and Haverhill, and Eastern railroads received aid from Massachusetts in 1836 and 1837. The line from Boston to Providence was opened to travel in June, 1835. The same decade saw the introduction of modern methods of wool manufacture in New England, the strict regulation of savings-banks in Massachusetts, and the opening of the marble quarries at West Rutland, Vermont. In 1834 the Massachusetts school fund was established, comprising the receipts from the sale of reserved lands in Maine, and the money received from the United States under claims for military services.[1] Joint-stock corporations, begun before the Revolution, multiplied after 1830.[2]

Political divisions in the states tended after 1830 to follow national lines. Maine, which voted for Adams in 1824 and 1828, gave majorities for Jackson and Van Buren in 1832 and 1836, and as a rule chose Democratic members of Congress. The leadership of Isaac Hill and Levi Woodbury brought Democratic success in New Hampshire. In Vermont the National Republicans and Anti-Masons so far united as to choose presidential electors under the latter name in 1832; and the combination, shortly known by the name of Whigs, continued thereafter to con-

[1] *Laws of Mass.*, XIII., 241.
[2] Johnston, *Connecticut*, 367; *Public Laws of Conn.* (1836–1840), 49–53; Baldwin, *Am. Business Corporations before 1789* (*Am. Hist. Rev.*, VIII., 447).

trol the state.   Massachusetts had Whig governors
from 1834 to 1839.   Connecticut, on the other hand,
was an anti-Democratic state, save in 1836, when
Van Buren captured the electoral vote by a majority
of 542 in a total of 38,040.   In Pennsylvania the
Anti-Masons kept up a separate organization longer
than elsewhere, and in 1835 elected the governor.
The New Jersey governors were generally Whig, and
the legislatures generally Democratic.[1]

Ohio elected a Clay governor in 1829, notwithstanding its vote for Jackson the previous year; and
the state government continued to be National Republican or Whig until 1838.   In Indiana, party
divisions followed geographical lines, the northern
counties being National Republican or Whig, the
southern counties Democratic.   With the exception
of the Wayne congressional district, the state was
counted in the Democratic column from 1828 to
1836.   Illinois chose Democratic congressmen until
1834, after which time one of the three districts was
usually Whig by a small majority.[2]   Kentucky,
under the influence of Clay, went with the Whigs.
A State Rights party got control of Tennessee in
1835, and secured the electoral vote of the state in
1836 for Hugh L. White.

The legislature of Maryland was controlled by the
Whigs from 1820 to 1852, and until 1837 the governors were of the same party.   North Carolina showed

[1] Johnston, in Lalor, *Cyclop. of Polit. Science*, II., 1015.
[2] *Ibid.*, 477, 496.

a Whig majority in 1836. In Georgia the chief political issue, from 1825 to 1835, was the removal of
the Indians, and the State Rights or "Troup" party
retained its organization until 1837, though before
that time it had become practically Whig. In number of votes, however, the Whig and Democratic
followings were pretty evenly divided, with the
Democrats slightly preponderant.[1] The members
of Congress, who were chosen on a general ticket,
were as a rule Democrats. Mississippi had a strong
Whig minority until 1837, when the minority became a majority. The sugar interests of Louisiana
favored the growth of the Whigs in that state, although the French and English elements of the
population were commonly found on opposite sides
of political questions.[2]

The activity of the states was strikingly shown in
the increase of state debts. For a number of years
after the War of 1812 the states were largely free
from debt, but with the development of the west and
the demand for internal improvements, bonded indebtedness rose rapidly. From 1825 to 1830 the
debts contracted aggregated $13,079,689; from 1830
to 1835, $40,012,769; from 1835 to 1838, $107,823,-
808. Of the total state debt of $170,806,187 in 1838,
$52,640,000 had been incurred in aid of banks,
$60,201,551 for the construction of canals, $42,871,-
084 in aid of railroads, $6,618,868 for turnpikes and

[1] Johnson, in Lalor, *Cyclop. of Polit. Science*, II., 334.
[2] *Ibid.*, 785.

roads, and $8,474,684 for miscellaneous objects.[1]
To this was to be added the $28,000,000 received
from the United States as a loan through the distribution of the surplus revenue. The burden was
greater than the resources of the states warranted,
and after the panic of 1837 a number of states repudiated their debts in whole or in part.

The growth of cities between 1830 and 1840 devolved further responsibilities upon the state legislatures, particularly in the direction of charter making and suitable legal provision for the welfare of
compact masses of population. Municipal development showed the general adoption of manhood suffrage in place of a suffrage based on property qualification, and the election of the mayor by popular
vote. The bicameral city council, a reflection of the
state legislative organization, gained somewhat in
favor. There was a widening range of municipal activity in such directions as police and fire systems,
lighting, sanitation, and water supply. As a consequence, taxation and debt increased, and municipal finance assumed special importance. A considerable volume of special legislation developed
through the action of city councils and state legislatures in reference to these new activities.[2]

Finally, the decade of the thirties saw substantial
gains in humanitarian and educational directions,
due in part to the increased diffusion of culture and

[1] Tenth Census (1880), VII., 523, 526.
[2] Fairlie, *Municipal Administration*, 81–85.

wealth, in part to the financial hopefulness which accompanied a period of business speculation. The prison systems of Pennsylvania and New York, the one distinguished for its use of solitary confinement, the other for its rule of silence imposed on all prisoners, attracted much attention as marked advancements in the humane and disciplinary treatment of criminals. Boston, New York, and Philadelphia had reformatories for children, in which state aid supplemented private benevolence. Stephen Girard, who died in 1831, left the bulk of his fortune for the establishment of the orphan school which bears his name. The total-abstinence movement which began in 1824, and which numbered more than a thousand societies in 1829, contributed immeasurably to the health, good order, and prosperity of the people.[1] The establishment of Oberlin, Mount Holyoke, Randolph-Macon, Haverford, Knox, Muskingum, Lafayette, Wabash, and Marietta colleges, Tulane, Wesleyan, and New York universities, the state universities of Michigan and Alabama, and Hartford, Lane, and Union theological seminaries, met and strengthened the growing demand for higher education. Even religion felt the democratic impulse, for while the non-liturgical sects everywhere predominated, there was a softened regard for Episcopalians, and a decline of the discrimination and petty persecution to which Roman Catholics had long been subject.

[1] Schouler, *United States*, III., 524.

CHAPTER XVI

PUBLIC LANDS AND THE SPECIE CIRCULAR
(1829–1837)

AT the time when Jackson entered upon his first administration, the law and practice of the United States in reference to the public domain had crystallized into something like a system. The system of rectangular survey had been long accepted, and in its extension was more than keeping pace with the settled area. In the development of local government, the township, with its subdivisions of school districts and road districts, represented a natural adoption of the nomenclature and form of the survey, while the county, when it came to be organized, was a combination of townships.[1] The process of quieting the Indian title had been going on for many years, and the removal of the Indians westward was under way. The annual expenses of the department of Indian affairs, including the charges for annuities and other obligations resulting from the surrender of the occupancy - title of lands to the United States, were from $275,000 to $750,000 in the years from 1815 to 1829.[2] A General

---

[1] Howard, *Local Const. Hist.*, I., 155.
[2] *House Exec. Docs.*, 46 Cong., 3 Sess., No. 47, pt. iv., 20.

Land Office, for the issuance of patents and other purposes, was created in 1812 as a bureau of the treasury department.[1]

In 1820 the minimum price of land was reduced from two dollars to one dollar and twenty-five cents per acre, and sales for cash in quantities of not less than eighty acres provided for.[2] Land sales, aggregating 781,213 acres in 1821, reached 1,244,860 acres in 1829. Receipts from the sales of lands from 1815 to 1829 averaged a million to a million and a half dollars a year. From 1830 to 1837 inclusive, 57,-294,834 acres were sold, over 36,000,000 acres, however, being disposed of in 1836 and 1837. Grants to states and corporations for internal improvements amounted to 1,780,505 acres between 1827 and 1838, although but 29,552 acres were so granted during Jackson's presidency. Grants to states for other purposes than internal improvements reached 2,138,-117 acres, and grants to individuals 2,459,373 acres, between 1829 and 1837. Altogether, 63,166,736 acres of the public domain were disposed of during Jackson's time.[3] The notion that the public lands were a great potential source of national revenue was still held by many, though in practice the United States had never been much governed by it, but instead had disposed of its lands on easy terms, with the object of inducing early settlement. Down to 1829, at least, the idea of a liberal land policy

[1] *U. S. Statutes at Large*, II., 717.   [2] *Ibid.*, III., 566.
[3] Hart, *Practical Essays on Am. Government*, 256.

found favor in all sections of the country, while the high protectionists, aware that their system would be jeopardized by a surplus, were not anxious to see a new source of revenue developed in the west.[1]

Save as regards the removal of the Indians, Jackson's earlier messages do not indicate any policy concerning the public lands. Foot's resolution, in 1829, apparently intended to equalize sales in different districts and insure the disposal of lands already on the market, provoked a debate in which nullification, and not the land system, was the subject discussed. The existing system, however, was not satisfactory, especially to those who resented the continuance of federal authority over any part of the area of a state. There was discussion of the propriety of reducing the price of land, and of ceding unsold lands to the states. A bill, introduced by Benton, providing for the sale of lands at graduated prices, and reducing the price of land which remained unsold after three years, was passed by the Senate, May 7, 1830, by the close vote of 24 to 22, but was laid on the table in the House.[2]

March 23, 1832, Clayton presented a resolution directing the committee on manufactures to inquire into the expediency of distributing the public lands, or the proceeds of their sale, among the states, "on equitable principles."[3] The reference of the resolution to the committee on manufactures, which had in

---

[1] Dewey, *Financial Hist. of the U. S.*, 217.
[2] *Debates of Congress*, VI., 427, 1148.   [3] *Ibid.*, VIII., 638.

charge the tariff bill, was embarrassing to Clay, who was chairman of the committee, because of the bearing upon the tariff of the revenue from the sale of lands. In a report on the resolution, April 16,[1] Clay argued against the policy of the resolution, and recommended that, since the revenue from customs was sufficient for ordinary purposes, the revenue from the public lands, after deducting fifteen per cent. as a dividend for the states in which the lands were situated, be divided for five years among the states "according to their federal representative population, to be applied to education, internal improvement, or colonization, or to the redemption of any existing debt contracted for internal improvements, as each state, judging for itself, shall deem most conformable with its own interests and policy." The estimated amount of such annual distribution was $2,550,000.

The bill which accompanied the report of the committee on manufactures went to the committee on public lands, which in a report, submitted May 18 by King of Alabama, took issue with Clay at every point.[2] The report recommended a reduction of the price of new land to one dollar per acre, and of land, much of it comparatively worthless, which had been on the market five years, to fifty cents per acre; together with an increase of the allowance to the new states to twenty instead of fifteen per cent. The

---

[1] *Debates of Congress*, VIII., App., 112–118.
[2] *Ibid.*, VIII., App., 118–127.

Senate passed Clay's bill, but the House by postpone-
ment declined to consider it.   The opinion of the administration was probably represented by McLane,
the secretary of the treasury, in his annual report in
December, 1831,[1] in which he suggested the sale of
the public lands to the states in which they lay, and
the apportionment of the proceeds among the states
"according to such equitable ratio as may be consistent with the objects of the original cession."   The
alleged reasons for the proposal were that the revenue would thereby be reduced and all causes of difficulty between the states and the general government removed.

In his message of December, 1832, Jackson expressed the opinion that the true policy was "that
the public lands shall cease as soon as practicable to
be a source of revenue, and that they be sold to
settlers in limited parcels at a price barely sufficient
to reimburse to the United States the expense of the
present system and the cost arising under our Indian
compacts."   Clay's distribution bill of the previous
session was renewed, and debated at length until
January 25, when, by a vote of 24 to 20, it passed
the Senate, a substitute reducing the price of lands
being rejected.   The bill passed the House March
1, after a heated debate in which there was much
disorder.[2]

[1] *Debates of Congress*, VIII., App., 20.
[2] Richardson, *Messages and Papers*, II., 601; *Debates of Congress*, IX., 1920.

Jackson pocketed the bill, and then took the extraordinary course of sending to the Senate, on December 4, 1833, a message explaining his action.[1] Jackson's objections to the bill were that it "begins with an entire subversion of every one of the compacts by which the United States became possessed of their western domain, and treats the subject as if they never had existence and as if the United States were the original and unconditional owners of all the public lands"; that it appropriates the money of the United States to objects of a local character within the states, thus reasserting the principle of the Maysville turnpike bill which Jackson had vetoed; and that, instead of returning to the people "an unavoidable surplus of revenue paid in by them," it creates a surplus for distribution. "A more direct road to consolidation," Jackson declared, "cannot be devised."

The action of the president was vigorously denounced by Clay as "unprecedented and alarming."[2] The subject, he declared, had been long before Congress and the country. The bill had been made the subject of comment in the annual message at the beginning of the previous session, and presumably the president had had sufficient opportunity to make up his mind as to its merits. It was not to be expected, therefore, that he would take advantage of the shortness of the session, and the late date on

---

[1] Richardson, *Messages and Papers*, III., 56–69.
[2] *Debates of Congress*, X., 15–18.

which the bill had been sent to him, to retain the bill so long. Instead of promptly approving or vetoing it, however, he had "despotically kept silence." To Benton's defence that the number of bills passed on the last day of the session was so great as to preclude proper consideration of them, much less the preparation of an elaborate statement of reasons, Clay rejoined that the president had apparently found time to approve most of the bills so presented, and that his course in withholding the land bill was "arbitrary and unconstitutional."

On December 10, Clay again introduced the bill, modified by removing the restrictions on the states in the application of the proceeds of the lands—a restriction which he considered unnecessary. The report of the committee to which the bill was referred, submitted May 2, 1834,[1] contended that the failure of the president to return the bill to the Congress which passed it practically converted the qualified veto granted by the Constitution into an absolute veto, by depriving Congress of its constitutional right to reconsider a bill and determine whether it ought not to pass notwithstanding the president's objections. It is obvious that the effect of such a doctrine would be to destroy the veto power altogether.[2] As to the objection, upon which Jackson had dwelt at length, that the bill violated the agreement under which the lands were ceded to the United States, it was

[1] *Debates of Congress*, X., 24; App., 205–212.
[2] Mason, *Veto Power*, 113.

insisted that there was nothing in the acts of cession, or in the treaties under which still larger tracts of land had been acquired, which interfered with the right of Congress to dispose of the public lands; and such disposition had been, in practice, unrestricted. If Jackson's proposal to grant all the lands to the states were constitutional, might not Congress also grant, for a limited time, one-eighth of the net proceeds of the lands to the states in which they were situated?

A committee of the House of Representatives had already reported, December 27, in favor of reducing and graduating the price of such lands as had been offered at public sale, and remained unsold, in proportion to the time the lands had been on the market.[1] Benton got some memorials and statistics relating to the same subject printed by the Senate. No further action was taken by either House, however, and the matter dropped.

Clay brought forward the distribution bill once more, in December, 1835.[2] The proposition now was to distribute the proceeds of the land sales for the years 1833 to 1837 inclusive, the amount for the years 1833, 1834, and 1835 aggregating a little over twenty - one million dollars. The bill passed the Senate, May 4, by a vote of 25 to 20. The House laid the bill on the table, and the agitation for the distribution of the revenue from the public lands

---

[1] *Debates of Congress*, X., App., 213–215.
[2] *Ibid.*, XII., 48.

among the states came to an end. It was at this point that Calhoun successfully urged his scheme for the distribution of the surplus revenue as a whole, embodied in the deposit act of June 23, 1836.

The public land question shortly became involved with the question of the currency. Down to the time of the removal of the deposits, Jackson had been supposed to favor paper money,[1] while Benton, his chief spokesman in Congress, earned the sobriquet of "Old Bullion" for his insistent advocacy of hard money. Various propositions for the revision of the coinage laws and the establishment of a metallic currency were considered in Congress during Jackson's first administration: and new interest was given to the subject by the increased production of gold in the southern Alleghanies. An act of June 23, 1834, fixed the standard and weight of gold coins so as to make the ratio to silver sixteen to one. In 1835, branch mints were established at Charlotte, North Carolina, Dahlonega, Georgia, and at New Orleans, the two former for gold coinage only. The act of 1834 did not alter the weight of the silver dollar, but no silver dollars were coined from 1805 to 1836, and those of the latter year could not be kept in circulation, inasmuch as the overvaluation of silver made that metal a commodity.[2]

Jackson's later messages show increasing interest

---

[1] Sumner, *Jackson* (rev. ed.), 371.
[2] *U. S. Statutes at Large*, IV., 699, 774; Sumner, *Jackson* (rev. ed.), 392.

in the establishment of a specie currency and the withdrawal of bank-notes. For a few months after the removal of the deposits the currency was in sound condition.[1] The deposit banks felt the necessity of maintaining an adequate specie reserve, and the Bank of the United States managed its affairs with discretion. In 1834, however, banks began to multiply at a dangerous rate. A year later, the country was fairly embarked on an era of speculation. The payment of the public debt, the abundance of free capital in the United States and Europe, the development of canal transportation, and the building or projection of railroads, combined to produce the ambitious and reckless confidence which attends a speculative fever. Prices and rents rose, and business enterprises based on credit were extensively launched. To the ordinary observer, the United States seemed to be floating on a wave of wonderful prosperity.

The speculative spirit showed itself particularly in the sales of public lands. The opening of the Erie Canal, together with the projection or construction of other canals and the building of roads, had given a powerful impulse to the economic development of the west. As a consequence, the receipts from the sale of lands increased: in 1834 they were $4,857,000; in 1835, $14,757,000; in 1836, $24,877,-000, being greater in the latter year than the receipts from customs.[2]

[1] Sumner, *Jackson* (rev. ed.), 372.
[2] *House Exec. Docs.*, 46 Cong., 3 Sess., No. 47, pt. iv., 17.

The government found itself embarrassed, however, by the variety of currency received in payment for public lands. In 1834, Jackson had proposed to the deposit banks a plan for the gradual
withdrawal of notes of less than twenty dollars, and
the substitution of specie.[1] By October, 1836, more
than half the states had forbidden the further issue
of notes under five dollars, although the circulation
of such notes of earlier issues continued.[2] But the
increasing local demand for money, strikingly evidenced by the high rates of discount in the fall and
winter of 1835–1836, the temptation offered by the
possession of the government deposits, the willingness to aid speculative enterprises by loans, and the
mania for banking, led to further inflation of the
volume of paper, and rendered useless all efforts to
force the circulation of specie. In June, 1836, the deposit banks, with a combined capital of $46,400,000,
and a circulation of $27,900,000, owed to the United
States $37,200,000, to other depositors $16,000,000,
and to other banks $17,100,000; while their gross
assets of $147,000,000 comprised $71,200,000 in
loans, $37,100,000 in domestic exchange, $17,800,000
due from other banks, $10,900,000 of notes of other
banks, and $10,400,000 in specie.[3]

The probable course of the administration was
foreshadowed by the issuance, in 1835 and 1836, of a
number of treasury orders to the receivers and dis-

---

[1] Sumner, *Jackson* (rev. ed.), 371.   [2] *Ibid.*, 379.
[3] *Niles' Register*, L., 313.

bursers of the public money and to the deposit banks. An order of April 6, 1835, prohibited the receipt, after September 30, 1835, of bank-notes of a denomination less than five dollars.[1] A further order, February 22, 1836, prohibited the payment of such notes to any public officer or creditor, or the receipt after July 4 of bank - notes of a denomination less than ten dollars, unless otherwise provided by law.[2] In the payments by the deposit banks of sums less than five hundred dollars, creditors were empowered to demand one-fifth in gold.   The banks were further requested not to issue notes under five dollars after July 4, nor under ten dollars after March 3, 1837. The latter part of the request was interesting in view of the fact that it would not become operative, if acceded to, until after the expiration of Jackson's term.

These orders were followed, July 11, 1836, by the "specie circular," addressed to receivers of public money and to the deposit banks.[3] The order forbade the receipt, after August 15, in payment for public lands, of anything save what was directed by existing laws—viz., gold and silver, and in certain cases Virginia land-warrants; exception being made, until December 15, of payments for parcels of land "not exceeding 320 acres to each purchaser, who is an actual settler or bona fide resident in the State

[1] *House Exec. Docs.*, 24 Cong., 1 Sess., No. 3, p. 54.
[2] *Niles' Register*, L., 10.
[3] *Senate Docs.*, 24 Cong., 2 Sess., No. 2, p. 96.

where the sales are made." The receipt of drafts or certificates of money or deposits, though for specie, was prohibited unless they bore the signature of the treasurer of the United States. The purposes of the circular were declared to be "to repress alleged frauds, and to withhold any countenance or facilities in the power of the government from the monopoly of the public lands in the hands of speculators and capitalists, to the injury of the actual settlers in the new States, and of emigrants in search of new homes, as well as to discourage the ruinous extension of bank issues and bank credits, by which those results are generally supposed to be promoted."

Benton is authority for the statement that he himself drew the rough draught of the circular at the request of A. J. Donelson, Jackson's private secretary; that a majority of the cabinet were opposed to it; and that it was not issued until after the adjournment of Congress, "for the fear that Congress would counteract it by law." [1] The circular added greatly to the difficulties of the banks, particularly in the west, where banks were numerous, paper money plenty, and specie scarce. Most of the banks whose notes had provoked the circular did not pay specie. [2] Further, the deposit banks were under obligation to pay out to the states on January 1 the first instalment of the surplus revenue to be distributed under the act of June 23. The specie circular was only one of the

---

[1] Benton, *Thirty Years' View*, I., 676–678.
[2] Sumner, *Jackson* (rev. ed.), 393.

causes, however, of the panic of 1837. The progress
of speculation and inflation had about reached its
limit, and the circular did little more than administer the blow that brought on collapse.

Jackson defended the specie circular in his annual
message in December, declaring that it had "produced many salutary consequences," checked the
career of the western banks, cut off the means of
speculation in land, "tended to save the new States
from a non-resident proprietorship," kept the public
lands open for entry by immigrants at government
prices, and caused the transfer to the west of large
quantities of gold and silver, "there to enter perma-
nently into the currency of the country and place it
on a firmer foundation." [1]   The circular was at once
attacked, however.   Ewing of Ohio introduced a
resolution in the Senate, December 12, to annul the
circular, and to prohibit the secretary of the treasury
"from directing what funds should be receivable in
payment for public lands, and from making any
discrimination in the funds so receivable, between
different individuals, or between different branches
of the public service." [2]

The debate which followed savored of an approaching presidential election.   Benton defended Jackson
with his accustomed exuberance of rhetoric.   "After
forty years of wandering in the wilderness of paper
money, we have approached the confines of the con-

[1] Richardson, *Messages and Papers*, III., 249.
[2] *Senate Journal*, 24 Cong., 2 Sess., 31.

stitutional medium. . . . If reform measures go on, gold and silver will be gradually and temperately restored; if reforms are stopped, then the paper runs riot, and explodes from its own expansion." [1] Crittenden of Kentucky, on the other hand, ridiculed the notion that specie could be forced out of the commercial centres where it was most needed and most used; while Webster deemed it remarkable "that these evils of frauds, speculation, and monopoly should have become so enormous and so notorious, on July 11, as to require this executive interference for their suppression, and yet that they should not have reached such a height as to make it proper to lay the subject before Congress, although Congress remained in session until within seven days of the date of the order." [2]

The resolution was referred to the committee on public lands, which reported, January 18, 1837, a bill providing for the reception by the government of the notes of such specie paying banks as should discontinue the issue of notes of denominations less than five dollars, and after December 30, 1839, of less than ten dollars. [3] The bill applied to receipts from customs and other sources as well as to those from lands. With amendments cutting off notes under twenty dollars after 1841, and rescinding the specie circular, the bill passed the Senate, February

[1] Benton, *Thirty Years' View*, I., 697.
[2] Webster, *Works* (ed. of 1851), IV., 268.
[3] *Niles' Register*, LI., 356.

10, by a vote of 41 to 5. Calhoun, who was convinced that the currency was "almost incurably bad," declined to vote. In the House, March 1, the bill passed without division, the large majority, however, in its favor being indicated by the vote of 143 to 59 on engrossment for a third reading. Butler, the attorney-general, to whom the bill was referred, found it so obscure that Jackson vetoed it.[1]

The specie circular was finally disposed of by a joint resolution of May 21, 1838, which forbade the secretary of the treasury "to make or to continue in force, any general order, which shall create any difference between the different branches of revenue, as to the money or medium of payment, in which debts or dues, accruing to the United States, may be paid."[2]

---

[1] Richardson, *Messages and Papers*, III., 282–288.
[2] *U. S. Statutes at Large*, V., 310.

CHAPTER XVII

THE ELECTION OF 1836

(1836–1837)

THE presidential campaign which terminated with the election of 1836 was in one respect unique. The nomination of Van Buren, foreshadowed from the time of his withdrawal from the cabinet, was part of a carefully wrought plan which was intended to give the Jackson party control of the executive department of the federal government for years to come.[1] Yet the central figure throughout the canvass was not Van Buren, but Jackson. Although Jackson apparently recognized the force of the third-term tradition,[2] and wisely took no steps to break it, it was he who chose his successor, and forced him upon a reluctant electorate with all the energy and power which personal and official prestige, joined to control of the federal patronage, could give. Of all those who took a prominent part in the contest, Van Buren was one of the least consequential, and the Democratic victory at the polls was the triumph of Jackson, not of his candidate.

[1] Parton, *Jackson*, III., 297.
[2] Sumner, *Jackson* (rev. ed.), 440.

So far as the Democrats were concerned, the issues of the campaign were furnished by the administration. The events of Jackson's second term had a curious effect upon the Democratic following of the president. At no time was the personality of Jackson more aggressively dominant. The victory over the nullifiers in the winter of 1832–1833 was followed by the arbitrary removal of the deposits, with its accompanying forcible reconstruction of the cabinet. The strained relations with France reached a crisis early in 1836. The annexation of Texas was persistently, though covertly, fostered by the administration. In April, 1836, Benton's expunging crusade reached its spectacular culmination. In July came the specie circular. There could be no doubt that these bold strokes, defiant of precedent and opposition, had alienated many of Jackson's more intelligent supporters. There was no evidence, however, that they had shaken in the least his popularity with the masses or lessened the confidence of his political allies in their ability to carry things through. John Tyler affirmed that the world never saw a "more perfectly unprincipled set of men" than Jackson's advisers;[1] and it was upon their efficient aid that Jackson relied to bring success at the polls.

It was the good fortune of Jackson that he did not have to contend with a well-organized and united opposition. The majority of the anti-Jackson forces who in 1834 took the name of Whigs, represented a

[1] Tyler, *Tylers*, II., 414.

combination of factions which agreed only in opposition to the administration and its candidate. As described by Horace Greeley in 1838,[1] the Whigs comprised: " (1) Most of those who, under the name of National Republicans, had previously been known as supporters of Adams and Clay, and advocates of the American system; (2) Most of those who, acting in defence of what they deemed the assailed or threatened rights of the States, had been stigmatized as Nullifiers, or the less virulent State-Rights men, who were thrown into a position of armed neutrality towards the administration by the doctrines of the proclamation of 1832 against South Carolina; (3) A majority of those before known as Anti-Masons; (4) Many who had up to that time been known as Jackson men, but who united in condemning the high-handed conduct of the Executive, the immolation of Duane, and the subserviency of Taney; (5) Numbers who had not before taken any part in politics, but who were now awakened from their apathy by the palpable usurpations of the Executive, and the imminent peril of our whole fabric of constitutional liberty and national prosperity."

It was manifest that such a combination lacked the elements necessary to the formation of a permanent national party. The Whigs were united only in opposition to what they characterized as "executive usurpation." The fundamental political

[1] Whig Almanac, 1838, quoted in Stanwood, *Hist. of the Presidency*, 180.

question before the country was whether, in the development of the governmental frame - work of the constitution, the legislative or the executive departments should dominate. Down to the time of Jackson the whole tendency had been towards the absorption of power by Congress, and the consequent minimization of executive independence. It was against this tendency that Jackson fought, and fought, as it turned out, successfully. The Whigs, accordingly, stood for the old order, and claimed that they alone represented original republican principles. They drew to their ranks men of property and social position, who naturally sought to curb the executive through the legislature,[1] together with the dissatisfied of all parties. Their creed, however, was largely personal, and they lacked organization. In the history of American parties they bridge the chasm between the decadent Federalism of the first quarter of the century and the principled Republicanism of the fifties.

To the Whig combination the Democrats — or Democratic Republicans, as they were still often termed—could oppose a programme which had at least historical force. They stood in general for a strict construction of the Constitution and the maintenance of the rights of the states as against federal encroachments. They were in favor of popular suffrage and direct participation of the people in legislation and the choice of public officials. They

[1] Burgess, *Middle Period*, 282.

were opposed to paper money, to banks, to monopolies and special privileges. To a creed were now added an effective organization, developed by Kendall, Blair, Lewis, and others on the model of the Albany Regency; and a leader of unprecedented popularity. It remained to be seen whether the machine and the president could dictate the succession to the throne of "King Andrew."

The strength of the opposition, joined to the hostility to Van Buren within the Democratic ranks, suggested an early nomination. The Democratic convention met in Baltimore, May 20, 1835. The chairman was Andrew Stevenson of Virginia, whose gross partisanship as speaker of the House of Representatives had made him especially odious to the anti-Jackson men, and whose nomination as minister to Russia had been rejected by the Senate. All the states except South Carolina, Alabama, Illinois, and Tennessee, together with the territories of Michigan and Arkansas, were represented by such number of delegates as they chose to send. Tennessee, Jackson's own state, was against Van Buren, and in January its legislature nominated Senator Hugh L. White for president, a nomination later seconded by Alabama and Illinois. A citizen of Tennessee, however, who happened to be in attendance at the convention, was allowed to cast the fifteen votes of that state.[1] Pennsylvania sent contesting delegations, both of which were admitted. A majority of the

---

[1] Stanwood, *Hist. of the Presidency*, 182.

six hundred and twenty-six persons present were office-holders.[1]

There was a wrangle over the two-thirds rule of 1832, which had been again reported by a committee, but the rule, after being once rejected, was finally adopted. As the convention was composed of Van Buren partisans, or of Jackson men who were ready to obey the commands of their chief, the nomination of Van Buren was assured, and he received a unanimous vote. The nominee for vice-president was Richard M. Johnson of Kentucky, a long-time Jackson worker, who received 178 votes as against 87 for Senator William C. Rives of Virginia, late minister to France. Virginia refused to support the nomination of Johnson, and later cast its 23 electoral votes for vice-president for William Smith of Alabama, who was not a candidate. Van Buren, in his letter of acceptance, declared his purpose "to tread generally in the footsteps of President Jackson," while Johnson asserted his agreement with Jackson in regard to the bank, the tariff, and internal improvements.[2] No platform was deemed necessary.

The opposition denounced the Baltimore convention as a packed caucus. The aim of the Whigs was to throw the election into the House of Representatives by nominating candidates of local strength, trusting thereby to prevent the choice of Van Buren.[3]

---

[1] Sumner, *Jackson* (rev. ed.), 442.
[2] *Niles' Register*, XLVIII., 257, 329.
[3] Schurz, *Clay* (rev. ed.), II., 98.

The nomination of White, who would have, it was believed, the support of three states, would contribute to this end. The Anti-Masons, who were still of some local importance, met at Harrisburg, December 16, 1835, and nominated William Henry Harrison of Ohio for president, and Francis Granger of New York for vice-president. Harrison had won a reputation for his services in the Black Hawk war, and his nomination was indorsed by the Whigs of Pennsylvania. Judge John McLean of Ohio, who had been prominently considered by the Anti-Masons in 1832, was nominated by the legislature of his state. The second place on the ticket with White was accepted by John Tyler of Virginia. The Massachusetts Whigs nominated Webster, who, it was thought, could carry New England. With the west, the south, and New England voting for different candidates, it was believed that the work of the Democratic machine could be circumvented. As for Calhoun and South Carolina, they stood alone.

The position of Webster and Calhoun calls for special notice. The break-down of nullification and the passage of the force bill marked the retirement of Calhoun from national leadership and party affiliation, but his hold upon South Carolina, and through South Carolina upon the south, gave unquestioned weight to his opinions. His confidence in the soundness of his opinions was only exceeded by his inability to read correctly the signs of the times. In February, 1834, he was "certain" of the overthrow of "Jacksonism" and Van Buren, and confident that "thousands who but a few months since execrated us, now look to the South, not only for protection against the usurpation of the Executive, but also against the needy and corrupt in their own section." In September he sharply criticised the course of the Richmond *Whig* for abandoning "the great right of State interposition, in favour of the phantom of strict construction—a thing good in the abstract, but in practice not worth a farthing, without the right of interposition to enforce it." In his opinion, the administration was "substantially overthrown." The defeat of the Jackson candidate in Maryland, in the state election of 1835, could not fail to have "an important bearing, in deciding the present struggle favourably to the cause of liberty." [1]

Webster, on the other hand, coveted the presidential office. Unfortunately for his chances, however, the Whigs of Massachusetts were as divided among themselves as were the opponents of Jackson elsewhere. In 1835, one faction preferred Clay; another preferred Webster and wished to make an immediate nomination; a third wished to take up the strongest Whig candidate who should appear; while a fourth was willing to follow any leader under whom they could personally become conspicuous. [2] The quarrel between Masons and Anti-Masons caused Webster much anxiety, and he urged upon Jeremiah

[1] Calhoun, *Corresp.* (Jameson's ed.), 331, 341, 348.
[2] Webster, *Letters* (Van Tyne's ed.), 192.

Mason, in February, 1835, his wish that "all fair means" might be employed to settle it. But for this, and the inactivity of Clay, who appeared to be waiting for some occurrence that would cause his friends to rally about him, Webster was confident that a union of Whigs and Anti-Masons could be achieved.[1] In November he put himself on record as opposed to freemasonry and all organizations whose members were bound by secret oaths and "extraordinary obligations," and politicly declared to the Pennsylvania committee which interrogated him that he had ever found the Anti-Masons of that state "true to the Constitution, to the Union, and to the great interests of the country."[2]

Of the twenty-six states which participated in the election, all except Maryland and South Carolina chose electors on a general ticket by popular vote. Arkansas, which was admitted as a state June 15, 1836, voted for the first time, as did Michigan, which, although not formally admitted until January 26, 1837, chose electors like the others. The popular vote was 762,978 for Van Buren, and 736,250 for the three Whig candidates, of which White received 145,396, and Webster 41,287; 549,567 were given for Harrison. This was an increase of 281,537 over the total vote in 1832, but a great decrease in the Democratic majority. Van Buren carried Maine, New

---

[1] Webster, *Letters* (Van Tyne's ed.), 193. But cf. Colton, *Private Corresp. of Clay*, 393.

[2] Webster, *Private Corresp.*, II., 12–14.

Hampshire, Rhode Island, Connecticut, New York, and Pennsylvania, all the southern states except Georgia and South Carolina, and the western and southwestern states of Illinois, Michigan, Arkansas, and Missouri.   Webster carried Massachusetts, while Georgia and Tennessee went for White.   The remaining states voted for Harrison, except South Carolina, in which there was no popular vote.   In a number of the states, notably Rhode Island, Pennsylvania, North Carolina, Mississippi, and Louisiana, the Van Buren majorities were small.   Harrison carried but one western state besides his own, however—Indiana—and no southern or south-western state except Maryland and Kentucky.[1]

When the appointment of a joint committee to count the electoral vote came before the Senate, January 27, 1837, Clay offered an amendment directing the committee "to inquire into the expediency of ascertaining whether any votes were given at the recent election, contrary to the prohibition contained in the second section of the second article of the constitution.[2]   And if any such votes were given, what ought to be done with them, and whether any, and what, provision ought to be made for securing the faithful observance, in future, of that section of the constitution."[3]   The next day Van Buren retired,

---

[1] Stanwood, *Hist. of the Presidency*, 185.

[2] "No senator or representative, or person holding an office of trust or profit under the United States, shall be appointed an elector."   [3] *Debates of Congress*, XIII., 617.

and William R. King of Alabama was chosen president pro tempore. A resolution of thanks to the vice-president, presented by Benton, was objected to by Calhoun, but the objection was withdrawn and the resolution agreed to.[1]

The report of the joint committee,[2] submitted February 4, stated that Isaac Waldron, an elector in New Hampshire, "was, at the time of his appointment as elector, president of a deposit bank at Portsmouth, and was appointed and acting as pension agent, without compensation, under the authority of the United States"; and that in two cases "persons of the same names with the individuals who were appointed and voted as electors" in North Carolina held the offices of deputy postmasters. Similar cases were found in New Hampshire and Connecticut. The committee had not, however, ascertained whether the electors in these cases were the same individuals who held the offices of deputy postmasters, though presumably they were; but even if the identity were established, the result of the vote would not be changed. The committee gave its opinion that the constitutional prohibition involved should be strictly observed, and urged that provision be made for determining the qualifications of electors should any dispute arise.

With regard to the electoral votes of Michigan, the committee recommended that, "if the counting or omitting to count them shall not essentially change

[1] *Debates of Congress*, XIII., 635.   [2] *Ibid.*, 1582.

the result of the election, they shall be reported by the President of the Senate in the following manner: Were the votes of Michigan to be counted, the result would be for A B for President of the United States, —— votes; if not counted, for A B for President of the United States, —— votes; but, in either event, A B is elected President of the United States. And in the same manner for Vice-President." The recommendations of the report were adopted. The count of the votes showed that Van Buren had received 170, counting the 3 of Michigan, against 73 given for Harrison, 26 for White, and 14 for Webster. For vice-president the vote stood 147 for Johnson, 77 for Granger, 47 for Tyler, and 23 for William Smith of Alabama. The vote of South Carolina was given to Willie P. Mangum of North Carolina, and Tyler.[1] As no candidate had received a majority of the electoral votes for vice-president, the choice devolved, for the first and only time, upon the Senate. The Senate, by a vote of 33 to 16, chose Johnson.

At the expiration of his term, Jackson issued to the people a farewell address.[2] The document, obviously inspired by the example of Washington, is characterized by an obtrusive paternalism and pious sentimentality which rob it of force. The issues of state rights, the preservation of the Union, the Bank of the United States, paper money, internal im-

[1] *Debates of Congress*, XIII., 739, 1657.
[2] Richardson, *Messages and Papers*, III., 292–308.

provements, and a vigorous foreign policy are reviewed at great length and in characteristic fashion, but without adding anything of consequence to the arguments already familiar. One misses the note of distinction which so often sounds through Jackson's state papers. The farewell address is rather the last utterance of an old man whose work is done, but who must needs recall once more the struggles and conflicts of a stormy and tempestuous career, and warn his countrymen that the future, like the past, holds not peace, but the sword. Only one new issue loomed into prominence as Jackson's administration drew to its close, but that issue was slavery, the greatest of them all. Jackson spoke truly when he said that, unless the agitation of this question ceased, it would divide the Union.[1]

March 4, 1837, Jackson rode with Van Buren to the Capitol, sat uncovered in the cold while the oath of office was administered and the inaugural address pronounced, and received the plaudits of the multitude as he withdrew, a private citizen.[2] Three days later he set out for his home in Tennessee, receiving everywhere the homage of an affectionate public as he proceeded. At the "Hermitage" he followed the life of a planter, continuing a keen interest in politics, and keeping up an active correspondence. He lived to see the overthrow of Van Buren, the victory of

[1] See Hart, *Slavery and Abolition* (*Am. Nation*, XVI.), chap. ii.
[2] Benton, *Thirty Years' View*, I., 735.

Harrison, the disastrous administration of Tyler, the election of Polk, and the annexation of Texas. He died at the "Hermitage" June 8, 1845, in the seventy-eighth year of his age.

CHAPTER XVIII

THE PERSONALITY OF JACKSON

OF all the men who have held the office of president of the United States, Jackson is the most difficult to characterize with either accuracy or impartiality. That he was the most notable figure in the public life of his day, and that his influence endured long after his term of office had run its course, is freely admitted; but the absolute contradictions of his personality have led to the most varied estimates of the man and his work. To some of his later critics, as to many in his own day, he has been a coarse, ruthless invader, embodying in his own person the uncivilized and even brutal elements of the frontier, playing havoc with the sober traditions of American politics, and, while working unquestioned benefit in certain directions, leaving, nevertheless, a dark stain on the page of American history. To others he has been the foremost representative of a great popular movement whose outcome, however violent the manner of it, was the overthrow of a theory and system of government which had become unquestionably corrupt, and the baneful influence of which threatened the subversion of most that was worthy in American politics.

To differences regarding the significance of his
public career are to be added differences equally
pronounced regarding his personal traits. Something of injustice has unquestionably been done him
at this point. Jackson had, indeed, little education
in the narrow sense of the term. He had few advantages of the schools, and never showed interest
in books. His study of the law never clarified his
thoughts or bred in him a judicial habit of mind, for
his acquaintance with law was of the slightest. Until
1829 he lived mainly on the frontier or in the wilderness, among associations rude and coarse, and in circumstances distinctly unfavorable to the development of the higher qualities of thought or conduct.
Born to command, he never, save once, in all his
military career encountered an enemy worthy of the
highest effort, and his long possession of military
power was attended by conditions which, in men of
common temper, inevitably gender tyranny. As for
his temper and his tongue, they remained throughout unsheathed weapons of offence and defence.

On the other hand, circumstances of some sort
developed in Jackson qualities of mind and manner
which stamped him as a superior person. In a coarse
and corrupt society, a society whose moral standards
were lax beyond anything that would be tolerated
now, Jackson retained a singular purity of life,
thought, and speech. Contemporaries are agreed in
commenting upon his striking dignity of presence.
In any society of gentlemen he was the most dis-

tinguished gentleman of all. He acquired an unusually clear and vigorous English style. So far
as formal construction goes, his state papers are
among the very best of the first fifty years of the constitutional period. No more than most men did
he always spell correctly, and his hastily written
memoranda contain the usual errancies, but his papers do not show a particularly illiterate, and least
of all an uneducated, man. A comparison of the
manuscript and printed copies of such of his papers,
from 1829 to 1837, as have been preserved in both
forms goes to show that not only the thought, but the
essential language as well, are usually his own; and
that the literary revision by his cabinet and friends
was no greater than has commonly been applied to
the state papers of other great men.

The limitations of Jackson's character were strikingly shown, however, in his relations with his
associates. Hardly any president has had so great
difficulty in getting on with those about him. He
was in a round of quarrels with his official associates,
with members of Congress, and with private individuals from the beginning to the end of his public
career. It is true that, while the combinations of
heads of departments which he made were, as a
whole, ill suited to work harmoniously for any length
of time, his cabinet changes were not greater than
those of most presidents; but he was not a good
judge of men, and some of the changes of personnel
were due to circumstances which did him no credit.

His quarrels which attained political significance, particularly the Eaton and Calhoun affairs, were such as only a mind at once narrow, vindictive, and intense could have prosecuted. To the general personnel of the civil service he seems to have been, on the whole, indifferent save where financial irregularity was charged or proven. In these respects his leadership is of the mass, not of individuals.

Jackson's second administration shows deterioration in personal ways. The homage and flattery of the first four years, joined to the triumphant vindication at the polls in 1832, had a demoralizing effect upon him. Irritability, impatience of opposition or dissent, and love of commendation increased. His supreme self-consciousness, verging always upon conceit, grew with the growth of power and the successful accomplishment of his plans. One can hardly avoid the impression that, during the latter part of his career, he not seldom posed before the public for mere popular effect. Yet he retained till the last, in the main, his extraordinary hold on the popular mind. He was still the great champion of the masses against the classes, the great exponent of popular government. What he did was applauded because he did it; what he wished was done because he wished it; and his last political victory—the election of Van Buren—was his greatest.

Jackson's state papers, taken as a whole, present a singular combination of direct and forcible expression and unclear thinking.   Abounding in passages of admitted soundness, one looks in vain in them for the development of an orderly body of sound doctrine.   On financial matters, especially banking and currency, the ideas of Jackson are in the main so crude as to be unworthy of serious attention save for the momentous consequences which followed their promulgation.   On the tariff he seems never to have reached any precise conclusion, and his attitude towards internal improvements is equally lacking in definiteness.   Only in the proclamation to South Carolina and the protest against the Senate resolution of censure does he show a firm, logical grasp of the theory which he is expounding.   Few presidents who have dealt largely in theoretical considerations have advanced arguments which, as a whole, stand less well the test of critical examination.

Yet one cannot but feel that, however unformed or contradictory his theories or his actions, Jackson nevertheless had hold of the right end of the matter in every one of the great issues of his administrations. His attack upon the bank was brutal, but the bank was nevertheless a gigantic monopoly whose abatement was of inestimable benefit to the political and economic life of the country.   His notions about hard money were visionary, but the paper-money situation was a grave menace to financial health. His treatment of France was brusque, but the claim of the United States was just, and there was but one language that France could understand.   His acquiescence in the aggression of Georgia upon the Cherokees was a direct encouragement of nullification in South Carolina, but the maintenance of the Indian pretensions was impossible. In his mental processes, Jackson showed the intuition of woman rather than the reason of man, but what he saw he saw directly, and from his main course he never varied.

It was this sure intuition that made Jackson, as a popular leader, at once so powerful and so dangerous. If there is one allusion which occurs more frequently than any other in Jackson's messages, it is the allusion to the will of the people. In the American system of government, the only authoritative method of ascertaining the will of the people is through an election. Jackson, however, always insisted upon his own right to interpret the popular will, whether there had been a formal expression of it or not. That he often projected his own notions into the range of his vision, and saw what he wanted to see rather than what was, is evident throughout his career. Yet no president ever had a clearer popular mandate than he. He came to the presidency the recognized exponent of a middle and lower class sentiment which, up to his time, had been largely ignored in the conduct of the federal government. That which was inarticulate in the mind of the many found concrete expression in him. It is the price of popular government, this predominance of the masses, but it is the foundation of American

democracy; and it was Jackson who first built successfully upon it.

The same irregular crossing of theoretical and
practical threads is apparent in Jackson's constitutional opinions. In the main he was a strict constructionist, a firm believer in the necessity of maintaining unimpaired the rights of the states. Yet
however much he cared for the states, he cared for
the Union more, and was prepared to resent at a
moment's notice any encroachment upon the pre-
rogatives of the federal government, particularly
the executive branch of it. In other words, he was
a strict constructionist so far as strict construction
did not interfere with his practical preconceptions of
the sphere of the federal powers; but in times of
crisis his view of the scope of the federal powers
would have done credit to the straightest sect of
Federalists. At one with Jefferson as regards the
general theory of democracy, Jackson's rough-and-
ready common-sense saved him from the impractical-
ity which marks in general the public life of Jefferson,
and made middle-class democracy what it had never
been before in the United States, a working scheme
of government.

Next to his theory of the will of the people, Jackson's conception of the relation of the three departments of government to one another is perhaps most
notable. Nowhere is the mixture of the good and
the bad more curious. Such a notion as that promulgated in his bank veto, regarding the respect due

to a decision of the supreme court, is as visionary as
the fancies of an unsound mind.   On the other hand,
his assertion of the essential independence of the
executive was a contribution of the first order.   The
office of president had grown less dignified and less independent under Madison, Monroe, and John Quincy
Adams.   Unquestionably there was real danger of
the establishment of a legislative oligarchy, under
whose influence the executive would be reduced to a
mere administrative agency, and the judiciary be
shorn of all substantial power.   Against this trend
Jackson successfully protested, albeit with an offensive arrogance which alienated some to whom the
theory otherwise appealed.

It is to the Jackson régime that we owe the modern
conception of political leadership and party affiliation.   The essence of that conception is the formulation of political opinion by self-constituted leaders,
the control of voters by a "machine," and absolute intolerance of dissent.   The importance of the
individual voter declines, but that of voters as a
mass is enormously enhanced.   Platforms are framed
to win votes, not to express definite opinions.   The
development of political organization was, of course,
necessitated by the growth of the electorate, but the
appeal was increasingly to the lower rather than the
higher sentiments.   Naturally, therefore, we have
in Jackson's time the beginning of a general withdrawal of the higher classes from active politics.
Men of consequence go out and men of the mass

come in. Family, education, experience, and high ideals find less and less place in the coarse, vulgar political life which Jackson represented. Only in the south, where there were no "bosses," and where the aristocracy of leading families and great planters dominated affairs, did the old order survive.

Finally, it is in the time of Jackson that the historian notes the emergence of the west as a distinct and influential factor in national politics. The growth of the west in population and wealth, reflected in the steadily increasing representation of that section in the House of Representatives, was shown still more in the demand for greater recognition in the federal councils. The west of the thirties was a raw, unformed region, abounding in natural resource, but dominated by a population appreciably lower in many of the essentials of culture than was to be found elsewhere in the United States. It is not surprising, therefore, that the irruption of such a society into the national field should have been temporarily disastrous, and that men of the older east, accustomed to consider politics as a somewhat serious business, should have resented the rule of what seemed to them only a mob. Undoubtedly, too, the appearance of the west accentuated the sectionalism which had been growing for a generation in American life. Yet it was through the west, and through Jackson who was the incarnation of its tone and temper, that the true nature of American democracy was to be made clear. Whatever the sphere

of an aristocracy in the United States—whether that
aristocracy be one of breeding or of intelligence or
of wealth—the destiny of the state is in the keeping
of the rank and file; and it is the greatest of all
Jackson's contributions to American politics that he,
first of all the presidents, gave to the people an
opportunity.

No single phrase suffices to characterize adequately either Jackson or his time.   In the great democratic revolution which came about between 1825 and
1840, Jackson is at most points the recognized and
trusted leader.   He embodied with rare perfectness
a political theory, at the same time that he spoke
only what the mass of men everywhere thought.
His public life exhibits at every point the profoundest limitations and the sharpest contradictions, yet
he is beyond question the most influential personality in American politics from the time of Jefferson to
the time of Lincoln.

CHAPTER XIX

CRITICAL ESSAY ON AUTHORITIES

BIBLIOGRAPHICAL AIDS

THERE is no special bibliography of the period covered by the present volume. The more important literature is classified in Channing and Hart, *Guide to the Study of American History* (1896), 366–374, and W. E. Foster, *References to the History of Presidential Administrations* (1885), 22–26. Numerous important works, with critical annotations, are listed in J. N. Larned, *Literature of American History* (1902), 181–204, 273–294, 302–331. The biographies of Jackson by James Parton (3 vols., 1861) and W. G. Sumner (revised edition, 1899) include extended lists of works consulted. The special studies enumerated below contain comprehensive references to authorities, both printed and manuscript. See the "Critical Essay on Authorities" in Frederick J. Turner, *The New West;* Albert Bushnell Hart, *Slavery and Abolition*, and George P. Garrison, *Westward Extension (American Nation*, XIV., XVI., XVII.).

COMPREHENSIVE SECONDARY ACCOUNTS

Hermann Eduard Von Holst, *Constitutional History of the United States* (Mason's translation, 8 vols., 1876–1892), contains the most thorough account of the period on its constitutional side. James Schouler, *History of the United States under the Constitution* (6 vols., rev. ed., 1899), is a well-balanced general narrative. The fifth volume of John Bach McMaster, *History of the People of the United States*

(5 vols. published, 1883–1900), enters Jackson's first administration: the work has special value for social and economic conditions. Jefferson Davis, *Rise and Fall of the Confederate Government* (2 vols., 1881); Horace Greeley, *The American Conflict* (2 vols., 1864–1867); E. A. Pollard, *The Lost Cause* (1867); Alexander H. Stephens, *Constitutional View of the War between the States* (2 vols., 1868–1870); Henry Wise, *Seven Decades of the Union* (1872), and St. George Tucker, *History of the United States* (4 vols., 1856–1858), are important for the r discussions of state rights, nullification, and kindred topics. A. W. Young, *The American Statesman* (1860) is an old-fashioned compilation, of some usefulness for its summaries of debates in Congress, but otherwise unimportant.

The most important single-volume works covering the period are Woodrow Wilson, *Division and Reunion* (1892); John W. Burgess, *Middle Period* (1897); and C. H. Peck, *The Jacksonian Epoch* (1899). Edwin E. Sparks, *Story of the United States* (2 vols., 1904), is an excellent summary.

Special mention should be made of several valuable signed articles by Alexander Johnston in J. J. Lalor, *Cyclopædia of Political Science*, etc. (3 vols., 1881–1884), especia ly those on "Bank Controversies," "Cherokee Case," "Internal Improvements," "Nullification," and "State Sovereignty."

POLITICAL BIOGRAPHIES

The biographical literature is very extensive. James Parton, *Life of Andrew Jackson* (3 vols., 1861), is the most elaborate account yet offered of Jackson's career, and the mine from which later writers have freely drawn. The work has remarkable wealth of incident, and is written in a lively, cynical style; but it is devoid of proportion and without critical worth. John H. Eaton, *Life of Andrew Jackson* (1842), is a glowing account of Jackson's early career, principally on its military side, written to further Jackson's presidential aspirations. Amos Kendall, *Life of*

Andrew Jackson (1843–1844), is a fragment, the narrative extending only to 1814. The best-known recent account is W. G. Sumner, *Andrew Jackson* (revised edition, 1899), in the *American Statesmen* series. The volume shows extended research, but is inaccurate in details, disproportioned, and pervadingly hostile to Jackson. B. M. Dusenbery, *Monument to the Memory of General Andrew Jackson* (1846), contains twenty-five eulogies and sermons on Jackson's death, together with a sketch of his life. A new life of Jackson based on the manuscripts is in preparation by John S. Bassett.

Elaborate biographies, often treating at length of the general history of the time, are: Calvin Colton, *Life and Times of Henry Clay* (2 vols., 1846); D. Mallory, *Life and Speeches of Henry Clay* (2 vols., 1843); James B. Swain, *Life and Speeches of Henry Clay* (2 vols., 1842); George T. Curtis, *Life of James Buchanan* (2 vols., 1883); Lyon G. Tyler, *Letters and Times of the Tylers* (3 vols., 1884–1896); George T. Curtis, *Life of Daniel Webster* (2 vols., 1870); J. P. Kennedy, *Memoirs of the Life of William Wirt* (2 vols., 1849); William W. Story, *Life and Letters of Joseph Story* (2 vols., 1851).

Noteworthy briefer biographies are: Josiah Quincy, *Memoir of the Life of John Quincy Adams* (1858); William H. Seward, *Life and Public Services of John Quincy Adams* (1849); I. C. Pray, *Memoirs of James Gordon Bennett* (1855); W. L. Mackenzie, *Lives and Opinions of Benjamin F. Butler and Jesse Hoyt* (1845); S. G. Brown, *Life of Rufus Choate* (1870); Ann M. Coleman, *Life of J. J. Crittenden* (2 vols., 1871); Epes Sargent, *Life and Public Services of Henry Clay* (1859); Cyrus P. Bradley, *Isaac Hill* (1835); George Bancroft, *Martin Van Buren* (1889); William Kent, *Memoirs and Letters of James Kent* (1898); C. H. Hunt, *Life of Edward Livingston* (1864); William E. Dodd, *Life of Nathaniel Macon* (1903); G. S. Hillard, *Memoir and Correspondence of Jeremiah Mason* (1873); H. A. Garland, *Life of John Randolph* (2 vols., 1850); Samuel Tyler, *Memoir of Roger B. Taney* (1876); J. S. Jenkins, *Life of Silas Wright*

(1847); J. D. Hammond, *Life and Times of Silas Wright* (1848).

The following biographies in the *American Statesmen* series are, in the main, admirable brief accounts: John T. Morse, *John Quincy Adams;* Carl Schurz, *Henry Clay* (2 vols.); A. C. McLaughlin, *Lewis Cass;* Theodore Roosevelt, *Thomas H. Benton;* Edward M. Shepard, *Martin Van Buren;* Henry Cabot Lodge, *Daniel Webster;* H. E. Von Holst, *John C. Calhoun.* The revised edition (1899) of this series is to be preferred.

MANUSCRIPT SOURCES

Most of the Jackson papers that have been preserved are in the Library of Congress. The collection is extensive, but the bulk of it consists of military papers, letters to Jackson, and copies of official documents. Many of the most important papers were intrusted to Amos Kendall for use in writing a life of Jackson, and were destroyed in a fire which consumed Kendall's library.

The Library of Congress also possesses large collections of the papers of James K. Polk and of Martin Van Buren. The latter contain numerous letters of Jackson. Another collection of Van Buren manuscripts remains in private hands. A transcript of the Polk diary is in the New York Public Library (Lenox Branch), and is soon to be published.

Brief accounts of these manuscript collections are given in Van Tyne and Leland, *Guide to the Archives of the Government of the United States in Washington* (Carnegie Institution of Washington, *Publication* No. 14, 1904), 197, 199, 200; and James Schouler, "The Jackson and Van Buren Papers," in *Atlantic Monthly*, XCV., 217–225.

A selection from the papers of Joel R. Poinsett in the library of the Pennsylvania Historical Society, edited by J. B. McMaster, is announced for early publication.

PRINTED DOCUMENTARY SOURCES

The chief printed documentary sources are the official publications of the United States government, usually referred to as *Congressional Documents*. From 1817 to 1847 these publications are classified as *Senate Journals*, *Senate Documents*, *House Journals*, *House Documents*, and, after 1819, *House Reports of Committees*. Many of the volumes of House documents, however, to 1830, have the binder's title *State Papers*, and, after that, of *Executive Documents*. The *Executive* or *Secret Journals* of the Senate, a separate series, extend to 1869.

Many of the most important documents to about 1838 are reprinted in *American State Papers*, classified as follows: *Foreign Relations* (6 vols.), *Indian Affairs* (2 vols.), *Finance* (5 vols.), *Commerce and Navigation* (2 vols.), *Military Affairs* (7 vols.), *Naval Affairs* (4 vols.), *Post Office* (1 vol.), *Public Lands* (8 vols.), *Claims* (1 vol.), *Miscellaneous* (2 vols.). This series is well arranged and indexed.

The debates of Congress from 1825 to 1837 are reported in the *Register of Debates* (29 vols.), otherwise cited as *Debates of Congress* or *Congressional Debates*. The *Congressional Globe* begins in 1833, the two series thus overlapping four years. Appendices contain the acts of Congress passed during the session, together with important documents. Thomas H. Benton, *Abridgement of Debates in Congress* (16 vols., 1857–1861), is a useful compendium.

The acts of Congress are published under the title of *Statutes at Large*. Volume VIII. contains an index to the series, to 1845. The most accessible collection of treaties is *Treaties and Conventions* (edition of 1889), with valuable historical and legal notes by J. C. Bancroft Davis. The decisions of the supreme court are referred to by the name of the reporter, those from 1828 to 1842 being cited as Peters (16 vols.). J. D. Richardson, *Messages and Papers of the Presidents, 1789–1897* (8 vols.), though unscientific in arrangement and apparatus, has superseded earlier collections in its field.

The maze of state documents is best explored by the aid of R. R. Bowker, *State Publications* (2 vols., 1899–1902), the annual *Reports* of the Public Archives Commission (in American Historical Association, *Annual Reports*, 1900–

1904), and the occasional catalogues or finding-lists of state libraries and historical societies.

COLLECTED WRITINGS OF STATESMEN

Of the writings of Webster there are three editions: one of 1846 (" 8th ed.," 3 vols.), one of 1851 (6 vols.), and one of 1903 (18 vols.). The first two were prepared under Webster's direction; the edition of 1903 includes the other two. To these are to be added the *Private Correspondence* (2 vols., 1857), edited by Fletcher Webster; and *Letters of Daniel Webster* (1902), edited by C. H. Van Tyne. The writings of Calhoun comprise his *Works* (6 vols., 1853–1855), and the *Correspondence*, edited by J. F. Jameson (American Historical Association, *Report*, 1899, vol. II.). Clay's *Works* (6 vols., 1863) and *Private Correspondence* (1855) have been edited by Colton. Levi Woodbury, *Writings* (3 vols., 1852), and *Writings of Hugh S. Legaré*, edited by his sister (2 vols., 1846), are important. Extracts from contemporary discussions of political and social questions are given in A. B. Hart, *American History told by Contemporaries* (1897–1901), III., 509–573.

BOOKS OF REMINISCENCE

The mass of autobiographic and reminiscent writing on this period is large. John Quincy Adams, *Memoirs* (12 vols., 1874–1877), and Thomas H. Benton, *Thirty Years' View* (2 vols., 1854–1857), are of pre-eminent importance. Other writers whose recollections include the Jackson period are S. C. Goodrich, *Recollections of a Lifetime* (2 vols., 1856); Lyman Beecher, *Autobiography* (2 vols., 1863–1865); James A. Hamilton, *Reminiscences* (1869); Peter Harvey, *Reminiscences and Anecdotes of Daniel Webster* (1877); Amos Kendall, *Autobiography* (1872), a collection of papers and memoranda edited by W. Stickney; Robert Mayo, *Political Sketches of Eight Years in Washington* (1839); Ben. Perley Poore, *Perley's Reminiscences* (2 vols.,

c. 1886); Josiah Quincy, *Figures of the Past* (1883); Nathan Sargent, *Public Men and Events* (2 vols., 1874); Winfield Scott, *Memoirs* (2 vols., 1864); William Sullivan, *Familiar Letters on Public Characters* (1834); John Trumbull, *Autobiography, Reminiscences, and Letters* (1841); John Wentworth, *Congressional Reminiscences* (1882). Charles A. Davis, *Letters of Major Jack Downing* (1833), often ascribed to Seba Smith, is a witty satire, much enjoyed by Jackson himself; the views of the satirist reappear in several sober publications of later writers.

NEWSPAPERS AND PERIODICALS

Of the many newspapers and periodicals, the following are of most importance: *Niles' Register* (76 vols., 1811–1849, also a reissue in 36 vols.), the most valuable single work; *American Annual Register* (8 vols., 1825–1833); *Political Register*, edited by Duff Green (8 vols., 1832–1833); *The Globe* (1831–1836), the Jackson organ, edited by Francis P. Blair; New York *Courier and Enquirer* (1828–1836); *National Gazette* (Philadelphia, 1820–1841), the organ of the Bank; *Southern Review* (1828–1832); *New York Evening Post* (1801); *National Intelligencer* (1800–1870); *Richmond Enquirer* (1804); *Boston Daily Advertiser* (1813); *Charleston Mercury* (1822–1868); *New York Herald* (1802). The *American Almanac* (33 vols., 1830–1862) is a mine of social and political information. The *North American Review* discusses many of the current questions.

SOCIAL AND ECONOMIC CONDITIONS

In addition to the foregoing works, most of which treat in general of all the subjects covered by this volume, the following books on special topics are of importance:

Comprehensive statistics are to be found in the decennial *Census of the United States*, particularly that of 1830. The *Statistical Atlas* accompanying the census of 1900 has many instructive comparative charts and maps. Timothy Pitkin,

Statistical View of the Commerce of the United States (1835), is a very useful compendium. The best financial history is Davis R. Dewey, *Financial History of the United States* (1903). A. S. Bolles, *Financial History of the United States* (3 vols., 1883–1886), is still of value, though ill digested. James L. Bishop, *History of American Manufactures* (3d edition, 3 vols., 1867), is a storehouse of facts collected by a strong advocate of protection.

Accounts of travellers are important sources under this head, although great caution is necessary in using them. An unusually full list will be found in Channing and Hart, *Guide to the Study of American History* (1896), 78–86. The literature of slavery is described in A. B. Hart, *Slavery and Abolition* (*American Nation*, XVI.).

Works of a descriptive character are: Alexis de Tocqueville, *Democracy in America* (first edition, 1835; several translations; new edition by D. C. Gilman, 2 vols., 1898); F. J. Grund, *The Americans in their Moral, Social, and Political Relations* (2 vols., London, 1837); T. Brothers, *The United States . . . as They Are*, etc. (London, 1840), very hostile; T. Macgregor, *Progress of America* (2 vols., London, 1847). Recent writers on the conditions of the time are John Bach McMaster, *History of the People of the United States;* Thomas W. Higginson and William MacDonald, *History of the United States* (1905); E. E. Sparks, *Expansion of the American People* (1900).

INTERNAL IMPROVEMENTS AND PUBLIC LANDS

Official reports of works of internal improvement projected or undertaken, with the annual expenditures thereon, are given in *House Reports*, 21 Cong., 2 Sess., No. 11; *Senate Documents*, 22 Cong., 2 Sess., No. 44; and *House Reports*, 24 Cong., 1 Sess., No. 850. References to resolutions of state legislatures will be found in H. V. Ames, *State Documents on Federal Relations*, IV. (1902). The only special treatise is H. V. Poor, *Sketch of the Rise and Progress of Internal Improvements* (1881). On canals and railroads, A. Trotter, *Observations on the Financial Position and Credit of Such of the States . . . as have Contracted Public Debts* (London, 1839); H. L. Tanner, *Description of the Canals and Railroads of the United States* (1840); Emory R. Johnson, *American Railway Transportation* (1903); A. B. Hulbert, *Historic Highways of America* (16 vols., 1900–1905). See also E. R. Johnson, "River and Harbor Bills" (American Academy of Political and Social Science, *Annals*, II.).

On the public lands, *Report of the Public Land Commission* (*House Executive Documents*, 46 Cong., 3 Sess., No. 47, 1871), often cited as Donaldson, *Public Domain:* an unintelligent compilation, to be used with the greatest care, but containing information not easily got elsewhere; Shosuke Sato, *History of the Land Question in the United States* (*Johns Hopkins University Studies*, IV., Nos. 7–9); A. B. Hart, "Disposition of Our Public Lands," in his *Practical Essays on American Government* (1893), No. vii.

BANKING AND CURRENCY

All other accounts of the bank controversy have been superseded or corrected by Ralph C. H. Catterall, *The Second Bank of the United States* (1903). The author has used the papers of Nicholas Biddle; the foot-notes and appendices contain full bibliographies. Clark and Hall, *Legislative and Documentary History of the Bank of the United States* (1832), is a valuable collection of documents. The account of the bank in W. G. Sumner, *Andrew Jackson*, is suggestive and informing, but prejudiced.

On currency and banking questions, besides the references in Catterall, *Second Bank*, 513–526, see Albert Gallatin, *Considerations on the Currency and Banking Systems of the United States* (1831); J. J. Knox, *United States Notes* (3d ed., 1892); J. L. Laughlin, *History of Bimetallism in the United States* (4th ed., 1897); W. G. Sumner, *History of Banking in the United States* (vol. I. of *History of Banking in all the Leading Nations*, 4 vols., 1896); D. K. Watson,

History of American Coinage (2d. ed., 1899); H. White, *Money and Banking* (2d ed., 1902). D. R. Dewey, in his *Financial History of the United States* (1903), chaps. vii.–ix., sketches these questions with a select list of references. A number of important documents are reprinted in William MacDonald, *Select Documents illustrative of the History of the United States, 1776–1861* (1898).

DEBT AND SURPLUS

The history of the public debt and the surplus revenue is treated in all of the financial accounts of the period. Edward G. Bourne, *History of the Surplus Revenue of 1837* (1885), is the standard monograph in its field. See, further, R. A. Bayley, *History of the National Loans of the United States* (in United States Census, 1880, *Report on Taxation*, 295–486); J. Elliott, *Funding System* (1845); J. W. Kearney, *Sketch of American Finances* (1887); Charles J. Bullock, *Finances of the United States* (University of Wisconsin, *Bulletin, Economics*, I., No. 2, 1895).

TARIFF AND NULLIFICATION

The discussions of the tariff in Congress, to 1833, are conveniently summarized in C. W. Harris, *The Sectional Struggle* (1902). The best concise history is F. W. Taussig, *Tariff History of the United States* (4th ed., 1898). See, also, Edward Stanwood, *American Tariff Controversies* (2 vols., 1903); J. D. Goss, *History of Tariff Administration* (Columbia University *Studies*, I.); J. L. Bishop, *History of American Manufactures* (3 vols., 1867); O. L. Elliott, *Tariff Controversy* (Leland Stanford, Jr., University *Monographs; History and Economics*, I.); B. F. French, *History of the Rise and Progress of the Iron Trade of the United States* (1858); J. M. Swank, *History of the Manufacture of Iron in all Ages* (2d ed., 1892).

The general works already referred to, with the documentary sources, contain a vast array of material relating to nullification. The best special studies are David F. Houston, *Critical Study of Nullification in South Carolina* (*Harvard Historical Studies*, III., 1896), and Ulrich B. Phillips, *Georgia and State Rights* (American Historical Association *Reports*, 1901, II.). E. P. Powell, *Nullification and Secession in the United States* (1897), has a chapter on nullification in South Carolina, but the treatment, though keen, is partial and unscholarly. *State Papers on Nullification* (1834), published by the Massachusetts General Court, contains the replies of the states; see, also, for state documents, H. V. Ames, *State Documents on Federal Relations*, IV. (1902). A number of letters of Thomas Cooper and others, 1825–1834, are given in *American Historical Review*, VI., 725–765; VII., 92–119. For some letters of Jackson to Poinsett, see *Pennsylvania Magazine of History*, XII., 257–303. C. W. Loring, *Nullification, Secession* (1893), and A. C. McLaughlin, "Social Compact and Constitutional Construction" (*American Historical Review*, V., 467–490), are suggestive discussions of the theory of nullification. The most important documents are given in William MacDonald, *Select Documents* (1898).

INDIAN AFFAIRS

There is no satisfactory account of the relations between the federal government and the Indians. Information must be sought in the documentary sources, including state statutes and documents, and in the brief references in general histories and biographies. The Indian treaties, to 1845, are collected in *United States Statutes at Large*, VII., and *Indian Affairs, Laws and Treaties* (Kappler's ed., 1904), II.

FOREIGN RELATIONS

The diplomatic correspondence, so far as published, is in *American State Papers*, *Foreign Relations*, and the Congressional documents. A number of despatches regarding the negotiations with France are given in J. H. Richardson,

Messages and Papers of the Presidents, II., III., in connection with Jackson's messages. E. Schuyler, *American Diplomacy* (1886), is valuable for commercial negotiations. George P. Garrison, "First Stage of the Movement for the Annexation of Texas" (*American Historical Review*, X., 72–96), is a recent study of importance; see also the same author's *Westward Extension* (*American Nation*, XVII.).

CIVIL SERVICE

The most recent discussion of Jackson's civil service policy is Carl R. Fish, *The Civil Service and the Patronage* (*Harvard Historical Studies*, XI., 1905). Lucy M. Salmon, *History of the Appointing Power of the President* (American Historical Association *Papers*, I., No. 5, 1886), pays more attention to the constitutional aspects of the subject. Both works are admirable examples of sound scholarship. The foot-notes and appendices give full lists of authorities. The subject is discussed by all the general historians and by many biographers.

POLITICS AND ADMINISTRATION

The standard history of presidential elections is Edward Stanwood, *History of the Presidency* (1898), a revised and enlarged edition of the same author's *History of Presidential Elections* (1884). Besides historical data, the work gives the texts of party platforms and carefully compiled tables of electoral and popular votes. The platforms and votes are also collected in T. H. McKee, *National Platforms of all Political Parties* (1892), and Cooper and Fenton, *American Politics* (rev. ed., 1884).

The growth and organization of parties are treated in Martin Van Buren, *Inquiry into the Origin and Growth of Political Parties in the United States* (1867), extracted from the author's *Autobiography*, now among the Van Buren manuscripts in the Library of Congress; F. Byrdsall, *History of the Loco-Foco or Equal Rights Party* (1842); J. D.

Hammond, *History of Political Parties in the State of New York* (2 vols., 4th ed., 1850), continued by the same author's *Silas Wright;* James A. Woodburn, *Political Parties and Party Problems in the United States* (1903); R. M. Ormsby, *History of the Whig Party* (1859), strongly partisan; Anson D. Morse, "Political Influence of Andrew Jackson," in *Political Science Quarterly*, I., 153–162; J. P. Kennedy, *Memoirs of the Life of William Wirt* (2 vols., rev. ed., 1872), for the Anti-Masonic party; Lyon G. Tyler, *Parties and Patronage in the United States* (1891); H. J. Ford, *Rise and Growth of American Politics* (1898), a brilliant essay; McCarthy, *Anti-Masonic Party* (Am. Hist. Assoc., *Reports*, 1902, I.).

Works of prime importance in their respective fields are Edward C. Mason, *The Veto Power* (*Harvard Historical Monographs*, No. 1, 1891), M. P. Follett, *The Speaker of the House of Representatives* (1896); L. G. McConachie, *Congressional Committees* (1898); Clara E. Kerr, *The United States Senate* (1895).

THE WEST

The principal literature, other than documentary sources, on the westward expansion, 1828 to 1860, is given with annotations in J. N. Larned, *Literature of American History*, 206–213. Aside from some chapters in the secondary works, the best authorities are the biographies of western statesmen. See Frederick J. Turner, *Rise of the New West* (*American Nation*, XIV.).

STATE HISTORY

The state constitutions and enabling acts are collected in Ben. Perley Poore, *Federal and State Constitutions* (2 vols., 1877). The journals and debates of constitutional conventions are also important. State histories are not, as a rule, of a high order. An elaborate list is given in Channing and Hart, *Guide*, 57–78; another, with annotations, in J. N. Larned, *Literature of American History*, 358–394.

The best brief works are those in the *American Common-wealths* series, of which Frank B. Sanborn, *New Hampshire* (1904); Alexander Johnston, *Connecticut* (1887); E. N. Roberts, *New York* (2 vols., 1887); Rufus King, *Ohio* (1888); J. P. Dunn, *Indiana* (1888); Thomas M. Cooley, *Michigan* (1885); and Nathaniel S. Shaler, *Kentucky* (1885), are useful for the Jackson period.

INDEX

LEE, HENRY, manages Jackson's canvass, 37; and Jackson's inaugural, 44; electoral votes for, 197.

Legaré, H. S., and tariff of 1828, 83.

Legislature, state, constitutional changes, 261–266; term lengthened, 267. *See also* Congress.

Lewis, W. B., manages Jackson's canvass, 29, 37; and Jackson's inaugural, 44; in kitchen cabinet, 51.

Lincoln, Levi, and railroads, 270.

Livingston, Edward, secretary of state, 128; nullification proclamation, 160; minister to France, 206, 207.

Local government, character (1830), 14. *See also* Cities.

"Loco-Focos," 270.

Louaillier, Louis, and Jackson, 19.

Louisiana, population (1830), 9; politics and sugar, 273.

Louisiana purchase, west boundary, 6, 211.

Lowndes, William, tariff of 1816, 72.

McCULLOCH *vs.* Maryland, 115, 131.

McDuffie, George, and tariff, 83; and bank, 122, 130; and force bill, 166.

McLean, John, appointed justice, 48; presidential candidate, 298.

McLean, Louis, secretary of treasury, 128; and West Indies trade, 202–204; and bank, 220, 222, 228; secretary of state, 223, 252; on public lands, 280.

Madison, James, veto of bonus bill, 135.

Maine politics, 271.

Mallary, R. C., woolens bill, 67.

Mangum, W. P., electoral vote for, 303.

Manufactures, displace trade in New England, 15; wool, 271.

Marcy, W. L., politician, 269.

Marshall, John, on implied powers, 108; doctrine of the "people," 108; on bank, 115; and Cherokees, 175–177; and Jackson, 177, 178; death, 248.

Maryland politics, 272.

Maryland *vs.* Bank, 114.

Mason, Jeremiah, branch bank, 121.

Massachusetts, population (1830), 9; political organization, 269; established church abolished, 267, 268; wool manufacture, 271; savings-bank regulations, 271; school fund, 271; aid for railroads, 271; politics, 272, 299.

Maynard, W. H., politician, 269.

Maysville road veto, 139.

Mecklenberg, tonnage duties, 210.

Mexico, commercial treaty, 210, 213; independence, 212; anti-slavery, 212; claims against, 216. *See also* Texas.

Michigan, territorial boundary, 5; admission, 5, 257–259; population (1830, 1840), 9; Ohio boundary, 258; alien suffrage, 258; constitution, 262; electoral vote (1836), 302.

Militia, reforms, 247.

Mississippi, population (1830), 9; tariff protest, 88; Indian lands (1825), 169; incorporates Indians, 173; constitution (1832), 264; politics, 273.

Missouri enlarged, 7.

Money, coinage act (1834),

END OF VOL. XV.

END OF VOL. XV.